ON TRIAL

ON TRIAL

America's Courts and Their Treatment of Sexually Abused Children

Second Edition

Billie Wright Dziech and Judge Charles B. Schudson

Beacon Press
Boston

Beacon Press
25 Beacon Street
Boston, Massachusetts 02108

Beacon Press books
are published under the auspices of
the Unitarian Universalist Association of Congregations.

98 97 96 95 94 93 92 91   1 2 3 4 5 6 7 8

Text design by Hunter Graphics

Library of Congress Cataloging-in-Publication Data

Dziech, Billie Wright, 1941–
    On trial : America's courts and their treatment of sexually abused
children / Billie Wright Dziech and Charles B. Schudson. — 2nd ed.
        p. cm.
    Includes bibliographical references and index.
    ISBN 0-8070-0415-4
    1. Sexually abused children—Legal status, laws, etc.—United
States. 2. Criminal courts—United States. 3. Children as
witnesses—United States. 4. Sexually abused children—United
States. I. Schudson, Charles B. II. Title.
KF9323.D97 1991
344.73'03276—dc20
[347.3043276]   90-23545
                                                              CIP

Judge Schudson has assigned a portion of the royalties from this book to
the National Committee for Prevention of Child Abuse,
the National Council of Juvenile and Family Court
Judges—Child Sexual Abuse Judicial Education Project,
the State of Wisconsin Children's Trust Fund, the
Children's Outing Association, and the Milwaukee Boys
and Girls Club.

In loving memory of my mother
BWD

For my children, Benjamin and Joel
CBS

Contents

Introduction to the Second Edition

In the two years since its publication, *On Trial* has produced the impact we had hoped and received critical acclaim beyond our most optimistic expectations. It has become the "textbook" for numerous multidisciplinary conferences and judicial colleges and, in some states, has been provided to every judge. We have received comments from lawyers, judges, and professionals who work with children, from parents of abused children, from adult survivors of abuse, and from offenders—all confirming our belief that a single book could cross professional lines and enhance understanding among all who seek fairness for children, their families, and their offenders.

In preparing this second edition we have listened to those voices. We have accepted the advice to build upon our original structure, with detailed attention to the most important recent developments in criminal law. We also have accepted the invitation to comment on additional subjects of critical concern, including several civil law issues arising from abuse cases and custody disputes. Thus this second edition of *On Trial* is strengthened by added experience and by the encouragement of so many, to whom we express our gratitude.

BILLIE WRIGHT DZIECH
CHARLES BENJAMIN SCHUDSON
1991

Preface

During a recent summer break, I was trying to decide about my next book project. I had just published a book on sexual harassment on college campuses, and as the euphoria of seeing it in print subsided, I began to worry about what would come next. I had been dedicated for so long to an obscure, unpopular cause that I wasn't certain how to proceed once it attracted public recognition and concern. I also feared I would succumb to the ivory-tower mentality of literature professors, who have fewer opportunities than most of their colleagues to work in the "real world" beyond the campus.

Looking back, I think that reality intruded upon me almost too forcefully. My sister had been talking for months about a friend whose child had been sexually abused, but I had dismissed her discussion because, like most people, I found the subject too repugnant. Then the case came to trial, and I became interested in not only what happened in that courtroom but in others like it. As I began following cases, I was shocked to discover again and again that when parents made criminal allegations against those they believed guilty of child sexual abuse, the legal system would almost invariably add insult to injury, would reabuse the children and demoralize their parents. That injustice made me angrier than I ever recall.

That anger was not directed toward the defendants. It was reserved for the lawyers, the judge, and most of all, "the legal system"—a system that seemed more interested in establishing a verdict than in discovering the truth. No one appeared to recognize that the children and the parents were on trial as much or more than the defendants, and no one seemed to care that they had no protection against even the most unreasonable and unsubstantiated accusations. The damage to the defendants was clear. But what of the children? How could anyone justify putting a child on trial for something others, whether defendants or parents, had caused? And the parents? If they were not, as the defense so often claimed, encouraging their children to fabricate stories, how could anyone justify the legal system's adding to their agony?

Having seen the legal process in action, I came away from the trials I had followed believing that something terrible had happened to the children in those courtrooms. And with that recognition, this book was born.

Eventually my interest in the predicament of sexually abused children began to grow. I realized it was a logical outgrowth of my experience with the issue of sexual harassment, which is itself a kind of psychological rape. The similarities between the situations of sexually harassed college students and sexually exploited children are obvious. Both involve abuses of power and psychological and sometimes physical violence. Both have been "closet" concerns; victims tend to endure their traumas in silence and are seldom believed when they disclose their victimization. Their reactions are surprisingly similar, just as the responses of the institutions to which they turn for help have been alike in their hesitancy to reform.

The legal system's treatment of children and their parents challenged all the comfortable notions upper-middle-class status had taught me about justice in America. I began to read books describing the disenfranchisement of minorities and the poor in systems that evaluate people almost exclusively by their verbal skills and their ability to articulate white middle-class values. And I wondered if the authors of those books had ever considered the isolation and vulnerability of children, a seriously abused minority in the legal system.

I couldn't fully define what distressed me until my husband gave me the analogy. "You don't like what happens to children in courtrooms because it's too much like a football game to you. The teams are lawyers, the ball is words, and the kids somehow get lost in all the competition and maneuvering."

While I believe his analogy was appropriate, my response was probably less so. I went through a stage in which I too became combative. I began arguing with the lawyers I know, hoping to prove somehow that the legal system is too much of a game, too competitive, too rigid, and often too violent in its insensitivity to human beings. The more I argued that the law was not written with children and sex abuse in mind, the more attorneys countered that the law is omnipotent and beneficent, above reproach, the "best system there is."

This was what I now call my Antigone phase, the period during which I viewed myself as a lone crusader in a hopeless fight against the ignorance and injustice of the judicial system. The chorus in Jean Anouilh's play *Antigone* describes the actions of tragedy as I perceived my approach to a book on the courts' treatment of child victims.

> You can shout aloud; you can get all those things said that you never thought you'd be able to say—or never even know you had it in you to say. And you don't say these things because it will do any good to say them: you know better than that. You say them for their own sake; you say them because you learn a lot from them.[1]

In time I discovered that the parallels between the playwright's concept of tragedy and my writing a book on children in the courts were limited. I recognized that if a book were to succeed, I would have to write it for more than its "own sake." It would not be enough to write a book because I had discovered a sudden need to "shout aloud," because I personally could "learn a lot" by writing it. You write a book because you believe, because you must believe, that what you have to say will be heard and will make a difference. Ultimately I discovered that you write a book like this for others, not for yourself.

One year after I began investigating child sexual abuse I attended a national conference on the problem. Such events usually attract social workers, therapists, physicians, researchers, and members of the legal profession. This was somewhat different, however, because parents of sexually abused children had come from around the country to tell their stories to the professionals. The meeting they held attracted a smaller audience than the sessions presented by well-known experts, but for me, it was the most instructive. Listening to mothers and fathers describe what had happened to them and their children was painful. It wasn't simply that descriptions of individual incidents were so horrifying. I had anticipated that. The greater difficulty was the reaffirmation of what I already suspected—that the agony of the abuse was often eclipsed by the trauma that followed when families turned to the legal system for help.

What impressed me about most of the parents was not just their courage but their lack of self-indulgence, their desire to turn their pain into something positive. They too were angry and frustrated, but they were not there for themselves. It was not self-interest that motivated them to plan education and prevention programs in their communities, to work for legislative reform, and to establish legal aid funds for sexually abused victims. They were working to protect children—mine as well as their own.

And so I realized that I needed to redirect my anger. Change can occur only with objective appraisal of the legal system and its traditions and with careful analysis of the needs, rights, limitations, and abilities of children. Change means refocusing our attention on what matters most—children, defendants, and the search for justice.

As I became more familiar with child abuse trials, I tried to imagine what it must be like to be five or six years old, seated where my feet couldn't touch the floor, trying to talk through a microphone to a room full of strangers. Sometimes I have talked with media people covering trials. Once a radio announcer praised the tactics of one defense lawyer who, he said, "really knows how to go for the jugular." The announcer and a lawyer observing the proceedings spent almost thirty minutes analyzing legal tactics in the case. I kept wanting to ask what their discussion had to do with the human beings involved, and later I realized that was the point—in a sense, none of it was concerned with the children or the truth or even with the defendants. It was like a football game, only it was far more brutal than the contests I have watched between my son and his friends.

I don't think that what I have observed in the courtroom is what anyone ever intended American justice to be; and I will never believe that in order to protect defendants, one must "go for the jugulars" of children. Ultimately, I learned from people like my co-author, Judge Schudson, that the trials I have witnessed may be the exception if people have the courage and commitment to work for change. There can be a better way for children if we care enough to find it.

BILLIE WRIGHT DZIECH

Before becoming a judge, I prosecuted a nursing home's owners and administrators for reckless homicide and patient neglect. Despite their knowledge of the resulting harm to patients, the defendants had reduced staff and services in order to increase profits. Throughout the six years of investigation and trial preparation, my colleagues warned that one factor would preclude successful prosecution: the victims could not testify.

By the time of trial, many of the fifty-nine victims had died. Others were developmentally disabled and could not speak. All the rest were either unable to recall the events or were physically unable to appear in court. In a five-week jury trial that gained national attention, we presented evidence from nursing home inspectors, nurses and aides, and medical and business records that allowed the jury to "see" and "hear" these special victims.

Without calling a single patient to testify, the prosecution still was able to try the case successfully. We developed special trial methods not by departing from legal traditions, but by understanding those traditions and the flexible methods they allow. We understood that the trial traditionally has been a search for truth. We knew that the unavailability of victims must not deny justice.

Throughout the case, my colleagues' cautious and conventional warnings troubled me. Since almost none of these patients had relatives involved in their lives, public officials had to be their advocates. If prosecution would be impossible because these victims could not testify, how could we protect nursing home patients? If an entire group of victims could gain no justice because of their unique vulnerability, what did that say about our system of justice?

Less than a year later, I was a judge presiding over juvenile and criminal cases, many of which involved child victims of abuse and sexual assault. I watched children freeze in court and learned of others who would not appear. Again lawyers told me cases could not be prosecuted because victims could not testify. What I found, however, was that many children could not do so because they were expected to testify like adults—with adult language in intimidating adult settings.

Twenty years earlier I had taught creative dramatics for children and trained YMCA day camp counselors in adult-child communication skills. I had studied the unique emotions, perceptions, and communication skills of children, and the techniques that adults need to work sensitively with them. Now those same techniques could help produce justice for children.

Alexander, one of the first victims to appear before me, was six years old when a babysitter ordered him and his three- and four-year-old brothers to their basement. The sitter threatened them with a knife and sexually assaulted the younger boys. During the trial, Alexander's brothers were unable to describe the assault. Then Alexander was called to testify. When he had visited the courtroom for orientation by the district attorney an hour earlier, he seemed bright and articulate. Now, before the jury, he said nothing. He appeared confused and frightened, his small body lost on what must have seemed an enormous chair. He nodded quickly when I asked, "Would you be happier right now if you were sitting on your dad's lap?" His father sat in the witness chair, put Alexander on his lap with an arm around him, and Alexander testified.

Kelly was also six years old when her mother, drying her after a bath, discovered Kelly's oozing vaginal discharge. "He hurt me, he hurt me! Kevin stuck his finger in me!" she cried. Doctors confirmed that Kelly had suffered penetration and had gonorrhea. At the trial Kelly testified, but not in person. She became the first child to testify under a new law permitting videotape depositions. She gave her deposition in the comfort of judicial chambers while the incident was fresh in her memory. She was able to move about the room from couch to floor, holding toys and munching crackers, as she answered prosecution and defense questions.

Despite the seriousness of the crimes and the strong evidence supporting Alexander's and Kelly's accounts, neither of these cases could have gone to trial without enlightened laws and techniques to assist children. These laws and techniques facilitate a child's communication; they do not tell a child what to say. In some ways, they are analogous to providing a translator for a Spanish-speaking or hearing-impaired witness or to allowing a disabled veteran to testify from a wheelchair. The techniques did not give unfair advantage to Alexander and Kelly, but removed discrimination that would have denied the jury the chance to search for truth.

These legal "advances," whether for nursing home patients or children, depended not so much on sophisticated legal skills as on caring—caring deeply about people to be served and justice to be pursued. That these efforts proved both unprecedented and successful tells us important, apparently contradictory, things about the criminal justice system.

The system often is consumed by "business-as-usual" officials, lawyers, and judges. Their failure to examine themselves and the legal principles that should guide their work is discouraging and harmful. Yet even they see the

system's inadequacies and welcome improvements. And many others have initiated important changes and continue to seek creative solutions to some of the system's most difficult problems. Thus while in many ways the criminal justice system seems bogged down by inertia, it is also ready for release. Innovations that appear controversial at first will be accepted if they build on America's best legal traditions.

In the last five years, I have traveled to more than forty states to help judges and other criminal justice professionals understand laws and techniques that can provide fairness to children in courts. Throughout, I have been impressed by two things: (1) the profound lack of understanding of children, evidence law, and trial traditions; and (2) the sincere and enthusiastic readiness to learn and change in order to enhance justice for children. As one judge told me after my presentation, "Making Courts Safe for Children," to the 1986 Tennessee Judicial Conference, "When you started out, I thought you were crazy as hell. But you made sense."

Although my primary experience with children in courts has been as a prosecutor and judge, the rights of defendants are crucial to the legal concepts we will consider. For two years, I worked for Legal Assistance to Inmates in jails, prisons, and mental hospitals. I have no illusions about the consequences of criminal conviction. I have also seen the suffering caused by unjust prosecution. I have an uncompromising reverence for the constitutional rights that preserve the presumption of innocence and protect all citizens from unfair prosecution and conviction. As Dr. Dziech and I will show, fairness for children in courts will help prevent unjust prosecutions, as well as produce just convictions.

CHARLES BENJAMIN SCHUDSON

The audience we hope to reach is diverse—police, lawyers, judges, legislators, social workers, therapists, sociologists, psychologists, psychiatrists, pediatricians, nurses, victims, their families, and the general public. For this reason, we avoid highly specialized language and exhaustive references that would have meaning for only a few. At the same time, we do not shy away from legal concepts essential to our themes. The best hope for resolving the problems confronting sexually abused children in the courts is to expand multidisciplinary understanding and to emphasize the common interests and goals of all concerned.

Because the criminal justice system has failed victims of both intrafamilial and extrafamilial abuse, our analysis of children as witnesses is relevant to the predicaments of both. Unfair and insensitive court procedures intimidate a child raped by a stranger just as much as one molested by a parent. Still, while all children confront similar obstacles in the justice system, intrafamilial and extrafamilial abuse involve different circumstances, dynamics,

effects, and even legal considerations. Until very recently researchers assumed that most child sexual abuse occurred within the family. Recent studies demonstrate, however, that abuse by nonfamilial offenders is far more frequent than once supposed. By concentrating in chapter 4 on a case study that involves extrafamilial abuse, we hope not only to focus attention on this equally serious problem, but also to avoid issues in child development and law that would divert attention from our basic themes—themes valid for both intrafamilial and extrafamilial sexual abuse victims.

The courts have failed both kinds of victims. In an ironic way, they have also failed defendants. Some will argue that the legal reforms and innovations we propose are departures from constitutional protections for the accused, but we will demonstrate that they are true to the best traditions of the law and the purposes of a trial. Moreover, we believe that the reforms are essential because the legal system does not serve defendants any better than it does victims. A significant number of Americans are convinced that the system overemphasizes the quest for proof beyond a reasonable doubt and, in the process, abandons any genuine search for truth. Thus a defendant found not guilty by a court may be branded for life if people believe that verdict was reached by depriving a victim of his or her rights in the trial.

If the system works as it can and should, the rights of two vulnerable groups—children and defendants—will be respected. The legal system evolved, in part, from a commitment to provide justice for the vulnerable. It is time to renew that commitment by providing sensitive and fair responses to children who are the victims of sexual abuse.

BWD
CBS

Acknowledgments

Most books belong as much or more to people other than their authors. This one would not exist without the following:

Joanne Wyckoff, my editor and friend, and Beacon Press for believing in yet another of my ideas.

The professionals—people like Lucy Berliner, Don Bross, Jon Conte, David Finkelhor, Gail Goodman, Kee MacFarlane, and Roland Summit—whose lives of commitment make the contributions of others so easy.

The parents and children whose suffering and courage I will never forget.

David Hartleb, whose understanding and encouragement make life beyond the university possible, and Sharon Snow, whose loyalty and endurance helped ward off insanity.

My husband and our family, smaller now, but bound together by love, strength, and laughter that somehow see us through.

BWD

Writing a book to help gain justice for children is a humbling challenge. I felt fortunate to have the chance, but fearful that I might fail. So in writing, I called for help from many special people. They responded with constructive critiques of early drafts, and with encouragement. While any failure is my own, any success must be shared with Priscilla Ahlgren of the *Milwaukee Journal*, Judge Ralph Adam Fine, Attorney Charles F. Kahn, Jr., Eve Lipchik, Attorney Richard J. Podell, and Professor Martha L. Minow of the Harvard Law School.

Others gave me the chance to teach at child abuse conferences and judicial colleges throughout the country, where I came to understand many of the questions this book would seek to answer. Much of that teaching was sponsored by the National Judicial College, and by the National Council of Juvenile and Family Court Judges with the support of Nancy M. Lick, Director of Curriculum Development, and M. James Toner, Associate Director of Training. Wisconsin's Director of State Courts, J. Denis Moran, and Director of Judicial Education, V. K. Wetzel, enthusiastically allowed my time to be shared with the judiciaries of other states.

My understanding could not have developed without early sensitization to the needs of victims. Jo Kolanda, Director of Victim/Witness Services for the Milwaukee County District Attorney's Office, and Bobbi Moebius, Director of Victim/Witness Services for the Milwaukee County Juvenile Court, showed me the very best that the criminal justice system can offer victims.

Without the chance to become a public servant, I could not have contributed to the cause of America's children. Two extraordinary men allowed me to serve. By their examples, they showed me that public officials truly can be independent, compassionate people who seek nothing except justice for future generations. Milwaukee County District Attorney E. Michael McCann and former Wisconsin governor Lee Sherman Dreyfus will always have my admiration and gratitude.

I have been blessed by an extraordinary family filled with amazing abilities and love. My parents and grandparents instilled the idealism that motivates all my thoughts and actions. My two older brothers provided examples of excellence that continue to inspire me. Hod's fierce determination and Mike's stunning scholarship set standards I could barely hope to approach, but that encouraged every page. Mona, Steve, and Tom joined in preserving and enriching the fullness of family despite tragedies. My wonderful wife Karen, despite the demands of her own career, carried added burdens to help maintain our family's vibrant love through three years of writing. As a psychotherapist, she viewed child sexual abuse from a different perspective, thus sharing and enhancing my commitment to this book. Finally, my magnificent children, Benjamin and Joel, were the most motivating of all. As I took time from them to write, I knew that this book would be for them and their future.

                                                                    CBS

ON TRIAL

1

Children in Jeopardy: Sexual Abuse and the Legal System

"This must be the wood," she said thoughtfully to herself, "Where things have no names. I wonder what'll become of my name when I go in? I shouldn't like to lose it at all—because they'd have to give me another, and it would be almost certain to be an ugly one."

—Lewis Carroll,
Alice's Adventures in Wonderland

THE latest statistics indicate that one American female in every three or four is likely to be sexually victimized before she is eighteen years old. Data for males is more sparse and less reliable, but most experts agree that the lowest frequency is between one in ten and one in six; and there is growing suspicion that male children may be as often involved in sexual activity with adults as females because they are the preferred victims of habitual pedophiles. The American Humane Association's latest figures, which are from 1986, indicate that 132,000 cases of child sexual abuse were substantiated in that year.[1] The first nationwide study of the extent of child molestation was conducted by the *Los Angeles Times* in 1985.[2] That poll, the largest to date, found that at least 22 percent of Americans (27% of women and 16% of men) were sexually victimized during childhood. The *Times* poll and studies by other researchers indicate that at least half of adult perpetrators are unrelated to the children they victimize.

1

These statistics are conservative when compared to two other studies regarded by experts as more methodologically rigorous. Diana Russell, a sociology professor at Mills College, reported that 38 percent of women in her 1978 survey indicated they were victimized before eighteen.[3] In a 1985 study Gail Wyatt, a professor of medical psychology at the Neuropsychiatric Institute at UCLA, found that in cases involving some form of body contact, one in approximately two females had experienced sexual abuse prior to age eighteen.[4] Statistical discrepancies in research surveys and reports from legal jurisdictions occur because there are no universal definitions for terms like child sexual "abuse," "assault," "misuse," or "molestation." The ambiguity is increased by lack of consensus about acts or behaviors that constitute child sexual abuse and about the age limits that should be employed to designate victims and perpetrators. Additional discrepancies may derive from variations in researchers' sampling and interview techniques.[5]

The National Center on Child Abuse and Neglect defines "child sexual abuse" as "contacts or interactions between a child and an adult when the child is being used for the sexual stimulation of that adult or another person. Sexual abuse may also be committed by a person under the age of 18 when that person is either significantly older than the victim or when the abuser is in a position of power or control over another child."[6] The authors of *Sexual Assault of Children and Adolescents* describe it as "forced, pressured, or stressful sexual behavior committed on a person under the age of seventeen."[7] Some recent definitions are more specific. Wyatt describes child sexual abuse as "contact of a sexual nature, ranging from those involving non-body contact such as solicitations to engage in sexual behavior and exhibitionism to those involving body contact such as fondling, intercourse and oral sex."[8] She uses seventeen as the upper age limit for victims and defines perpetrators as those five years older than the victim. If perpetrators are less than five years older but the situation involved coercion, the behavior is defined as sexually abusive. Her definition does not include "consensual, exploratory behaviors between minors," and willingness of a subject twelve or under to participate was not considered because "children do not understand what they are consenting to and are really not free to say no to an authority figure."[9]

The point on which experts agree is that child sexual abuse is one of the most underreported of all crimes. Fewer than half of the respondents to the *Los Angeles Times* poll told a close friend or relative about their victimization within a year, and only 3 percent reported the incident to legal authorities or public agencies. This statistic is similar to Russell's findings that only 2 percent of intrafamilial and 6 percent of extrafamilial incidents were reported to the police.

This means that in a culture frequently described as "child centered," the agony of thousands of children goes unheard each year. The results are devastating—not simply for the victims but for everyone who comes in contact with them. The trauma of victimization is not confined to the child and his or her family. The *Chicago Tribune* interviewed some of the most prominent professionals who work with convicted intrafamilial and extrafamilial sexual abusers and concluded from "a sampling of recent or ongoing clinical studies in different cities . . . that a clear majority of males who sexually abused children were sexually abused as children."[10] Although the numbers are difficult to determine, and the percentages may differ widely for males and females, researchers do agree that a very substantial percentage of child victims become sexual abusers themselves. In addition, other social ills — rape, prostitution, drug addiction, and crime — have been attributed to former victims of child sexual abuse. Thus the silence of the abused is eventually broken and their despair and rage are acted out in ways that threaten not only other children but all of society.

The magnitude of that threat may be what causes society to deny the problem. If at least one in five children is being sexually abused and half or more than half of the victimization occurs outside the family, then no one's child is really safe. In a society in which children are increasingly exposed to extrafamilial caretakers and acquaintances, the danger seems unavoidable. And so it becomes more comfortable not to know. Not knowing is easy to accomplish. The average person cannot fathom how or why someone could sexually abuse a child. There is usually little or no physical evidence to support victims' claims, and the initial effect on the child is often impossible to discern. The resulting dilemma has been most accurately described by Donald Bross, associate professor in pediatric family law and legal counsel for the Kempe National Center for the Prevention and Treatment of Child Abuse and Neglect: "If all this has supposedly happened to a child and if no one can prove it and no one can demonstrate its effect on the child, then where's the harm? One of the difficulties we have in dealing with child sex abuse is that it's more difficult to establish a 'body' count than it is in the case of physical abuse."[11]

Victims themselves unknowingly aid in society's denial. Most disclose the incidents slowly and reluctantly over a period of weeks, months, or even years. Some live all of their lives without admitting to anyone what happened to them. Of former victims responding to the *Times* poll, 42 percent replied they told someone within a year, 21 percent said they waited more than a year, and 36 percent reported that they had told no one until asked by the interviewer. This response is indicative of the process that psychiatrist Roland Summit, after thousands of first-hand observations and consultations with professionals dealing with victims, described as the "child sexual abuse accommodation syndrome."[12]

Summit noted that sexually abused children generally reveal five characteristics in coping with their dilemmas: secrecy, helplessness, accommodation (seeing oneself as responsible for the victimization), delayed disclosure, and retraction or recantation. Although he originally defined these patterns in terms of incest, increased experience with and understanding of child sexual abuse has led professionals to recognize that the syndrome appears in victims of extrafamilial abuse as well.

> If a respectable, reasonable adult is accused of perverse, assaultive behavior by an uncertain, emotionally distraught child, most adults who hear the accusation will fault the child. Disbelief and rejection by potential adult caretakers increase the helplessness, hopelessness, isolation, and self-blame that make up the most damaging aspects of child sexual victimization. . . . Without professional or self-help group intervention, most parents are not prepared to believe their child in the face of convincing denials from a responsible adult. Since the majority of adults who molest children occupy a kinship or trusted relationship . . . the child is put on the defensive for attacking the credibility of the trusted adult, and for creating a crisis of loyalty which defies comfortable resolution. At a time when the child most needs love, endorsement, and exculpation, the unprepared parent typically responds with horror, rejection and blame.[13]

Parents are not the only culprits, of course. Frequently, their ineffectuality is linked to their reluctance to seek redress for their children through the legal system. Such hesitancy is understandable, for the American courts have generally regarded child victims with indifference and disbelief. So pervasive are these attitudes that the legal system has often precluded the entry of children as witnesses in the courts and has thus increased their victimization by adults.

Society's indifference is revealed in its self-imposed ignorance about the crime. Government statistics on child sexual abuse are sparse. The authors of *When the Victim Is a Child,* a publication of the Department of Justice's National Institute of Justice, observe, "It is a sad commentary on modern society that children, like adults, become victims of crime. . . . What is perhaps even more appalling is the fact that so little is known about the incidence and types of crimes committed against children. We do not even know the true magnitude of the problem."[14] Government, legal, and social service agencies have made sporadic and uncoordinated attempts to accumulate data about child sexual abuse. The FBI's Uniform Crime Reports, which provide the most comprehensive information about reported crime in the United States, painstakingly record the number of yearly auto thefts in America, but they contain almost no information about crimes against children except when they are the victims of murder. Data accumulated by the Department of Health and Human Services' National Center on Child Abuse and Neglect include only incidents of child maltreatment inflicted by a parent or caretaker and known to child protection agencies in each state. Even the data the center do possess are unreliable because states report voluntarily, and the quality of information they provide is uneven. Child protective services and other social agencies attempt to compile a national overview of the problem, but they too are limited by inadequate reporting at various levels of government.

The result is that although we recognize that we're dealing with an enormous problem, we know too little about it because there are few large-scale attempts to analyze more complex facets of the issue. The American Humane Association, the Westat Corporation, and the Family Violence Research Program at the Universities of Rhode Island and New Hampshire are among those that have attempted nationwide surveys of violence against children, but the full extent of sexual abuse of the young remains obscure.[15] Few legal agencies maintain records on the number of complaints in comparison to the number of arrests, indictments, convictions, and acquittals of defendants. There is almost no data on the number of parents who withdraw complaints or on their reasons for doing so; yet this can be one of the single most revealing indications of the legal system's success or failure. We have little information about the frequency with which child victims appear in courts, the impact of their testimonies upon verdicts, or the effect of the courtroom experience upon their emotional recovery. This is not surprising since we know so little about children as witnesses—about their abilities and limitations in testifying and about their special vulnerabilities when they do so.

Our willingness to invest time, effort, and money in record keeping and research may be a measure of our genuine commitment to fighting sexual abuse of children. Almost twenty years ago in a pioneer study of the problem, Vincent De Francis commented on the need for national data and suggested that one of "the most common" elements mitigating against reliable research was "resistance." He observed: "This may consist of resistance to the implications of the findings or resistance to such change as the findings make necessary. . . . Resistance to change is insidious, and difficult to counter, because the status quo is so much more comfortable and so much less demanding."[16]

Ignorance and indifference to the problem, acceptance of the status quo, are comfortable and undemanding. If the public doesn't realize how pervasive the problem is, it won't feel compelled to learn about children, about their capabilities and limitations, their powerlessness in society and especially in the legal system. If the public doesn't know about children in courtrooms, it can abandon the legal system to police, attorneys, judges, and legislators, who have little motivation to question it. If acceptance of the status quo prevails, society won't have to analyze legal misinterpretations that often render the justice system incapable of providing justice for child victims. Comfortable in its ignorance, the public can avoid the challenge of Suzanne Sgroi, whose *Handbook of Clinical Intervention in Child Sexual Abuse* is a classic in its field. Sgroi reminds us that "we tolerate sexual abuse of children in our society because we continue to process cases through an adversary system that is overwhelmingly weighted against the child victim at virtually every level."[17]

Such tolerance and subsequent refusal to alter inequities in the system have occurred throughout history as people tended to disbelieve children's accounts of sexual abuse. Depending on the age, location, and cultural norms of the societies in which they live, people have discovered methods to explain away the words and behaviors of sexually abused children. Florence Rush's work *The Best Kept Secret* analyzes and documents the ways in which sexual abuse has been ignored and even condoned by Jewish, Catholic, and Protestant cultures. She contends, for example, that many of the children tortured and murdered for consorting with the devil during the witch hunts in sixteenth-century Europe were actually sex abuse victims. Citing case after case of children who described being raped by the devil in the guise of a man, Rush concluded,

> In a society where sexual abuse went unhampered and people believed in evil spirits, it was not difficult to attribute a sexual offense to a supernatural spirit. . . . Victims of sexual abuse, without a recourse, found it simpler to blame or even believe that spectral demons rather than flesh and blood men had violated them.[18]

Adults accepted the children's interpretations and were bolstered by their ignorance of child psychology. During the Counter-Reformation, Nicholas Remy, prominent demonologist and Inquisitor, found "no lack of examples to prove that their age does not restrain children from committing deeds of witchcraft."[19] In his treatise on demonology he recorded the story of one young "witch":

> Although Catherine Latomia of Mache at Harcourt, February 1587, was not yet of an age to suffer a man, [the devil] twice raped her in prison being moved with hatred for her because he saw that she intended to confess her crime; and she very nearly died of the injuries she received from that coitus.[20]

Even the development of modern psychology did little to alter the distress of sexually abused children and adults who had been victimized in childhood. While there is still controversy surrounding the issue, many now acknowledge that Sigmund Freud and his disciples did much to denigrate child sexual abuse victims and to retard progress toward relieving their plight. Despite his indisputable contribution to the modern age, Freud either misunderstood or intentionally rejected evidence about sexual abuse of female children. Although he originally identified sexual abuse in childhood as the trauma leading to "hysteria" in his female patients, he—for reasons still being debated—later abandoned faith in their accounts. Despite considerable professional and private commitment to the seduction theory, which described seduction by fathers as essential to manifestations of hysteria, he turned instead to the Oedipal theory, which relieved incestuous fathers of guilt but incriminated female children. Rush points out the devastating effects of his reversal.

When Freud arrived at the seduction theory, he did so by listening carefully and intently to his female patients; when he arrived at his Oedipal theory, he did so by listening carefully and intently to himself. His monumental *Interpretation of Dreams* (1900), the result of self-analysis and the basis for all his later theories, came from *his* memories, *his* dreams and *his* experiences, and, unfortunately, *his* theories strongly bear the stamp of *his* personality and *his* time, sex and class. In his attempt to shape a particular personal conflict into a universal mold, he reverted from a cultural to a biological determination of neurosis. This shift was damaging to the female, for it was she, not the abuser, who bore the brunt of her own seduction. This so-called "seduction fantasy," this myth of incestuous wish for the father, became integral and inevitable to the woman's nature, and therefore, even if she had been actually assaulted, the problem was not the assault but the result of her innate compulsion to possess a penis. . . . Freud therefore cautioned the world never to overestimate the importance of seduction and the world listened to Freud and paid little heed to the sexual abuse of the young.[21]

Against all conflicting evidence about the pervasiveness of child sexual abuse and the trauma it inflicts, generations of psychologists, psychiatrists, and researchers have built upon Freud's theory. Nearly a half century before the *Los Angeles Times* poll, Alfred C. Kinsey reported in *Sexual Behavior in the Human Female* almost identical findings about the prevalence of sexual abuse of female children. In Kinsey's survey, one woman in four reported some sort of unwanted preadolescent sexual experience with an adult male. Amazed that 80 percent of his respondents expressed fear over their experiences, however, Kinsey rejected the validity of that fear and blamed those who supported the victims:

It is difficult to understand why a child, except for its cultural conditioning, should be disturbed by having its genitalia touched, or disturbed by seeing the genitalia of another person. . . . Some of the more experienced students of juvenile problems have come to believe that the emotional reactions of the parents, police and other adults . . . may disturb the child more seriously than the contacts themselves. The current hysteria over sex offenders may well have serious effects on the ability of many of these children to work out sexual adjustments some years later in their marriages.[22]

Startling as it now seems, Kinsey was not alone in denying the trauma of child sexual abuse. Psychiatrist Karl Menninger, another highly esteemed "authority," raised no public protest when he observed that adult-child sex relations are not often harmful and that "when the experience actually stimulates the child erotically, it would appear . . . that it may favor rather than inhibit the development of social capabilities and mental health in the so-called victims."[23]

Today we are less vulnerable to fears about demons and the supernatural. We are less ignorant about children and sexual abuse. Nevertheless, many still blame the victims, continuing to believe that seductive children—especially adolescents—account for the increasing reports of sexual activity between children and adults. The assumption that adolescents are responsible for most adult-child sexual interaction is not, however, supported by research. The American Humane Association defines the average age of child sexual abuse victims as 9.3 years. It reports that 27 percent of victims are 0–5 years old, 35 percent are 6–11, and 38 percent are between 12 and 17. Former victims responding to the *Los Angeles Times* poll indicated even younger ages for their first encounters with sexual abusers: 0–6 years, 14 percent; 7–12 years, 61 percent; and 13–18 years, 25 percent.

As Freud himself declared, age is no barrier to seductiveness, and thus child victims are caught in an impossible situation. They can do nothing against those who choose to view them as seductive. Children do like and need to be held, touched, and cuddled. They do respond readily to gestures of affection. They are willing to return love in unconditional, nonjudgmental ways. They are physically attractive; and if one wants to interpret their beauty as sexually stimulating, there is little the young can do to alter the perception. They do offer limited resistance to abusers, especially those they know and trust; and since only about 25 percent of perpetrators are strangers, children are in particularly vulnerable positions.[24]

Confronted with denial that rests upon either excusing the behavior as normal or blaming the victims, the public needs to be reminded of the ways in which normal men and women behave so that it can differentiate their responses to children from the behaviors of sexual abusers. Healthy adults are not stimulated to erotic activity by child beauty. Healthy adults do not molest children simply because children are demonstrative and like being touched. No matter how sexually frustrated they may be, healthy adults do not take advantage of children. Healthy adults are protective rather than abusive of children precisely because children seek and display affection so readily.

Their behaviors differ radically from those of child sexual abusers, who fabricate excuses to normalize the behavior or to blame the victim in order to alleviate or deny their own guilt. There are several models for describing perpetrators. One of the most often cited is that of A. Nicholas Groth, author of *Men Who Rape*.[25] He differentiates offenders into two categories: fixated and regressed. Groth's approach is somewhat similar to that of Park Elliot Dietz, whose typology is employed in *Child Molesters: A Behavioral Analysis for Law Enforcement Officers Investigating Cases of Child Sexual Exploitation,* a work published by the National Center for Missing and Exploited Children in conjunction with the FBI.[26] Dietz also divides offenders into two broad categories, situational and preferential, and then further subdivides the two groups. The preferential child molester is what people commonly refer to as a pedophile. He definitely prefers sex with children and often exhibits a need for frequent and repeated sexual activity with them. He becomes very adept at manipulating children. It is absolutely illogical to blame the victim of a pedophile because even if the child were sophisticated enough to try, he or she could do nothing to become less alluring to an individual who simply prefers sex with children.

Situational child molesters, in contrast, do not prefer child partners exclusively but become involved with them for varied reasons. Dietz subdivides this group into four categories: regressed, morally indiscriminate, sexually indiscriminate, and inadequate. In all cases the victims of situational child molesters are powerless to alter their fates. Regressed molesters take advantage of the child's availability. They probably prefer peer sex partners, but their self-esteem and coping skills are so limited that it is easier for them to coerce children. Thus any child who is available to serve as a substitute becomes a desirable partner. Similarly, the individual characteristics of the victim have little bearing on the inadequate molester, who is a social, psychological, or mental deviant who turns to children out of insecurity or curiosity. The code of the morally indiscriminate molester is, "Why not?" Sexual abuse of children is simply one aspect of a life pattern of abuse and experimentation; thus the abuse depends upon the perpetrator's urge and access to the child. Who the child is or what the child does is secondary. The same criteria apply to sexually indiscriminate molesters, who may nevertheless be morally discriminating in other areas. However, because children are considered off-limits by society, they are all the more attractive to this kind of offender, whose primary motivation is sexual experimentation; but again, the choice is made by the offender, not the child.

If offenders' motivations are so obviously divergent from the mainstream, why has denial of child sexual abuse flourished throughout history? One reason is, of course, that adults do not readily understand or trust children. Another, perhaps more significant, reason is that apart from their aberrant sexual activities, those who exploit children are not easily differentiated from the "normal" population. People prefer to think of child sexual abusers as "dirty old men" lurking in deserted buildings and alleys, but the truth is that they are teachers, lawyers, politicians, clergy, and judges as well as welfare recipients and alcoholics. Their only commonality is gender; adults who sexually exploit children are usually male.[27]

Even this indisputable fact has been perverted by some into a form of denial. A psychiatrist closely aligned with those who oppose legal reforms to protect child victims observes, "There's no question that this whole thing is mixed in with an anti-male bias. There's no question about it."[28] A California attorney also hostile to legal reform, contends that one "common thread" in "all" preschool sex abuse scandals is that "they're using female judges and female prosecutors."[29]

These statements are inaccurate, perhaps even absurd, when one considers that a large percentage of victims are male and that the majority of law enforcement personnel involved in child sexual abuse cases also are male. Furthermore, many women have been prosecuted for abuse and many others have lost custody of children because of their failure to oppose or report abuse by husbands or boyfriends.[30]

Child sexual abuse is a moral, not a gender issue, and despite centuries of indifference and denial, more people than ever before are willing to listen to victims and are capable of understanding them and their predicaments. This is true partly because the media have encouraged the public to recognize the plight of abused children.

In the United States, the process began with newspaper coverage of the case of Mary Ellen Wilson, a little girl severely abused by her guardians. Publicity about the child resulted in the 1874 founding of the Society for Prevention of Cruelty to Children in New York. Similar situations led to a sudden rise in the number of child protective societies, but the issue waned as emphasis on family rehabilitation grew. Professionals assumed that abused children were better off remaining with their natural parents and that effective reform for adult offenders and recovery for victims occurred most successfully if the family remained intact.

While valid in some respects, the family rehabilitation approach placed children at risk and allowed the public to deceive itself about the extent of child abuse. Teachers, doctors, and other professionals dealing with children often disregarded the symptoms of physical abuse either because they did not recognize them or because they knew little could be done for abused children. This era came to an end in 1962 when C. H. Kempe published "The Battered Child Syndrome" in the *Journal of the American Medical Association*.[31] Kempe's work resulted in the rediscovery of child abuse as a critical problem in American society, and subsequent studies revealed that it was far more widespread and less understood than most people imagined. The growth of interest in the issue was phenomenal.

In 1969 special attention was extended to child sexual abuse as a result of Vincent De Francis's survey of child sexual abuse victims and their families in New York City. Pioneering works like those of Kempe and de Francis were supplemented by media coverage and led ultimately to the passage of the federal Child Abuse and Neglect Prevention Act of 1974. Action against sexual abuse was incorporated into that legislation in 1978, and almost all states now have statutes concerning the offense.

In *Making an Issue of Child Abuse*, Barbara J. Nelson points out that during the decade prior to the Kempe article, all the relevant professions (medicine, law, education, and the social sciences) produced only 9 articles on child abuse. In the decade following Kempe's publication, 260 articles appeared, and during the 1980s there have been thousands of publications and media presentations on the issue. Nelson observes that public concern was finally aroused because the media "created and responded to the urgency over child abuse."[32]

Explicitly detailed stories about sexually abused children continue to raise the consciousness of American society. But if accounts in print seem removed from daily reality for most Americans, television brings child sexual abuse directly into their homes. The public has been educated by documentaries, talk shows, and made-for-television movies like "Adam" and "Something about Amelia." In addition, parents and schools have introduced a variety of preventive programs and materials to help children recognize, resist, and report sexual abuse. The results of this education process have been overwhelming. According to statistics released by the Child Welfare League of America, reports of child sexual abuse increased 58 percent from 1984 to 1986.[33]

Greater public awareness has resulted in much less indifference to the issue, and many Americans are now speaking out about the need for improvements in the ways in which child sexual abuse is treated in our society. Increased sophistication has also led to greater scrutiny and criticism of the legal system. Dissatisfaction with the system is documented in the *Los An-*

Question 32: Do you think that the laws we have on the books are adequate to deal with the problems of sexual abuse, or not?

| | Former Victims | | Nonvictims | |
	Men	Women	Men	Women
Yes	20%	16%	19%	20%
No	69%	69%	61%	59%
Not sure	11%	15%	19%	21%
Refused	0%	0%	1%	0%

Question 39: Sometimes in cases of childhood sexual abuse, innocent people are tried for crimes they did not commit. Other times, guilty people are never brought to trial. In your opinion, which of these two situations worries you the most?

| | Former Victims | | Nonvictims | |
	Men	Women	Men	Women
Innocent	23%	17%	25%	18%
Equal	14%	11%	14%	10%
Guilty	58%	68%	54%	66%
Not sure	4%	4%	7%	6%
Refused	1%	0%	0%	0%

Question 40: When children testify in court about sexual attacks, which do you think is more important: that the child who is testifying be protected from psychological damage, or that the legal rights of the defendant be protected?

	Former Victims		Nonvictims	
	Men	**Women**	**Men**	**Women**
Child	66%	81%	66%	79%
Both	16%	10%	16%	9%
Defendant	13%	4%	11%	5%
Not sure	3%	4%	7%	6%
Refused	2%	1%	0%	1%

geles Times survey, which reveals a startling mandate for change in the legal process—as is clear from the responses outlined above.

It is not difficult to understand why the public is concerned about the laws governing sexual abuse of children and about the treatment they receive in the legal system. Vincent de Francis's 1969 report provides insight into the frustrations confronting victims. Based on 256 documented cases of sexual abuse of children by 250 offenders, the analysis establishes that 76 of the cases were dropped because families found dealing with police processes too frightening for their children. After bringing formal charges, another 77 families dropped them once their children were exposed to the trauma of interrogations and court appearances. This left 97 out of 256 cases. The remaining victims found only limited redress in the courts. Of the 97 defendants, 39 were acquitted, their cases left pending, or escaped. This left 58 to be tried. Of these, 49 pleaded guilty to a lesser charge. Five of the 58 were sent to mental institutions, 5 received indeterminate sentences, 18 were sentenced to jail from six months to a year, and 30 received no jail sentences.

Why do so many families refuse to report sexual abuse of their children? Why do so many that do report the crime eventually withdraw charges? The answer is obvious. For most victims, confrontation with the legal system is a second and separate trauma, a process of revictimization. Families that turn to authorities for relief quickly discover that the judicial system is no haven for their children. The courts are likely to add insult to injury, agony to anguish. Parents who expose their children to the system overwhelmingly regret their decision because the legal process so often becomes as devastating a trauma as the sexual assault.

In *Reconstructing Reality in the Courtroom*, W. Lance Bennett and Martha S. Feldman advance a theory that clarifies the predicament of children.

Our search for the underlying basis of justice and judgment in American criminal trials has produced an interesting conclusion: the criminal trial is organized around storytelling. When people say that trials are an objective and impartial means of producing legal judgments, what they really mean is that trials rely on a standardized means of packaging and analyzing information: the story. . . . The courtroom is a classic example of a setting that places speakers of an elaborated (verbal) code at an advantage because of their ability to reconstruct information more broadly through stories. . . . There are two ways in which systematic bias might result from differences in storytelling practices. First, some people may lack shared cognitive routines for presenting information in story-coded forms. The inability to produce a conventional story would leave individuals vulnerable to having truthful accounts . . . rejected. Second, even the construction of a coherent story may not guarantee a just outcome if the teller and the audience do not share the norms, experiences, and assumptions necessary to draw connections on story elements.[34]

Bennett and Feldman analyze the ways in which race, class, and lifestyle differences unobtrusively but radically alter jurors' responses in criminal cases. Their emphasis is on the difficulties minorities and the poor encounter as defendants in trials, but their discussion is equally applicable to children. If minorities and the poor are disadvantaged because they speak different languages and reconstruct reality according to different social and intellectual norms than does the white middle class, how much worse off are children in such a system. With little social experience of any kind and limited verbal skills and cognitive development, many sexual abuse victims find it impossible to produce a "conventional story." A significant number of complaints never reach the courts because prosecutors fear that child witnesses will not be able to withstand the pressure of the courtroom. Many share the opinion of David Lloyd of the Children's Hospital National Medical Center in Washington, D.C., who contends that our criminal justice system was "designed in the year 1215 for adults accusing adults under the Magna Carta, not for children accusing adults."[35]

It takes months, and in some cases years, for child victims to traverse the maze of questionings and interviews, preliminary hearings, grand jury appearances, pretrial hearings, plea bargainings and delays before their cases actually come to trial. Again and again they are forced to repeat their stories, not comprehending that the defense lawyers are often trying to provoke or expose the slightest error in testimony—perhaps a minute discrepancy in time, place, or circumstance—that will help to disprove their experiences or at least place reasonable doubt in the minds of jurors. As Jerome Frank explains,

> The lawyer aims at victory, at winning in the fight, not at aiding the court to discover the facts. He does not want the trial court to reach a sound educated guess, if it is likely to be contrary to his client's interest. Our present trial method is thus the equivalent of throwing pepper in the eyes of a surgeon when he is performing an operation.[36]

Parents of the abused are more passionate in their condemnation of the way in which the legal system sometimes works. The mother of a four-year-old assaulted at a preschool observes:

I believe the criminal justice system failed my daughter and all the other children who were victimized. . . . I no longer have any faith in the system. I am very angry about the secondary victimization my child has experienced. As one of the children determined to be "courtworthy" (a condescending phrase that I absolutely hate!), my daughter was questioned on many occasions by investigators who were only interested in building a case, not in hearing what she had to say. Agencies involved in the investigation were not effectively coordinating interviews, which meant that she had to be questioned first by police, then by social service representatives and again by prosecutors. Telling her story over and over again was unnecessarily exhausting and left her with the impression that they doubted her word. On several occasions she had to wait a long time before her interview in rooms with no toys, food or other diversions. By the time investigators talked to her, she was tired, hungry and restless. Bear in mind that she was only four years old at the time and she was also scared to death. Investigators were not always prepared for the interview; for instance, on one occasion an interviewer had to leave the room to go get the anatomically correct dolls he should have had available from the outset.

The biggest obstacle for our daughter and our family, however, arose not from procedural errors but rather from the denial of investigators themselves. My child told her story as best she could, directly to investigators, to me, and in therapy, but no action was taken. Teachers were never arrested or prosecuted. The message this has given my little girl is that she was not believed. One of the threats used by her abusers to keep her silent was "No one will believe you." With the exception of her family and her therapist, the threat was true.

For the past two years we have lived in a state of suspended horror; we have had to listen to our child's accounts of abuse and torture that are almost too terrible to believe. But we believe it because we know a young child has no frame of reference from which to make such reports unless it is from actual experience. As parents, we had more reason than anyone to want to doubt our child's allegations of abuse. After all, we have more invested emotionally in wanting not to believe that these horrible things happened to our child.

It has been very difficult to accept the fact that the legal system will not acknowledge or address what happened to our child. Every agency we turned to let us down. We have a system that cannot or will not validate and support her. To experience that kind of victimization is to be left with a feeling of powerlessness; once again, we are unable to protect our child. The healing process for our child and our family has been severely hampered by the fact that we have encountered denial at every front.

Our daughter has been in therapy for over two years. She is making progress and has made an excellent adjustment to school. She is a straight-A student, popular with both her peers and her teachers. I believe that she will eventually lead a normal, productive life. But I know she will never be the same trusting person she was before she was abused and the system failed her. Neither will I.

When the fairness and methods of an institutional system are questioned, there are always those with political, economic, philosophical, and personal reasons to argue for its preservation and to reject reforms. As public concern about child sexual abuse has heightened, denial of the problem and resistance to legal reform have increased in some quarters. Indeed, there are even national and international organizations that advocate legalization of sex between children and adults. In the United States the Childhood Sensuality Circle (CSC), Better Life and Boy Love (BL), the North American Man-Boy Love Association (NAMBLA), and the René Guyon Society defend the rights of adults to child-adult sex.[37]

These organizations have motivations that are quite different from those of VOCAL, Victims of Child Abuse Legislation, a group which claims to be composed of several thousand people falsely accused of child molestation and abuse. VOCAL and its supporters oppose legal reform and, to some extent, public education about child sexual abuse. Many of their arguments are variations on the denial approach; others are more sophisticated.

Perhaps VOCAL's least credible contention is that there is a child sexual abuse industry financially dependent upon discovery, prosecution, and conviction of offenders. The view that innocent people are being destroyed in vast numbers by bureaucrats and politicians seeking to score "points toward a promotion, a pay raise, or a federal grant" is developed in *The Politics of Child Abuse*. This book contains primarily remarks by child sexual abuse defendants, their relatives, and attorneys and records a series of personal attacks on professionals working with child victims. One attorney quoted in the book contends:

> These people [working with victims] are afraid of losing money. The real explosion [in reporting of child abuse] is related to money. It took a few years for it to crank up, but with all this money going into the system, that's what makes the social workers so anxious to start new cases. It's their job that's on the line. . . . And then you have the ripple effect. [The social workers] send [children] to one of their favorite agencies or doctors, some of whom—without mentioning any names—have a reputation among attorneys doing juvenile law, as being *professional child abuse finders*. . . . And these agencies then make a lot of money from the

county. They not only get paid per case or per child, but they get grants!
. . . Look for the profit motive if you really want to know what this thing
is all about. Most of these schools carry liability insurance of one million
dollars per child. And all these militant parents are pushing and pressur-
ing the District Attorney's office to convict these people so they can sue
for millions.[38]

The facts belie these claims. Social workers' jobs are hardly "on the line"
because they lack work. From the largest cities to the most remote rural
areas, social workers are overworked and underpaid. The 58 percent increase
in reports of child sexual abuse over a two-year period demonstrates only one
facet of the ever-increasing demand on their time and energy. The vast majority of social workers are civil service employees whose salaries are constant
and not affected by caseloads or grants; the annual minimum salary recommended by the National Association of Social Workers for a beginning
professional with a bachelor of social work degree was $20,000, and many do
not receive that much.

The physicians treating sexually abused children are usually pediatricians. They too are in short supply relative to the demand for their services,
and they are among the lowest paid of medical specialists. Pediatricians
charge their patients, including sexual abuse victims, fees. The decision to
accept pay for court appearances is personal; but physicians who do so usually suffer loss of revenue because their fees are seldom commensurate with
those they receive for treating several children per hour in their offices.

Grants are not avenues to personal wealth; grant revenue generally goes
to institutions that can prove their needs in exacting detail and account for
every dollar they spend. Grants are always precarious sources of income and
most last no longer than three years, an inadequate amount of time to study
long-term consequences on human subjects. In 1990 the total expenditure on
research and program development by the National Center on Child Abuse
and Neglect, the federal government's primary agency for assisting state
efforts to address abuse and neglect, was only $20 million.

Unfortunately, contrary to the argument in the *Politics of Child Abuse*,
the "agencies" or special treatment centers for child sexual abuse victims are
far from numerous. Even the most prestigious operate on a relatively small
scale. For example, the Kempe National Center for the Prevention and
Treatment of Child Abuse and Neglect is located in an old house near the
campus of the University of Colorado School of Medicine, with which it is
affiliated. The center diagnoses only 400–600 cases per year at the university's hospital; it runs a diagnosis and treatment program for twelve to fifteen
families per month, a preschool for ten to twelve children, and a third-party
treatment group for another ten to twelve children. It provides approximately 500 case consultations, processes approximately 5,000 information

calls, and maintains a forensic group that deals with approximately 100 serious crimes against children per year. The center administers the Adolescent Perpetrators Work Network, runs a pilot program for the treatment of adolescent perpetrators, and houses the National Association of Counsel for Children and the International Society for the Prevention of Child Abuse, which publishes the journal *Child Abuse and Neglect*. The center has fourteen to thirty employees, depending upon its funding—90 percent of which derives from private contributions, contracts, and occasional federal grants. The other 10 percent of its funding comes from the state of Colorado because the center is affiliated with the University of Colorado Hospital. The budget of the Kempe Center has never exceeded $1.2 million a year. On occasion, it has been able to anticipate only sixty days of remaining operating expenses. If the "profit motive" drives employees of the Kempe Center, they are apparently easily satisfied. Some do, of course, provide consulting services for which they receive at most $750 a day, $500 of which they must return to the center to help maintain it.

The "militant parents" hoping to "sue for millions" are virtually unknown to professionals in the field of child sexual abuse. Almost no families bring law suits in civil courts; instead they seek redress in criminal courts where they may gain protection and punishment, but not money. While an occasional action has been brought against institutions where children have been abused, there have been few major settlements on behalf of children. Until the very recent developments discussed in Chapter 7, the largest award in a child sexual abuse civil law suit was $10,000.

Another defense used by opponents of legal reform and better education is that as the public grows increasingly sensitive to the issue, children will suffer because adults will become too apprehensive to maintain close contact with them. It sounds like a rational argument, and occasionally there will be a letter to Ann Landers or a newspaper or television interview that lends this argument support. Nevertheless, research indicates that the vast majority of Americans are not intimidated by new knowledge about child sexual abuse and that they do not believe it has altered their behaviors with children.

The *Los Angeles Times* poll asked, "Has all the talk about child sexual abuse nowadays made you change the way you treat children? For example, do you find that you are less likely to want to be alone with other people's children, or to offer to babysit, or don't you hug children as much as you used to, or are you careful how you hold children, or are you less likely to help a lost child, or to smile at children you don't know? Have any of those things happened to you—or other things similar to that?" Eighty-five percent replied that their treatment of children had not changed.

Similarly unsubstantiated upon close examination is the claim that there is somehow a parallel between current concern over child sexual abuse and witch hunts of previous historical eras. The only similarity is the presence of children making accusations against protesting adults; and even here the parallel is limited, since most child sexual abuse victims do not eagerly disclose their plights.

The witch-hunt analogy does not work for several other reasons. In the past people became hysterical about witches because ignorance and lack of education led them to believe in a nonexistent evil, whereas current concern about child sexual abuse results from increased education and sophisticated research, and a growing body of medical and psychological proofs that validate the existence of a very real evil. Witch hunts flourished because the authoritative force of society, the Church, encouraged them and supported the accusers. In our society, however, validation of child sexual abuse victims has occurred despite the failure of our authoritative force, the legal system, to encourage the accusers. Witches were tortured, hanged, and burned. Child abusers are rarely reported to authorities, and those who are seldom see the inside of a jail or even a psychiatrist's office. National statistics on child sexual abuse indicate, for example, that judges see only 15.4 percent of sexual abuse cases.[39]

From one perspective, however, the analogy may be distressingly apt. Witch hunts occurred because the priority for those in power was to establish guilt or innocence rather than to engage in an open, methodical search for truth. The question our society has yet to answer is whether our commitment to our symbols of authority is any less blind than the loyalties and prejudices of our predecessors, whether we too will deny justice and allow people to suffer because of our own misunderstanding of our legal traditions.

Opponents of child abuse legislation argue that innocent people are being punished because of false allegations by children. But a major purpose of the new legislation is to provide better means of communicating with child witnesses to help assure more informed judgments about their veracity. Once an accusation is made, it is vital to an innocent suspect that the system use every means possible to communicate with and encourage responses from the accuser. The reforms—using anatomically correct dolls and hand puppets in questioning children, allowing children to be seated on the laps of trusted caretakers, permitting them to be questioned via closed circuit television or by an impartial court representative—do not threaten the innocent. They facilitate discovery of truth.

A child intimidated into silence by the traditional court process is a far greater danger to an innocent defendant than is one who communicates confusion or untruth. Silence can be interpreted as fear of the defendant when it may, in reality, be reluctance of the child to be trapped in a lie. The best defense against false allegations by children is implementation of procedures that will increase their participation in the legal process. To establish that the innocent are being persecuted because of malicious stories from devious children, one must first allow the children to tell their stories; and if the telling is contingent upon puppets or laps or even a television camera, it is preferable to little or no testimony at all.

There is also no validity to the claim by VOCAL and other opponents of legal reform that attention to child victims' rights somehow threatens the constitutional rights of defendants. Child advocates have not argued that American courts should abandon traditional protections for defendants. Responsible professionals have not advocated rejecting the constitutional principle that the accused is innocent until proven guilty. They have not maintained that defendants be denied the right to confront their accusers. They have argued only that sometimes in order to facilitate discovery of truth, confrontation of a child must occur in ways not usually employed in courtrooms. Child advocates have not maintained that hearsay evidence should be admitted to give special favor to children in sexual abuse cases. They have argued only that most hearsay properly should be allowed under traditional rules and enlightened interpretation of evidence law. Respect for the rights of child victims does not limit the rights of defendants; it helps to balance the scales of justice so that the system can foster the quest for truth.

The legal and judicial profession has recognized the need for greater equity between children and defendants. In its publication *Deprived Children: A Judicial Response*, the Metropolitan Court Judges Committee, comprising judges from the nation's forty largest cities, asserts,

A child's physical or mental health can be threatened through . . . the insensitivity of rigid legal or administrative systems which have no regard for delay as a detrimental impact upon a child's life. The justice system tends to be over-formalized at the expense of the child victim.

Sensitivity to the needs of child victims, evidentiary and procedural reforms, specially trained attorneys and court workers, special volunteers, priority for abuse cases, reasonable caseloads and victim and family participation in the disposition of cases are required. The judicial process must reflect a greater awareness of the child as a child, and the child's treatment and service needs. . . .

All judges of all courts must ensure sensitivity in the courtroom and encourage sensitivity out of the courtroom to minimize trauma to the child victim. . . . The legal system must treat children with special courtesy, respect and fairness. Judges must work with attorneys, law enforcement, child protection agencies and state and local funding sources to improve facilities, services, and procedures affecting children who appear in court.[40]

In a 1986 issue of the *Juvenile and Family Court Journal* devoted to child sexual abuse, Judge L. G. Arthur observes "It has been said that 'the court is the second trauma.'" He then argues that this is true of the system as a whole, not just the courtroom itself:

> The system may interview the child time and again, each time making her relive the experience, keeping the wound open. It may force her down to court waiting rooms where she sits uncomfortably without even the accoutrements of a dentist's office for hours . . . often to be told that the case [has been] continued and to come back next week. She may be put on a witness stand, in a big formal room, with what seems like a thousand eyes staring at her, and a bailiff in full uniform ready to lock her up, and a judge in a black robe towering above her. She may find that the newspapers and television are full of her name and pictures and stories about what happened to her which they obtained from the official records.
>
> The system is always more concerned with the well-being of the criminals than of the victims. When children are the victims, surely change can be made.[41]

Change must be made. We have come too far in our knowledge about the crime, about its victims, and about the perpetrators to accept and perpetuate the false assumptions of the past. The legal system is not a fixed reality. It was never intended to be inflexible. At the very heart of the American experience lies the conviction that when laws and traditions are unjust, they must be changed. That theme dominates our legal traditions from the Declaration of Independence to the Constitutional Convention to countless Supreme Court decisions and reminds us—indeed, requires us—to reexamine our laws to assure that they provide justice for all. We cannot forsake that history; if in our passion to protect one individual's rights, we ignore those of another, especially those of a child, we cannot claim to be a just society.

2

Yesterday and Today: A Brief History of Children in the Courts

"I don't know what you mean by your *way," said the Queen. "All the ways about here belong to* me—*but why did you come here at all?"*

—Lewis Carroll,
*Through the Looking Glass
and What Alice Found There*

DON'T talk to me about the legal system," says a father whose five-year-old daughter was raped by a neighbor. "I know all about the legal system. The legal system lets the guy who used to live next door get up and leave the house every morning after we've been up all night dealing with [Jenny's] nightmares. He saw a psychiatrist once a week for six months, and now life is back to normal for him. [Jenny's] been in therapy for years, we had to move across town because she was so afraid he'd come and get her, and sometimes I think she'll never be able to lead a happy life. That's the way the legal system protected us."

How did we reach a point where America's cherished legal system has become an enemy of a five-year-old rape victim? Stinging critiques of the system are as familiar on television talk shows as they are in lengthy scholarly treatises. Citizens, social critics, and journalists locate injustice in the very place where justice should be pursued. The critique is predictable: courtroom justice is a "sometimes thing" in which conservative rich men make the rules and play the game for the benefit of conservative rich men. The rest—elderly, poor, women, minorities, and children—are powerless.

Nevertheless, implicit in that angry critique is a measure of hope. Our impatience and outrage with the system's treatment of child victims reflects an ironic optimism: courts, of all places, should provide justice for children; and when they fail to do so, courts, of all places, can and should change. Beneath the frustration and despair that child advocates endure lies an awareness that courts sometimes *do* provide justice for the powerless. More than any other American institution, courts have become the great equalizer—the place where the powerless have gained power. Journalism, literature, television, and movies offer daily accounts of the underdog succeeding in court: the individual battling the corporation; the innocent gaining acquittal; the civil rights plaintiff, ignored or denied everywhere else, winning before judge or jury. Thus child advocates steadfastly refuse to write off the criminal justice system.

Of course, they really have no alternative. Where else would they turn? Whatever the inadequacies of the system, the courtroom remains the one place where children can hope to have society validate their claims and redress the wrongs they have suffered. The child advocates striving for change in the legal system, however enraged they may seem, are really reformers at heart. Most are not advocating abolition of the system but are expressing frustration over faith betrayed.

Increasingly they are discovering that they are not alone, that people do hear children and do care enough to demand reform. Gail Goodman, a professor of psychology and law at the University of Denver, observes, "Courts and legislatures are now reassessing the laws that govern child witnesses and looking to psychologists, psychiatrists, attorneys, and social workers for information and advice. The openness of the contemporary justice system to social science research, in addition to its concern for the rights of victims as well as the accused, has helped spark new interest in the child witness."[1] Like Goodman, Lucy Berliner and Mary Kay Barbieri, social workers at the Sexual Assault Center in Seattle, believe that the legal system can be adapted to meet the needs of sexually abused children: "We argue that the current system is out of balance in ways that do not always do full justice to the interests of the child victim/witness. The imbalance needs to be redressed, and we believe it can be done in ways that do not seriously threaten the legitimate interests of the other parties."[2]

To locate that balance, we might begin by asking why the courts have succeeded in serving the interests of some at the same time they have ignored and failed others. There is nothing to be gained from attacking the system for its historic biases. They existed. We cannot deny them, and our anger cannot change them. While it at first seems valid to evaluate courts as institutions with hostility toward children, it may be more accurate to view that seeming hostility as an unintended result of courts' original adult-designed purposes.

Despite the complex and elaborate history of the American legal system, its immediate and most influential ancestor is clearly identifiable. The roots of American law are heavily entrenched in English common law, which Lawrence Friedman has described as "utterly obsessed by two central topics: formal legal process and the law relating to land."[3] In *A History of American Law,* he goes on to note:

A second's thought tells one, however, that these two topics could not have been *all* of the living law of England, any more than the life of great lords could have been the life of everyone in England. Common law was, essentially, the law of the royal central courts. Common law handled the legal problems of a tiny group of people. . . . It was an aristocratic law, for and of the gentry and nobility. The masses were hardly touched by this system and only indirectly under its rule. There was law on the manor—law that controlled the common people and bound them to their betters. This was largely subterranean law and made little impact on the treatises. Lawbooks were written at the seat of power; they dealt with the king's kind of law. Day-to-day law of the lower orders was barely chronicled.[4]

Children, even those of the gentry and nobility, were in a very real sense among the "lower orders" in early British society. Most of their day-to-day problems lay far beyond the scope of common law, and the absence of interest in children that characterized British common law continued in the colonies.

Historical examination of the American legal system reveals little about children in the courts. What it does disclose is that they had no role. They were never expected to be a force in the legal system. Even when their existence was acknowledged in court records, it was for reasons related to the status or welfare of adults. For example, proceedings of the county court of Prince Georges County, Maryland, on November 24, 1696, mention children three times. In the first case George Hutcheson, impoverished because of physical disability, requested that he be "excused . . . from paying his leavye" because he received only "a poore maintenance in teaching of Children to reade." In the second James Paine, a seven-year-old, was with his father's consent bound as an apprentice until he reached twenty-one. And in the third instance, a grand jury convened and made presentments against a servant woman, Elizabeth Pole, "for haveing a bastard."[5]

Added to the habitual indifference to children were the practical realities governing development of a legal system in a new country. Like their English counterparts, American courts originally existed for two purposes: to settle disputes and to redress wrongs.[6] A young society divided into states with widely divergent cultures and economies needed an efficient, nonviolent forum for resolving differences among citizens. The commerce of a growing nation depended on business knowing that contracts could be written and honored or could be satisfied through legal action. Thus the actors, or the "consumers," of the American court system were (1) those of legal status (adults, not children); (2) those with legal interests recognized by society (white male property owners, not children); and (3) those who, on their own behalf or through lawyers, could express their interests in courts (the articulate and the wealthy, not children).

The second function of the courts was to provide a nonviolent method for redressing wrongs, a way to ensure public safety without relying on "frontier justice." With a Constitution that pledged to "promote justice" and ensure "domestic tranquility" for the new nation, America's courts concentrated on acts that most obviously endangered public safety and offered the best potential for arousing community outrage. Crimes like theft and burglary became important because they threatened fundamental privacy and property interests. Readily perceived and reported, such property crimes allowed for relatively easy investigation and prosecution since thieves and burglars often were caught in the act or discovered with stolen property. Most confessed or pleaded guilty, obviating the need for a trial and thus efficiently providing the community with displays of contrition that were important to the emerging social order.

In his study of crime in Puritan America, Kai Erikson observes that during periods of community creation or change, crime serves an essential function, with confessions or guilty pleas providing important confirmation of emerging social values:

> The deviant act . . . creates a sense of mutuality among the people of a community by supplying a focus for group feeling. Like a war, a flood, or some other emergency, deviance makes people more alert to the interests they share in common and draws attention to those values which constitute the "collective conscience" of the community. Unless the rhythm of group life is punctuated by occasional moments of deviant behavior, . . . social organization would be impossible.[7]

Child sexual abuse could supply no comparable "focus for group feeling." It lacked all the "advantages" of theft or burglary. It did not threaten obvious community interests. It was not easily perceived, understood, or reported by the victim or witnesses. People did not assume that its dangers could move beyond the neighbor's house to endanger them. Apprehension of offenders was virtually impossible. Evidence, before development of the forensic sciences, was almost nonexistent. And with little or no concrete proof, confessions or guilty pleas would have been rare.

Thus recognition of child sexual abuse provided no apparent advantages to an emerging society. Reporting, apprehension, and trial of sexual abusers would contribute nothing to the developing country. Moreover, in a nation struggling to reconcile its diverse cultural and religious traditions and to locate the proper place for God in government, such a "moral wrong" was not necessarily appropriate for redress in the public forum. Sexual abuse, if it was known at all, was a private offense not to be aired before strangers in public courtrooms.

In settling disputes and redressing wrongs, children almost never had anything to do with the courts. They were not needed, were not relevant, and could not contribute anything to arguments before the courts. The courts did not set out to ignore children, but rather, to pay attention to those who were their primary consumers. More than one hundred years passed before children became legal consumers, and even then the results were ironic.

In 1899, America's first juvenile court was established in Chicago. "Regarded as 'one of the greatest advances in child welfare that has ever occurred,' the juvenile court . . . system was part of a general movement directed toward removing adolescents from the criminal law process and creating special programs for delinquent, dependent, and neglected children."[8] An integral part of the "progressive" agenda, juvenile court legislation was enacted in all but three states by 1917. Most social and legal historians view the foundation of these courts as one of the nation's stunning accomplishments, providing children with protection and opportunity previously unavailable in the legal system.

Reformers believed that separation of children from the adult justice system was critical for three reasons: (1) Children committed crimes not from a sense of evil or malice, but rather from a sense of need. A child's crime was an expression of pain, a signal that something was not right with the individual or family. The child needed help, not criminal court punishment. (2) Children suffering abuse or neglect might have to be removed from the family, an action that required special procedures to evaluate the circumstances of the family and the needs of the child in order to balance their respective rights. (3) Those responsible for decisions about delinquent, abused, or neglected children should have the special inclination and expertise needed to understand the young.

While social reformers were sincere in these beliefs, other, less altruistic, motivations also influenced the establishment of juvenile courts:

> The efforts to establish juvenile courts . . . in the early twentieth century were part of a broader social movement. . . . The juvenile court served not only as a symbolic proving ground but as a literal dumping ground. It was the place where children and parents landed who could not, despite much institutional revamping in their behalf, perform in the larger society on terms the reformers considered acceptable.[9]

Steven Schlossman concludes from this that the juvenile court movement "was ill-conceived in its main objectives."[10] Anthony Platt reaches a similar conclusion: "Although the child savers were rhetorically concerned with protecting children from the physical and moral dangers of an increasingly industrialized and urban society, their remedies seemed to aggravate the problem."[11]

However one assesses the success or failure of this innovation in the nation's justice system, one ironic result is clear. The existence of juvenile courts encouraged the exclusion of children from adult criminal courts even when children needed to be there. Juvenile courts allowed child abuse and sexual assault to remain behind closed doors. With the best intentions of preserving confidentiality for the child, juvenile courts became the only American courts to require closed proceedings. The fundamental American concept of open courts was compromised so that troubled children and families could address their problems uninhibited by a curious public or probing press.

Juvenile courts became "anti-legal" in that they "encouraged minimum procedural formality and maximum dependency on extra-legal resources."[12] Proponents believed that they worked best when they moved toward a medical model in which the judge searched for all circumstances affecting the condition of the child/patient.[13] In addition, the judge's role could be reduced by the preventive "nursing" efforts of juvenile probation staff.

> The creation of juvenile courts altered the nature and purpose of courtroom appearances for children. Indeed, if possible, the child was to be kept out of court entirely. . . . The probation officer, it was expected, would obviate judicial intervention by resolving many difficulties with the personal advice and services he offered, and by mediating between the child's family and available . . . resources in the community.[14]

Thus, without intending to do so, the juvenile courts prevented child sexual abuse from coming to public view. Although they provided the first formal intervention in cases of abuse or neglect, they did so by conceding that most of these were family problems, not crimes. The irony was that these courts designed to protect children also protected those who abused them.

Abusers benefited in two ways. First, and most obvious, they enjoyed confidentiality. The law prohibited disclosure of juvenile court proceedings even when neighbors or relatives might have been able to protect children had they known the identity of the abuser. (Even in the 1980s, when some jurisdictions have relaxed confidentiality rules to allow journalists to cover juvenile courts, disclosure is limited to "what happened," rather than "who." Elaborate statutes or court orders assure that media use no names or descriptive data that could identify those in court.)[15] Less apparent but more significant is the fact that once juvenile courts became the primary place for child abuse cases, adult criminal courts could ignore the issue.

Thus, on the one hand, the juvenile court system benefits the sexually abused child. It protects the child's privacy; and if physical and circumstantial evidence clearly demonstrate that a family member has assaulted a child too young to identify the offender, juvenile laws and courts afford protection for the victim. The child can be removed from the home with proof that sexual abuse has occurred, despite absence of proof to identify the abuser beyond a reasonable doubt. Moreover, if it feels shielded from criminal prosecution, the family may identify the abuser within the confidential proceedings of the court.

On the other hand, when cases are handled in this way, the criminal justice system can deceive itself. It avoids sensitive, unsavory, embarrassing offenses because they are handled elsewhere, quietly. In that sense, the Schlossman critique seems less cynical and more incisive: "Most striking to me in retrospect is the superficiality of the 'progressive' viewpoint [toward juvenile courts]. Advocates generally ignored or hedged basic questions: What is punishment? What is rehabilitation? . . . What is crime?"[16] The establishment of juvenile courts inadvertently allowed child sexual abuse to continue as serious and unfortunate "incidents" handled with psychology, social work, and only a bit of law. As a result, sexual abuse of children did not have to be aired in open, public courts. It did not have to be called "crime."

In the late 1970s, however, greater awareness of the dangers of child sexual abuse pushed it to the fore of America's consciousness. In part, heightened sensitivity to child victims was the result of dramatic and unprecedented social forces that altered the life styles of Americans and their children. Some of those forces had been building gradually for years; but for most, their impact came with extraordinary power and speed. And it was only a matter of time before they blended to produce new sets of court consumers and a new outcry over the legal rights of children.

One of the most significant forces was the changing character of the family. Until the 1960s, Americans considered divorce an exception to the rule of normal family life. A painful acknowledgment of failure, divorce was relatively rare for many reasons, including the emotional costs it exacted from spouses, extended family, and most of all, children. But the frequency of divorce and attitudes about divorce quickly changed. Prior to 1965, there were approximately 2 divorces per 1,000 people. By 1979, the rate increased to 5.2 per 1,000, the highest in the world.[17] More than two million children are now involved in divorce every year; and by 1990, it is predicted, only 40 percent of American children will live their entire childhoods with both natural parents.[18] In *The Divorce Revolution*, Lenore Weitzman notes that the more normal divorce appears, the more acceptable it becomes: "The divorce revolution is the culmination of three trends: more people are getting divorced, divorce has become more socially acceptable than ever before, and more states have no-fault divorce laws. Each of these trends intensifies the effect of the others. Together, they have transformed both the perception and the reality of divorce in our society."[19]

Family courts were originally established to consider whether and under what conditions the marital contract should end. They analyzed the basis for divorce, attempted to place blame, determined property division, alimony, child custody, support, and visitation. Suddenly that changed. No-fault divorce law came to California in 1970 and spread throughout the country by 1980, transforming family courts "from a position of protecting marriage (by restricting marital dissolution) to one of facilitating divorce."[20]

Just as suddenly, custody of children was no longer a foregone conclusion. Fathers, as well as mothers, love their children and want that love recognized and confirmed by the law. Automatic presumption of custody for mothers gave way to a standard that stressed the best interests of the child. Joint custody emerged as a common legal option, and contested custody became a painful but frequent reality in the courts. The transformation was captured in the 1979 Academy Award-winning movie *Kramer vs. Kramer.* Fighting to keep his six-year-old son, Ted Kramer pleads to the judge:

My ex-wife says that she loves Billy, and I believe she does. But I don't think that's the issue here. If I understand it correctly, what means the most here is what's best for our son—what's best for Billy. My wife used to always say to me, "Why can't a woman have the same ambition as a man?" I think you're right, and maybe I've learned that much. But by the same token I'd like to know, what law is it that says that a woman is a better parent simply by virtue of her sex? . . . What is it that makes somebody a good parent? You know, it has to do with constancy; it has to do with patience; it has to do with listening to him; it has to do with pretending to be listening to him when you can't even listen any more. It has to do with love. . . . And I don't know where it's written that says that a woman has a corner on that market . . . that a man has any less of these emotions than a woman does.[21]

With reluctance and feelings of inadequacy, judges began listening not only to the Ted Kramers but also to their children. Divorce had changed families, but it had also altered the courts. More and more, judges were compelled to ask, "Would you rather live with Mom or Dad?" Whether they liked it or not, and despite the fact that almost no one wanted it, children were empowered in court.

With divorce came new life styles for children that exposed them to more outsiders and potentially threatening circumstances. Through the 1960s, children with working mothers were often considered victims of family misfortune for whom special day-care or after-school arrangements were required. But in the 1980s, "latch-key" children and day-care centers were common. In 1950, only 11 percent of women with preschool children worked outside the home; by 1980, that figure had risen to 43 percent.[22] Divorce was not, of course, the only force responsible for the increase in working mothers. A changing national economy forced married mothers, often against their wills, out of the home and into the work force; others, influenced by feminism, determined to combine careers and parenting; and still others chose to have children without marrying.

Almost overnight there appeared a new norm—the working parent. Television, the mirror of American values, recorded the transition. Shows like "My Three Sons," "Bachelor Father," "One Day at a Time," and "Kate and Allie" portrayed the single, working parent with fascination and admiration. "Family Ties" and "The Cosby Show" romanticized working parents successfully combining careers and family. Even surrogate parental figures—from a British butler ("Mr. Belvedere") to an alien life form ("Alf") led some of television's nontraditional families. In fact, of the sixty-eight regular TV series in 1986, only three depicted the traditional nuclear family.[23] The Nelsons, Cleavers, Andersons, Petries, and Flintstones of earlier years were history.

On television these new familial arrangements always work. Children are never neglected; they are never confused and unhappy for longer than thirty minutes; and in the end love, understanding, and harmony sustain them and their families. Real life is quite different. With the phenomenon of the working parent came new demands and new compromises. In a society unprepared to cope with the enormous influx of mothers of young children into the work force, something had to give—or rather, someone had to give up something. With employers offering little flexibility in job demands and hours, parents had little choice but to leave employment behind, or leave their children behind with others. Their children, however, were not consulted. Children's time with friends, recreation, lessons, and most important, parents was compromised; and American society, in order to accommodate the social and economic demands of a new era, established a haphazard network of facilities and programs—some excellent, some dismal—to care for children. Infants and toddlers filled day-care centers. School-age children found themselves in after-school programs. Responsibility and exposure came early and sometimes at great cost.

During roughly the same period, unprecedented numbers of poor teenage children were having their own children. Unmarried, uneducated, unemployed, and emotionally immature, these teenagers were now attempting to be parents. Abuse and neglect of infants and toddlers increased so rapidly that, in some states, social workers could not even respond to cases within twenty-four hours, as required by law. They described the problem of teen pregnancy and resulting child abuse as "mammoth" and "overwhelming." One county social worker told of an eleven-year-old mother and thirty-four-year-old grandmother, "You ask them if they tuck little Joey in at night and they look at you like you're crazy. Those words don't mean anything to them." Another social worker explained, "I say, 'Does your mother tell you she loves you?' They've never heard those words before.' "[24]

By 1983, in many parts of the country for the first time, the birth rate of single women exceeded 50 percent. From 1981 to 1985, reported child abuse in America increased at unprecedented rates almost everywhere—445 percent in Arizona, 137 percent in Mississippi, 142 percent in Ohio, 367 percent in Oregon, 196 percent in Rhode Island. The actual numbers are even more frightening—for example, there were 18,000 substantiated cases of abused and neglected children in Wisconsin from 1985 to 1987, many involving sexual abuse.[25] While increased reporting undoubtedly accounts for some of the increase, child protection social workers relate most of that reporting to actual increases in child abuse and neglect, often in families with poor, young, unmarried parents.

Whether their working parents were unavailable to assure their protection, or their young, impoverished parents were unable to meet their needs, America's children became more vulnerable. In their own homes or day-care centers, during day or night or latch-key hours, with parents, sitters, or strangers, children were, as never before, likely to be witnesses to or victims of crime; and the courts could no longer afford to ignore them.

Although the legal system was increasingly compelled to acknowledge the presence of children, the courts remained ill-equipped to deal with child witnesses and victims. Since the original concerns of the criminal justice system were public offenses that threatened property rights, which usually involved clear-cut evidence, criminal courts had become settings for guilty pleas and sentencings rather than trials, and they had little need for testimony from victims—adults or children. In the 1970s the power of the women's movement produced radical changes in the character of the criminal justice system and forced courts to respond to victims of the most sensitive crimes. First rape victims and then battered women demanded their day in court; and the courts had to adjust in ways that would have an enormous impact on child victims of sexual abuse.

In its emotional impact, rape is perhaps the most complete humiliation and injustice to women, and feminists knew that the legal system had never adequately grasped that reality. Consequently, one of their major objectives was to force Americans to confront the truth about rape, rapists, and their victims. To this end, feminism exposed the worst inequities and absurdities in the legal system; and in responding to the outcry of women, the courts began to lay foundations for the treatment of sexually abused children.

Feminists changed America's view of rape by convincing the criminal justice system that the subjects of rape were tragic victims of violence rather than of their own sexual proclivities. They forced police and prosecutors to recognize that rapists must be prosecuted and incarcerated, no matter how difficult the investigation and trial. And they helped police and prosecutors understand that a rape victim requires support and sensitivity in order to withstand the delays, inconvenience, and trauma of court.

In rape cases prosecutors confronted crimes that were not public, did not involve property, had no witnesses other than the victims, and had few defendants willing to confess. As more women sought redress in the courts, authorities became increasingly aware of the plight of the victims. They discovered that preparation and counseling of victims, who would have to detail their experiences before judges, juries, and rapists, were essential if they were to succeed in court. The humiliations suffered by the relatively few rape victims who had braved the criminal justice system in the past were a secret no longer. Police and prosecutors gradually realized that the criminal justice and court systems had produced further victimization, and that fair and strong prosecution of rape would require alterations in both the form and substance of the criminal justice system and trial procedures.

Across the country, legislatures and courts responded. In the 1970s and 1980s, they constructed the framework on which fairer trials could be built. To many women it all seemed too little too late, but changing laws did reflect greater understanding of the myths that had prevented conviction of the guilty. Police, prosecutors, and judges became more aware of the emotional devastation of the victim who, for the first time, gained support essential to persevering through a trial.

To reduce the victim's courtroom exposure and trauma, some state laws closed rape trials to the public during the victim's testimony. Others prohibited news media from revealing the victim's identity. To rape victims and their advocates, these "innovations" reflected nothing more than common sense. Without them, many victims would not testify. Still, the apparent logic and simplicity of these laws should not suggest that they were merely mild intrusions into legal tradition. Indeed, by restricting public and media access to the trial, they were the first, sweeping compromise of the Sixth Amendment's guarantee of the right to a "public trial . . . in all criminal prosecutions."

State legislatures also enacted significant laws reflecting better understanding of rape. Recognizing that it was a crime of violence, not sexual passion, legislators came to understand that a victim could not "have asked for it." Accordingly, many states closed the evidentiary door to the most common and unfair line of victim cross-examination: prior sexual activity.[26] No longer could defense attorneys expose a victim's sexual history in order to persuade a jury that because she had had sexual relations with more than one man, her account of rape could not be trusted.

Just as the laws had previously assumed that prior sexual experience or promiscuity led to rape, it had insisted that victims resist and suffer physical injury to prove they had not consented. The women's movement confronted that myth, and the laws again changed. In 1986, for example, the California Supreme Court reversed a trial court decision that failed to apply the more enlightened view implemented by California law in 1980. Rejecting the "resistance requirement" imposed on rape victims, the Court explained the basis for its decision:

> The requirement that a woman resist her attacker appears to have been grounded in the basic distrust with which courts . . . traditionally viewed a woman's testimony regarding sexual assault. . . .
>
> This distrust was formalized in the law in several areas. . . . For example, juries were traditionally advised to be suspect and cautious in evaluating a rape complainant's testimony, particularly where she was "unchaste." . . .
>
> In most jurisdictions, corroboration of the complaining witness was necessary for a conviction of rape. . . . Skeptical of female accusers, the majority of courts . . . considered it appropriate that the "prosecutrix" in all sexual assault cases undergo psychiatric examination before trial. . . .
>
> Such wariness of the complainant's credibility created "an exaggerated insistence on evidence of resistance." . . .
>
> Recently, however, the entire concept of resistance to sexual assault has been called into question. . . .
>
> For example, some studies have demonstrated that while some women respond to sexual assault with active resistance, others "freeze." . . . The "frozen fright" response resembles cooperative behavior. . . . Indeed, . . . the "victim may smile, even initiate acts, and may appear relaxed and calm." Subjectively, however, she may be in a state of terror. . . . The victim may make submissive signs to her assailant and engage in propitiating behavior in an effort to inhibit further aggression. . . . These findings belie the traditional notion that a woman who does not resist has consented. They suggest that lack of physical resistance may reflect a "profound primal terror" rather than consent. . . .
>
> Additionally, a growing body of authority holds that to resist in the face of sexual assault is to risk further injury. . . .
>
> . . . A 1976 study of rape victims and offenders . . . found that over half of the sexual assault offenders studied reported becoming more violent in response to victim resistance. . . .
>
> On the other hand, other findings indicate that resistance has a direct correlation with *deterring* sexual assault. . . .
>
> Reflecting the foregoing uncertainties about the advisability of resistance, the [study] concluded: . . . "rape prevention is more possible through vigorous resistance; however, resistance incurs greater risk of injury. When confronted with attack, each woman must make a choice which is highly personal and may be affected by situational factors beyond her control." . . .
>
> . . . In so amending [the rape law in 1980], the Legislature has demonstrated its unwillingness to dictate a prescribed response to sexual as-

sault. For the first time, the Legislature has assigned the decision as to whether a sexual assault should be resisted to the realm of personal choice.

The elimination of the resistance requirement is also consistent with the modern trend of removing evidentiary obstacles unique to the prosecution of sexual assault cases.[27]

Other archaic legal biases regarding rape that had prevented prosecutions and convictions began to disappear from the courts. For instance, the Florida Supreme Court decided in 1986 to "bury" the words of the seventeenth-century Lord Chief Justice Matthew Hale. For hundreds of years in final instructions before deliberations in rape trials, judges had repeated Hale's warning to juries that "where no other person was an immediate witness to the alleged act [of rape], the testimony of the prosecutrix should be rigidly scrutinized." Rejecting that instruction, the Florida Supreme Court discerned "no unique reason" why those accused of rape "should occupy a status different from those accused of any other crime where the ultimate factual issue at trial pivots on the word of the victim against the word of the accused."[28]

Greater sensitivity to the plight of rape victims paved the way for increased understanding of battered women, another victim group with whom children were closely associated. Until 1975, not a single program for specialized prosecution of the cases of battered women existed in the United States. Battery of a woman within the home, family, or relationship was a "domestic dispute" relegated to family or social work solutions or simply ignored.

Like rape, wife-battering attracted the national consciousness with startling rapidity. Once regarded as "the secret crime," it was suddenly the focus of both the media and legislatures.[29] Increased attention to battered women encouraged the criminal justice system to understand the dynamics of family violence. Countless battery prosecutions, cutting across racial, cultural, and economic lines, forced police, prosecutors, and judges to open livingroom and bedroom doors. In horror, they discovered that just behind many battered women were abused or sexually assaulted children. No longer would property crimes be the most compelling concern of the criminal courts. America had redefined "serious" crime, and sexually abused children were an integral element in that redefinition.

These "new" serious crimes imposed unprecedented demands on the criminal justice system. Rape victims, battered women, and abused children required services rarely needed by theft and burglary victims. The "new" serious crimes frequently went to trial, and the victims needed sensitivity and support to see the process through. Of necessity, with support from government, private foundations, and volunteers, the movement to assist victims and witnesses in the criminal justice system was born. Whereas in 1970, no victim/witness programs existed, by 1980 America had over 1,300 rape crises centers, nearly 400 domestic violence centers, and over 500 victim/witness programs. In ten years, the number of states with victim compensation programs increased from two to twenty-eight. And even during times of economic austerity, some states expanded such programs by enacting victim/witness surcharge laws that required every person convicted of a crime to pay an additional fine to fund victim/witness programs. By the 1980s, victim/witness services provided to the courts by nonlawyers and volunteer advocates became an established part of the criminal justice system.[30] Finally, states began to follow the lead of Wisconsin, which enacted the country's first victim/witness bill of rights "to ensure that all victims and witnesses of crime are treated with dignity, respect, courtesy and sensitivity . . . and are honored and protected by law enforcement agencies, prosecutors, and judges in a manner no less vigorous than the protections afforded criminal defendants."[31]

And yet it cannot be forgotten that this new commitment to "dignity, respect, courtesy, and sensitivity" conflicts or at least shares little in common with legal tradition. The traditions, embodied in language and procedures, have cemented America's heritage of common law that "came down through the centuries with some of its past sticking to it, like a skin it never quite succeeded in molting."[32] Parts of that "unmolted" past deny fairness to children in court. If child victims of sexual abuse are to gain the chance for justice, those who control the courts must examine the extent to which legal traditions interfere with the discovery of truth.

Perhaps the "skin" of Anglo-American law most difficult to shed is the absolute adherence to adversarial trial procedures. Few question the origins of the adversarial system, which is sacrosanct to most who work in America's legal system. The English concept of adversarial trial by a jury of peers was preceded by a far older approach to discovery of truth, and the character of that approach remains in the American system even now. In twelfth-century England, when two litigants confronted each other, there was no such thing as trial in which accused and accuser met to offer testimony so that judge and jury could weigh the evidence and reach a decision. Instead the system relied on "proofs." One method was proof by ordeal, in which the accused attempted to suffer the red-hot iron or cauldron or to perform some other physical feat to prove innocence. Another popular form of ordeal was proof by battle. Although ignored for centuries, trial by battle was not officially abolished in England until 1819.[33] Two combatants would fight until one bettered the other; the combatant who lost was guilty. What really triumphed, of course, was not truth but force.

While both ordeal and battle formally disappeared long ago, the basic concepts linger in the adversarial system. Lawyers assumed the roles of combatants for their clients, and combat by physical battle became combat by verbal strife. The American legal system remains deeply, unalterably com-

mitted to the belief that in the clash between attorneys, the truth will ultimately emerge. Some, especially those outside the legal system, are not so
certain that truth necessarily follows from the verbal onslaught; and many,
both outside and inside the system, are convinced that victory often is gained
by the defendant or victim who best withstands the "ordeal" of court. Thus
even though there is no chance that the adversarial system will be abandoned,
it is worthwhile to recall its origins, understand that it is more an accident of
history than an act of God, and consider how it can be modified when it
clearly interferes with a trial's search for truth.

In the legal system, terminology is paramount. Lawrence Friedman
comments that "it is the business of the lawyer to tolerate and master artifice.
After all, technical difficulty is the sole social excuse for the lawyer's monop-
oly, his stranglehold on court work, on the drafting of documents, on the
counseling of clients."[34] One could suggest that lawyers do not deliberately
use language to manipulate witnesses but rather to "edge up" to a position
in incremental steps. Lawyers learn to think and speak in terms geared to
extraordinary precision. For example, a lawyer will substitute "not unimpor-
tant" for "important" in order to avoid committing to a particular point of
view until absolutely necessary. Attorneys speak and write in subtle, complicated terms in order to make the most careful possible case for their clients.

But another view would suggest that such "artifice" and "technical difficulty" tend to obscure rather than elucidate truth. One trial lawyer comments, "You learn by experience to manipulate your own witnesses with
words so that they are as effective as hell within the bounds of truth. But
remember—truth is a very wide road. Ten people can see an event and describe it in ten different ways, depending on who they are and how they see
the world. Manipulation really isn't supposed to be part of the system, but
every good trial attorney knows it is."

Another lawyer points out that where children are concerned, "manipulation is a crap shoot. The worst thing for a manipulator is to be seen as a
manipulator, and there's always that danger when you're working with child
witnesses. One of the things I remember best from law school is the phrase
'client control'; I guess that also implies 'witness control' for those hostile to
your client. Whether you're the prosecutor or the defense attorney in one of
these [child sexual abuse] cases, you have to know how to establish and maintain control in the courtroom."

Whether lawyers use complex language to manipulate or to establish
clarity is probably not the most important issue for child witnesses. After all,
the normal process of communication in the courtroom is difficult for most
adult witnesses. A successful witness must be able to listen carefully and
maintain attention for significant periods of time. He or she must have the
cognitive and verbal skills to decipher attorneys' questions, reconstruct
events, recall previous statements from various stages of the legal process,
and relate a story to a judge and jury. Ideally, he or she will not be intimidated

by a new environment, by the presence of an offender, or by the demeanors and legal tactics of hostile attorneys.

There are successful and unsuccessful adult witnesses as well as successful and unsuccessful child witnesses. But there is a critical difference. When an adult does not do well in court, he or she can normally still give testimony. Although the words may be halting or ambiguous, the adult can still speak to the jury. Children, on the other hand, often freeze or say almost nothing; and when the case hinges on the child's testimony, that failure is fatal. In sexual abuse cases, the child has to succeed at least in telling the substance of the story to the jury, or there usually is no case.

The reasons that sexually abused children freeze will become more obvious as we compare the demands of the courtroom with the needs and abilities of children. But first it is important to consider how and why cases do or do not reach the trial stage, how and why certain children are selected to be witnesses in court. Many people assume that when citizens make a complaint to police or when police make an arrest, a person is charged with a crime. In fact, while most criminal charges are preceded by such complaints and arrests, no criminal charge is issued without a decision by a prosecutor to charge or by a grand jury to indict a defendant. The decision whether or not to charge a crime is far from automatic. The prosecutor reviews police reports, interviews witnesses and suspects, evaluates the quality of the evidence, the legality of police conduct, and the intangible, human dimensions of the alleged offense before deciding whether to charge a crime. Before charging, the prosecutor is legally and ethically required to conclude that the crime was committed, and that the evidence is sufficient to prove guilt to a jury.

Day after day, police and prosecutors, victims and witnesses, agonize that they "know who did it" but cannot prove what they know. The burden for prosecutors is that they must resist the temptation to charge a case simply to appease an outraged victim, for to do so would be to cause additional injury. In a short time the victim would face the bitter experience of watching a defendant walk out of court when the case is dismissed for lack of evidence. Prohibited from charging cases that cannot be proved "beyond a reasonable doubt," prosecutors recognize the injustice of allowing the guilty to go free, but also know the equal injustice of subjecting both defendant and victim to a trial without evidence. This standard prevents prosecution of child sexual abuse cases even when sensitive and conscientious prosecutors would like to go forward. When the victim is too young to speak and when there are no other witnesses or strong circumstantial evidence, prosecution cannot follow, despite the certainty that "he must have done it."

Sometimes, even when the crime is certain and even when evidence is sufficient, prosecutors decide not to charge. They may conclude that some noncriminal process is better or that prosecution would bring counterproductive results. For example, if an eighteen-year-old celebrating his high school graduation damages school property and subsequently confesses his offense, the prosecutor may decide that since he has no record and is sincerely remorseful, the best course will be to "hold open" the case with a condition of restitution. If the offender complies, he saves his clean record and the school restores its property. If he does not, prosecution can still occur.

At times, a prosecutor may have to balance important public interests against certain private, human costs. A battered woman may plead with a prosecutor to dismiss a case against her husband, following his productive counseling efforts. She, her husband, counselor, and the prosecutor all may conclude that while the threat of prosecution served as a catalyst for meaningful counseling, continued prosecution now would harm the family. These kinds of considerations affect many child sexual abuse cases. While the exceptional severity of such crimes may lead some to urge prosecution in every case, the decision may not be so simple for those who must face tearful victims and family members asking that there be no prosecution.

This is not to imply that all prosecutors are dedicated, high-minded public servants who are never indifferent, inefficient, or personally or politically motivated. The point is simply that prosecutors, good and bad, for a variety of legal, ethical, humane, personal, and political reasons, operate according to this rule: Do not prosecute what you cannot prove. Thus if evidence depends on victims and witnesses who are uncertain, problematic, or likely to ask for dismissal later, the case probably will not be charged.

A practical consideration bolsters the prosecutor's "safe case" outlook. Strong cases rarely go to jury trial since most defendants plead guilty. The criminal justice system, forced to cope with overwhelming case loads, depends on almost all cases being resolved without trial. Thus for practical, as well as legal and ethical reasons, prosecutors cannot afford to take many risks. For each case that goes forward with only tenuous evidence and hesitant witnesses, there will be a defense determined to go to trial. Resources will be squeezed further, and the prosecutor's time and resources for other important cases will be reduced.

In another important sense, a prosecutor's psyche is not a risk-taking one. If successful prosecution depends on a novel legal theory, the prosecutor knows that if the judge does not accept that theory, the case will be dismissed. Even if the prosecutor persuades the trial judge and gains a conviction, the results may be reversed on appeal of the same issue. Consequently, prosecutors hesitate to charge cases when success depends on evidence that can be introduced only on an untested evidentiary theory.

Prosecution of some child sexual abuse cases may depend on evidentiary theories related to circumstantial evidence, which becomes critical because victim and witness testimony are so often difficult to obtain. "Circumstantial" evidence is evidence of certain facts or circumstances to prove the existence of other facts. It is distinguished from "direct" evidence, which is offered to prove the very facts it presents. For example, circumstantial evidence of a burglary could be scientific analysis of fingerprints from the scene, which are introduced to prove another fact—that the defendant is the burglar. Direct evidence, on the other hand, is a neighbor's observation that the defendant broke a window, crawled into the home, and exited carrying a TV.

Because there is a common misconception that direct evidence is always stronger than circumstantial evidence, many assume that in a sexual abuse case, prosecution is not possible without the victim's testimony. While in some cases that may be so, careful investigation and preparation may allow cases to go forward without such testimony.

In fact, in some cases circumstantial evidence is the most compelling. The burglary case demonstrates this. If the defendant was discovered with a stolen television weeks after a burglary, such evidence would help the prosecution; but it would be weak circumstantial evidence, falling short of proving guilt since the defendant might have purchased the TV at a second-hand store. However, fingerprints are strong circumstantial evidence—even stronger than the direct identification of the defendant by a neighbor who, cross-examination reveals, saw the break-in, but at night from a distance.

It may be, then, that even without direct testimony from the victim, a child sexual abuse case can be proved. Does medical evidence substantiate the allegation? Can other witnesses establish that the victim was within the exclusive care of the defendant at the time of the assault? Did the defendant make conflicting and refutable statements when interrogated? The surrounding "circumstances" may provide evidence sufficient for prosecution. The decision is the prosecutor's, whose analysis of child sexual abuse cases might be something like this:

1. A two-year-old child is sexually assaulted. Only the victim and offender were present; and although the parents are convinced of the suspect's guilt, there is little evidence. In this instance, the offender is not likely to be charged. The prosecutor does not want to penalize the child for being too young to identify the suspect, but the prosecutor also does not want to charge the suspect unfairly; and the dilemma is that the child is too young to explain who committed the assault. The prosecutor knows that the assumptions of others will not prove a suspect guilty.

2. A six-year-old is sexually assaulted. Only the victim and offender were present, but the child is able to describe the offense. The prosecutor may charge the suspect if the child is able and willing to testify; if the child can do so without trauma; if, in the absence of such testimony, someone else will be allowed to relate what the child described; and if the testimony will be sufficiently strong to prove guilt.

3. A ten-year-old is sexually assaulted. The child is able to testify, and additional evidence from witnesses and hospital reports strengthens

the case. The prosecutor will charge the suspect, but the anxiety of the victim and family may produce uncertainty in the preparation for trial. Such uncertainty may lead a prosecutor to consideration of a plea-bargain: a guilty plea to a reduced charge resolves the case, avoids the delays and uncertainties of trial and appeal, and guarantees conviction and some control over the defendant.

Thus when a prosecutor decides whether to charge a child sexual abuse case, a number of alternatives that may influence the likelihood of success at trial must be evaluated. Together with the feelings of the victim and family, the likelihood of a successful outcome usually controls whether a case will be charged. There is, however, one other factor that may control the course of a child sexual abuse case. A prosecutor may also consider another option: abuse proceedings through the juvenile court. There, while conviction of the suspect is not possible, protection of the child is. Instead of charging a defendant, the prosecutor may file a case "on behalf of the child," alleging that the child needs court protection and services.

Whereas the criminal court focuses on the defendant, on whether evidence proves guilt, and if so, on what should happen to the defendant, the juvenile court focuses on different subjects. Without requiring proof of who assaulted the child, the juvenile court asks whether the child was assaulted. If evidence proves there was abuse, the court gains authority to make orders for the child's protection, including removal from the home. The court can restrict or prohibit contact between the child and a suspect and can order conditions such as individual therapy or family counseling prerequisite to the child's return.

Furthermore, a juvenile court case, despite its enormous consequences, is not a criminal case requiring evidence beyond a reasonable doubt. Only a judge (and in a few states, a jury) must be convinced by "clear and convincing evidence" that the assault occurred. Even without a child's testimony, that standard often is met with relative ease, when medical experts testify that physical examination confirmed the sexual abuse.

Thus as the prosecutor contemplates the uncertainties of criminal charges, he or she does so realizing that the prosecution may fail; that even if it is successful, the sentence may not provide lasting protection for the victim (the defendant might not be incarcerated or might return to abuse the child after release); and finally that the juvenile court proceeding may provide better service to the victim, without requiring testimony.

The prosecutor is not compelled to choose one or the other option, and some successful cases have gone forward in both criminal and juvenile courts, achieving a fair sentence for the defendant and lasting protection for the victim. That, however, is the exception. After all, in most cases of sexual abuse by someone outside the family, the child does not need protection or services that would require removal from the home. And in most incest cases, the juvenile court seems to present a more appealing option when the victim and family do not seek incarceration of the defendant. Moreover, limited prosecutorial resources and concern for the stress a court case imposes on victims and families usually influence prosecutors to attempt as few court proceedings as possible.

Thus for very appropriate reasons relating to the purpose of prosecution, feelings of the victim and family, and quality of evidence, a prosecutor may decide not to charge sexual abuse. But for equally inappropriate reasons, traditional prosecutors might all too readily accept the apparent impossibility of prosecution. They might turn away from the challenge of new knowledge about children and evidentiary innovations. They might relegate too many cases to the legally more secure realm of the juvenile court, where cases are private and success more certain.[35] For some victims, that might prove the right course; for others, it will be tragic. In all cases, the decision must be made with careful attention to what the legal system demands of witnesses, whether or not the children can meet those demands, and whether or not the courts can adjust to meet the needs and abilities of each child.[36]

3

Children's Reality: Integrating Developmental Psychology into the Legal System

"I am real!" said Alice and began to cry. "You won't make yourself a bit realler by crying," Tweedledee remarked, "there's nothing to cry about."
"If I wasn't real," Alice said, "I shouldn't be able to cry."

—Lewis Carroll,
Through the Looking Glass
and What Alice Found There

IMPROBABLE as it may seem in a world of Barbies and action toys, childhood is regarded by most historians as a relatively recent invention, since it was not recognized as a distinct phase in the human life cycle until approximately four hundred years ago. Philippe Ariès's 1962 work, *Centuries of Childhood*, aroused the interest of subsequent scholars who began to document in detail the indifference, ignorance, and cruelty that have for centuries characterized adults' relations with children.[1] Ariès's central thesis is that prior to the late Middle Ages, children were free and happy because they were not socially or culturally differentiated from adults. He argues that once childhood was "invented" and parents and other adults developed more interest in the young, children were far more likely to be oppressed and victimized.

41

Lloyd DeMause's *The History of Childhood* strongly contests Ariès's thesis. DeMause and other authors contributing to his work maintain that throughout history children have almost never been free of indignity and abuse. Lacking understanding of the unique needs, capabilities, and behaviors of children, our ancestors progressed through a series of child-rearing modes that DeMause describes as "a nightmare from which we have only recently begun to awaken. The further back in history one goes, the lower the level of child care, and the more likely children are to be killed, abandoned, beaten, terrorized, and sexually abused."[2] Since they mirrored societal interests and values, the laws of most Western cultures did little to protect children from even the worst violence.

DeMause's work is valuable in examining the predicament of children in modern courts because it helps to explain, at least in part, society's hesitation and confusion in dealing with the young. While his approach tends to overgeneralize time periods and geographic and individual differences, it provides a frame within which to examine childhood. He divides Western culture into six periods that designate "the modes of parent-child relations which were exhibited by the psychogenically most advanced part of the population in the most advanced countries": the infanticidal mode, the abandonment mode, the ambivalent mode, the intrusive mode, the socialization mode, and the helping mode.[3] It is useful to trace these attitudinal periods along with DeMause, for child sexual abuse must be set in the larger framework of violence toward children.

Infanticidal Mode (Antiquity to Fourth Century A.D.)

By contemporary standards, life for children in antiquity was a long catalog of terrors. Infanticide was common, and other brutalities toward the young were widely accepted.[4] Physical imperfections, female gender, illegitimacy, or simply parental whim were approved standards for murdering children. Arguing that a man could do what he wants with his children, Aristippus maintained, "We . . . cast away from us our spittle, lice and such like, as things unprofitable, which nevertheless are engendered and bred even out of our own selves."[5]

Those who did not die at the hands of their parents were still in great danger from others. Sacrifice of children was not unheard of in Rome, and the practice of murdering the children of one's enemies was common. It was not until A.D. 374 that the law began to consider killing an infant a form of murder, and many historians contend that infanticide was probably punished only sporadically until well into the fifteenth century.[6]

Children who survived infancy were frequently sold or used as security for debts and political hostages, practices that extend as far back as Babylonian times.[7] Mutilation of the young was also common, as Seneca observed bitterly of child beggars:

> Look on the blind wandering about the streets leaning on their sticks, and those with crushed feet, and still again look on those with broken limbs. This one is without arms, that one has had his shoulders pulled down out of shape in order that his grotesqueries may excite laughter. . . . What wrong has been done to the Republic? On the contrary, have not these children been done a service inasmuch as their parents had cast them out?[8]

Discipline was harsh, "full of devices and practices unknown to later times, including shackles for the feet, handcuffs, gags, three months in 'the block,' and the bloody Spartan flagellation contests, which often involved whipping youths to death."[9] Ghosts and masks were used to frighten children into submission, and there were legions of threatening figures like Lamia and Striga who were supposed to eat children alive.[10]

Not surprising in light of the violent terror of life, sexual abuse of children was common during this period. The frequency of sexual abuse of both males and females has been well documented. DeMause argues that "the child in antiquity lived his earliest years in an atmosphere of sexual abuse. . . . The Greeks and Romans couldn't keep their hands off children."[11] Children of both genders were encouraged to touch and be touched by adults. They were sold as prostitutes and used sexually by friends and teachers. Homosexual exploitation of boys was an especially grave problem, and adult women were no less likely to participate in children's abuse than were men. Petronius, for example, recorded the rape of a seven-year-old girl that was witnessed by a line of women who stood clapping around the bed.[12]

Abandonment Mode (Fourth to Thirteenth Century A.D.)

As the influence of the Church increased, society grew less open in its defense of infanticide. But while child killings are not recorded from the Middle Ages, DeMause and others suggest that murder of illegitimate children and of infant girls, whatever their status, may have been frequent. Children who were not murdered by their own parents nevertheless had slim hope for survival. Until only the last few centuries, more than half of infants born died before reaching the end of childhood. Children were, in fact, so physically vulnerable that it was not unusual during the Middle Ages for siblings to be given identical names, distinguished only by their birth order.[13]

Although parents during this period may have been less likely to kill their offspring casually, many solved the problem of undesirable children in a more "humane" way—they abandoned them. Children of both rich and poor families were sent to wet-nurses for care for as long as five years. Noble parents offered children to convents and monasteries. As a result, many spent their lives "from infancy in the cloister, without home life, or the free society of other boys and girls."[14] Some were sent to serve as pages or ladies-in-waiting in the homes of strangers, and children of the poor became apprentices and laborers. Florence Rush observes that since most fathers could seldom provide dowries for more than one daughter, "the rest were packed off to convents. By age six, a girl's fate, marriage or a nunnery, was decided."[15] Marriage was hardly an attractive proposition since it was not uncommon for a ten-year-old to be married to a septuagenarian. Children continued to be used as political hostages and security for debts and were often sold outright. In the seventh century, for example, the archbishop of Canterbury ruled that a man could not sell his son into slavery after the age of seven; and a twelfth-century source reveals that the English were still selling their children as slaves to the Irish.[16]

Discipline remained strict, terrifying, and often violent. Witches, devils, and monsters were popular punitive figures. In thirteenth-century England it was decreed, "If one beats a child until it bleeds, then it will remember, but if one beats it to death, the law applies."[17] Even children in monasteries were severely abused, as an eleventh-century abbot's complaint to Saint Anselm indicates. Distressed about his inability to control the boys under his care, he protested, "We never give over beating them day and night, and they only get worse and worse."[18]

It was during the Middle Ages that the notion of the sexual innocence of childhood was advanced. Nevertheless, in monasteries "rigorous watchfulness" was exercised to prevent sexual temptation and to deter youth from this most dangerous of sins.[19] For all the emphasis on preserving children's innocence, adults were not overly concerned about the fates of children who were raped. Rush notes that "since copulation with or without consent established male possession of the female, vaginal penetration superseded all impediments. Gratian, twelfth-century Italian ecclesiastic and founder of canon law, set forth that while consent was desirable, conjugal union was rendered indissoluble, regardless of age or mutual consent by coitus. . . . If vaginal penetration had taken place, the female was bound to her husband for life."[20]

Although abandonment and abuse continued, the period was not without signs of hope for children. Infanticide and exploitation were increasingly condemned; and though children continued to be regarded as the property of their parents, there was modest recognition that they were human beings in their own right. Ironically, the concept of childhood was advanced during this period because of the problems posed by youth confined in religious institutions. The difficulties they created "fostered in, or forced upon, many [a] sense of the distinctiveness of childhood as a stage of life with its own needs and capacities."[21]

Ambivalent Mode (Fourteenth to Seventeenth Centuries)

Most historians of childhood agree with DeMause that the late Middle Ages and the period of the Renaissance were marked by an enormous ambivalence about children. Many contend that this was so because for the first time, children were recognized as more than miniature adults. In *Children in English Society*, Ivy Pinchbeck and Margaret Hewit describe what was developing as "a new consciousness of childhood."[22] Elaborating on the now popular theory that childhood was "invented" during the Renaissance, Neil Postman argues in *The Disappearance of Childhood* that the ever-widening gap between adults and children occurred as a result of the invention of print. Once adults' symbolic world became inaccessible to the young except by long formal schooling, they were increasingly separated from adults and placed in the company of peers; and the seeming commonality of the two groups diminished until it became apparent that children were not so similar to adults after all.[23]

Thus on the one hand, it was believed that children would be denied Heaven if they died before Baptism; on the other, they were symbols of innocence, joy, and even good luck. To wealthy sixteenth-century Englishmen they were convenient manifestations of status and conspicuous consumption.[24] Yet children in a variety of cultures were still sent out of their homes at a very young age to attend school or serve apprenticeships. Above all, children were regarded by most as objects to be molded and educated to fit the social, political, and cultural norms of their societies. The infant mind was, as John Locke contended, a "tabula rasa," an empty slate upon which responsible adults should write with care and discipline. Self-control, self-sufficiency, and strength of character were the ideals toward which parents were to direct their offspring.

To some extent, strong emotional bonding of the parent to the child was precluded because "high rates of infant and child mortality imposed a kind of 'tenderness taboo' preventing parents from becoming excessively attached to offspring whom they had no better than an even chance of preserving."[25] Often, of course, poor parents or those who had children (especially girls) out of wedlock made no attempt at "preserving" their offspring. As historian M. J. Tucker points out, "Infanticide was [still] woefully common."[26] Tucker's summary of a sixteenth-century analysis of infanticide in the Essex Quarter Sessions Records bears this out:

> Analysis of the causes of death in the thirty infanticide cases, including those already referred to, gives: strangled, five; smothered, two; suffocated—by pillow, one; in oven, one, in ditch, three; in haystack, one; drowned—in pond, four (one stillborn), in well, one; buried in a hole, one; broken or twisted neck, three; put in chest and then in dung heap, one; cut throat, two (one then drowned); struck against bedpost, one;

struck by a man, one; cause not stated, three. The verdicts, etc., were: guilty, seventeen [three women were remanded because they were pregnant again]; not guilty, five; John à Style guilty, one; guilty of homicide but not of murder, one; not proved that child was alive, one; killed by a man, one; inquests without verdict, three; "abortion," one.[27]

Attitudes toward punishment were changing, but violence and terror were still very much a part of most children's lives. Discipline at home and school was severe. Declaring that a large number of children prior to the eighteenth century could be described as "battered," DeMause catalogs the instruments used for beatings: "whips of all kinds, including the cat-o'-nine tails, shovels, canes, iron and wooden rods, bundles of sticks, the *discipline* (a whip made of small chains), and special school instruments like the flapper, which had a pear-shaped end and a round hole to raise blisters."[28] To the list of monsters, bogeymen, and witches, God himself was added as the ultimate disciplinary figure, the one who sent wicked children to Hell, where they would suffer eternal torment: "The little child is in this red hot oven. Hear how it screams to come out. . . . It stamps its little feet on the floor."[29] Usually the violence was carried out with the best of intentions, as when Italian Renaissance parents burned the necks of newborn babies with hot irons or candle wax to prevent "falling sickness," in other words, to prevent them falling out of their beds.[30] Probably most parents thought they were fulfilling their responsibilities—indeed, protecting the souls of the offspring in their care—when they took children to view corpses and witness public executions as a means of warning them about the dangers of wrongdoing. DeMause points out that these practices continued well into the nineteenth century when it was not at all unusual for children not only to be taken from school to attend hangings but later to be beaten by their parents so they would remember what they had seen. This was common despite the fact that "more and more children were being recognized as human beings with different developmental problems than adults."[31]

The issue of children and sex has become more complex as feminists have examined this period in history. On the surface at least, children were far less endangered than in previous times. Because the young were increasingly viewed as sexual innocents created in the image of the infant Christ, there were widespread taboos against copulation with children.[32] Indeed, children were exhorted to prevent adults from molesting them, because as Florence Rush argues, the taboo against sex with children was little more than a myth and terrified children were raped, diseased, and impregnated by people they either could not or would not identify.[33] The concept that the child is responsible for warding off sexual impositions by adults has survived to the present.

In a world of extraordinary change, the lives of many children did begin to alter. Suddenly they were considered important enough to write about, important enough to consume great amounts of attention as parents sought to live up to the Lockean ideal.[34] That children were different from grown-ups was increasingly obvious; how to accommodate their uniqueness was less apparent.

Intrusive Mode (Eighteenth Century)

The lives of typical eighteenth-century children had improved vastly over those of their predecessors. Abandonment and infanticide, especially in America, were rare; and while they were still frequently sent away to nurses, schools, or masters, "true empathy [with children] was possible."[35] Even more than their European counterparts, American mothers were in "closer and more constant contact with [their] children," and fathers took greater interest in them.[36] Perhaps the most significant proof of growing concern for the welfare of the young was the emergence of pediatrics as a separate discipline: "As early as 1727, the advocation of a careful and considered 'prudent government,' attuned to the needs of individual children, could be detected in Massachusetts Bay, in Pennsylvania, and in South Carolina. Moreover, there were signs parents were listening."[37]

Probably the most significant message directed toward parents in America was the need to rear godly children whose characters would reflect well on the parents and preserve their religious faith. Keeping children occupied and "at their books" was far more important than play, which was suspect and connected with sin in the minds of adults.[38] Submission and subordination to elders and God were stressed, though the means of achieving these ends were less violent than in the past. The eighteenth century witnessed a great decrease in regular beatings of children; but if they were not regularly whipped, children were still beaten when they were disobedient. John Walzer describes a case in which a boy's hand turned black and swelled considerably after a teacher hit it with a ruler. The child's father threatened court action, but the teacher was reassured that "the law was very favorable to schoolmasters."[39] Other forms of physical punishment were also common; William Byrd wrote of punishing a dependent child who wet the bed: "Made Eugene drink a pint of piss."[40] In societies so demanding of obedience from the young, corporal punishment was only one way to achieve submission. Fear and shame were most often used. Throughout the eighteenth century, children were taught to behave by being shut in closets and tied to bedposts.[41]

Despite the emphasis on godly behavior, children were probably in no less danger of sexual abuse than they had been in earlier times. Indeed, contemporary data confirm this assessment. DeMause notes, moreover, that in the eighteenth century adults developed "an entirely new twist [on the issue of child sexuality]: punishing the little boy or girl for touching its own genitals. . . . Parents began severely punishing their children for masturbation, and doctors began to spread the myth that it would cause insanity, epilepsy, blindness and death."[42]

Rousseau stands in direct opposition to the advocates of submission and subordination, fear and punishment. Believing both that children were innately good and that their virtue and reason would emerge with the proper encouragement of adults, he was to have a profound influence on subsequent attitudes toward childhood:

> If the philosophy of the Enlightenment brought to eighteenth-century Europe a new confidence in the possibility of human happiness, special credit must go to Rousseau for calling attention to the needs of children. For the first time in history, he made a large group of people believe that childhood was worth the attention of intelligent adults, encouraging an interest in the process of growing up rather than just the product.[43]

Socialization Mode (Nineteenth to Mid Twentieth Centuries)

Less likely to be abandoned, sold, mutilated, or murdered, children were generally more fortunate during the nineteenth and early twentieth centuries. DeMause describes these as periods in which "the raising of a child became less a process of conquering its will than of training it, guiding it into proper paths, teaching it to conform, socializing it. The socializing mode is still thought of by most people as the only model within which discussion of child care can proceed, and it has been the source of all twentieth-century psychological models from Freud's channeling all impulses to Skinner's behaviorism."[44]

Though debates about the advisability of corporal punishment continued, its popularity waned as experts and parents became increasingly committed to psychological means of control and training. Isolation and denial of food were two of the most frequent substitutes for beating children. During 1867–69, one English magazine solicited letters from parents expressing varied attitudes toward discipline: "Some felt that a quick whipping was cleanly done and soon over with, and actually created less resentment than prolonged isolation or bread-and-water. Others were certain whipping was a sure way to alienate children not only from their parents, but from their own sense of personal dignity and identity."[45] But there were punishments worse than beating. The concern over disciplining children who masturbated reached almost hysterical proportions during the nineteenth century—so much so that one "doctor whose book was the Bible of many an American nineteenth-century home, recommended that little boys be closely watched for signs of masturbation, and brought in to him for circumcision without anesthetic, which invariably cured them."[46]

The shift from an agrarian to an urban economy had profound effects on the life styles of poor children, who often found themselves employed for endless hours in factories or left homeless when their struggling parents could not survive the radical societal changes that were occurring. James Laver observes in *The Age of Optimism* that in 1876 there were more than twenty thousand young "street arabs" attempting to survive disease and starvation in the city of London.[47] Most nations gradually enacted child labor laws, and there were a great number of orphanages founded to care for homeless youngsters. Nevertheless, the works of authors like Charles Dickens reminded people that these acts of charity, however well-intentioned, did not always solve the plights of children.

Despite the improvements that had been made since antiquity, children clearly remained at the mercy of adults. This was especially evident in the Victorian idealization of and lust for young female children. Called "the cult of the little girl," the phenomenon resulted in unprecedented sexual abuse of children. Quoting an English medical journal, Florence Rush notes that "in London alone one house in sixty was a brothel and one woman in sixteen a whore. There were 6,000 brothels and 80,000 prostitutes, [many of whom were children]. One study estimated that 58 percent of the nonregistered prostitutes in Vienna were minors and another study claimed that more than half of the prostitutes in Stuttgart, Germany, had been 'deflowered' before they were seventeen. During the first part of the century, half the reported prostitutes in Paris were minors, some no more than age ten."[48] Some of the most prominent men of the period displayed the Victorian obsession with the child as a sexual being. As Rush notes, his piety did not keep Wordsworth from fantasizing about a young girl; Poe married his thirteen-year-old cousin; and Ruskin fell in love with a nine-year-old, whom he pursued for years.

Because there were never enough child prostitutes, an enormous international market for them developed; and the technological advances of the period encouraged the development of child pornography, which would become a major world industry by the latter twentieth century.[49] The sex merchants who traded in children relied on the Victorian male's "defloration mania," exemplified in the anonymous *My Secret Life*:

> She trembled. I pressed her and gave a tremendous thrust, and was on the right road. . . . She screamed "You hurt—get off—I won't let you!" She screeched loudly and struggled violently.
>
> I rose on my knees and looked at the girl who lay quiet with her thighs wide open and her hand over her face. . . . I was delighted beyond measure, she bled more than any virgin of her age which I ever yet have had I think.[50]

Thus although childhood had attained some "reality" by the nineteenth century, it still was not viewed as a stage of life with complete psychological, legal, and political significance. Children still "belonged" to adults, and they remained to many an enigma. Neil Postman believes that enigma to be best articulated in the works of Freud and John Dewey:

> At the end of the nineteenth century, the stage was set for two men whose work eventually established the mode of discourse to be used in all discussions of childhood in the present century. It is worth noting that the most influential book of each man was published in 1899, and each, in its way, led thoughtful people to pose the question: How do we balance the claims of civilization against the claims of a child's nature? Sigmund Freud's *The Interpretation of Dreams* and John Dewey's *The School and Society* . . . together represent a synthesis and summation of childhood's journey from the sixteenth century to the twentieth.
>
> Freud and Dewey crystallized the basic paradigm of childhood that had been forming since the printing press: the child as schoolboy or schoolgirl whose self and individuality must be preserved by nurturing, whose capacity for self-control, deferred gratification, and logical thought must be extended, whose knowledge of life must be under the control of adults. Yet at the same time, the child is understood as having its own rules for development, and a charm, curiosity, and exuberance that must not be strangled—indeed, is strangled—at the risk of losing mature adulthood.
>
> All of the psychological research on childhood that has been done in this century—for example, by Jean Piaget, Harry Stack Sullivan, Karen Horney, Jerome Bruner, or Lawrence Kohlberg—has been mere commentary on the basic childhood paradigm.[51]

Helping Mode (Mid Twentieth Century)

The "helping mode" is difficult to discuss in historical depth because it is still more an ideal than an actual approach to children. It requires recognition that children pass through a series of developmental stages that can be ignored only at great cost to the young and to society as a whole. It demands that adults guide their relations with children by responding to the children's needs and abilities rather than adult interests and capabilities. Children reared in the "helping mode" are not treated as inferiors or violently punished. They are not expected to behave as adults because it is obvious that they cannot do so. Their differences are respected, however, by those who recognize that children's abilities are not less than, only different from, those of adults.

"The helping mode," DeMause asserts, "involves an enormous amount of time, energy, and discussion on the part of both parents [and society], especially in the first six years, for helping a young child reach its daily goals means continually responding to it, playing with it, tolerating its regressions, being its servant rather than the other way around, [and] interpreting its emotional conflicts."[52]

The history of childhood is a record of neglect and violence by adults who learned too little too slowly about children's differences. Even at the end of the twentieth century, child libertarian Richard Farson can observe: "Our world is not a good place for children. Every institution in our society severely discriminates against them. We all come to feel that it is either natural or necessary to cooperate in that discrimination. Unconsciously, we carry out the will of a society which holds a limited and demeaned view of children and which refuses to recognize their right to full humanity."[53] Nowhere is discrimination against children more apparent than in the legal system's treatment of victims of sexual abuse. Because we do indeed hold "a limited and demeaned view of children," we cooperate in the discrimination they suffer in the system.

A legal system that is genuinely responsive to children must be able to "interpret children's emotional conflicts" and to be children's "servant" rather than their master. It must recognize that children are different from adults, that they have their own internal developmental mechanisms, and that these are often neglected in the frenzy to have them conform to adult standards of behavior.

Prosecutors' reluctance to pursue cases relying on children's testimonies is often reluctance born of misunderstanding—a misunderstanding of children corresponding to assumptions about children held by jurors. Significant numbers of child molesters are never brought to trial because prosecutors know that even when child witnesses do survive the rigors of the adversarial system in order to testify, juries are predisposed to doubt their testimonies.

> The mere *presumption* that a child will not be believed may persuade parents and attorneys not to pursue a case or to bring charges. Legal decision-making is influenced at many stages by the anticipated reaction of a jury. . . . A district attorney may be more likely to drop charges, a defendant less likely to plea bargain, and a judge more likely to dismiss a case if they believe a jury will not convict on the basis of a child's statements. In addition, parents may question why their child should be put through a potentially stressful experience if there is a strong chance that no one will believe the child anyway.[54]

To what extent are adults likely to doubt child witnesses? There is little research on adults' perceptions of children's cognitive abilities, but a recent study by A. D. Yarmey and H. P. T. Jones clearly indicates that adults often question children's credibility as witnesses.[55] In this study, groups composed of citizen-jurors, psychologists interested in eyewitness identification and testimony, legal professionals, law students, and college students were required to judge the reliability of a hypothetical eight-year-old's testimony. Asked how they assumed a child of this age would respond to questions by police or by attorneys in a court, fewer than 50 percent of any group believed the child capable of answering questions accurately. Sixty-nine percent of the citizen-jurors group felt that the children could not provide accurate testimony.

One might suppose that since 20 percent of Americans have suffered child sexual abuse in some form and since a portion of that population is likely to be represented on juries, their experiences as victims would predispose them to believe children testifying about sexual abuse. Surprisingly, this may not be the case. Unless the adults have analyzed their recollections of maltreatment and resolved the conflicts it produced, their judgments about children in similar situations may not be objective or appropriate.

People who have endured abusive treatment are less likely to recognize it as such than those who have not. In a 1987 study by Sharon Hershberger, a group of young adults was asked to react to a series of hypothetical "disciplinary interactions" between parents and children; the subjects were also asked whether or not they had experienced similar treatment when they were young.[56] The results indicated that a particular punishment was less likely to be defined as abusive if the respondent had experienced it as a child. Moreover, adults who had suffered a particular form of abuse were less likely to recognize its emotional damage to children and more likely to blame children for having created the need for punishment.

Research has also documented the importance, in varying degrees, of certain witness factors on juries' decisions. Jurors' perceptions of witnesses' truthfulness, accuracy, trustworthiness, consistency, certainty, confidence, objectivity, powerfulness, and even likeability and attractiveness affect their impressions positively.[57] Unable to meet most of these adult expectations, children thus face enormous odds in being believed beyond a reasonable doubt.

We demonstrate peculiar logic where children are concerned. Only in the last century have we learned much about them; and even though there are areas of ambiguity and controversy, there are points at which we can say of them, "Yes, this is known. This stage, this process, this behavior is true of most children." But sometimes when we are challenged to apply even these certain understandings about children in a situation involving adults, we tend to forget or reject our knowledge. Instead we disregard the facts of child psychology and development that teach us why children should not be expected to perform like adults.

Our children no longer work in textile mills and cotton fields; we build schools and amusement parks and spend billions of dollars each year on toys and games. We read books and watch television programs to learn about child nutrition, education, and moral development. We consider ours a "child-centered" society. And perhaps it is—until a child is pitted against an adult institution. Then somehow we forget children's separateness and uniqueness, and we treat them once again as if they were miniature adults.

If trials are genuine searches for truth, that truth must be sought in light of society's modern understanding of children rather than in subservience to age-old biases and ignorance. Adults who assume that their own perceptions, motivations, and fears are universal cannot empathize with children caught between the horrors of sexual abuse and the criminal justice system. Adults who doubt children because of false assumptions about their perception, memory, suggestibility, and truthfulness cannot fairly evaluate their testimony in the courtroom.

Yet there is a reliable body of information that could be used to establish a context for the evaluation of child testimony. While some of our knowledge of children is as yet inconclusive, we can differentiate with some precision the certainties from the areas of disagreement or lack of information. Although there are individual differences in children and although professionals have defined and described the various stages of child development in sometimes esoteric ways, it is possible to capture for the prosecutor, the judge, and the jurors the essential features of a child at a given stage of life. Many adult concerns about the child witness can then be addressed without pitting expensive prosecution and defense "experts" against one another in support of a particular position.

Below is a series of questions that a typical adult might ask about a child witness in a sexual abuse case. The discussion following each question outlines basic child development issues and explains why a child might respond to abuse in a particular fashion. Because the case study we examine in chapter 4 involved children of four and five, the question and answer segments here are based upon children at this point of development, the preschool stage.

1. Can I really believe this child's claims? Why would she allow herself to be assaulted? Why didn't she just resist?

The most fundamental understanding of child development would allow an adult to transcend such inaccurate perceptions of a preschooler's abilities. Psychoanalyst Erik Erikson observes that personality development is characterized by eight stages as the individual seeks to establish basic orientations to self and to the world.[58] While not every theorist identifies the exact same stages, most accept Erikson's basic observations about children.

In each of Erikson's developmental stages, the individual confronts a "crisis" between two opposed orientations to self and the environment. His first stage, "trust" versus "mistrust," corresponds to Freud's oral stage of psychosexual development and extends through approximately the first year of life. The crisis confronting the infant is learning to trust. To do so, he or she must feel that the environment is safe, nurturant, and need-satisfying. Basically passive in this process, the infant comes to trust the world and other people according to the quality and continuity of the care he or she receives.

Erikson's second developmental stage, which Freud called the anal stage, spans the second and third years. The child's primary "task" during this period is developing "autonomy." Once again the influence and behavior of adult caretakers are critical. Under the direction of adults, the child learns to walk, climb, manipulate objects, and control body functions. If there is proper reinforcement, the child gradually discovers the autonomy that derives from gaining control over both self and the environment.

The fourth and fifth years, roughly analogous to Freud's genital stage, are crucial to development of "initiative," as opposed to "guilt." This is the point at which the child's initiatives—motor activity, play, fantasy, intellectual inquiry—must be reinforced by caretakers if the child is to be prevented from feeling ludicrous or ignorant. If the child has developed a reasonably adequate sense of autonomy in the preceding stage, he or she possesses the reality of selfhood, the fact of being a real person. Now the issue is to clarify what kind of person that self will be. This is not an easy task. Thus Erikson notes that this particular period is characterized by rapid fluctuations between dependence and independence, maturity and infantilism, competence and ineptness, and social and antisocial behavior.

Thus with very brief explanation, the question "Why did the child do it?" can be moved out of adult misconceptions into the reality of childhood. Why does a child submit to intercourse with a relative or acquaintance? The most appropriate response to the query is obvious: How could a four- or five-year-old do otherwise? The preschooler's reality, the perception of self and the world, is inextricably linked to the attitudes and behaviors of adults. Adults possess free will and the right to self-determination because they appear to have developed the capacity of making rational choices. That ability and the rights it bestows are simply not available to a four- or five-year-old. Dependent for his or her very existence on adults, the child discovers trust, autonomy, and initiative only with their acceptance and acquiescence. Such achievements are almost always vulnerable to the decisions and whims of adults. Children admire and identify with the adults in their lives; and when sexual abuse occurs, the preschooler will often behave exactly as an abuser demands. A child submits precisely because "good" children follow the instructions of powerful, trusted adults—relatives, teachers, clergy, and family friends—who commit approximately 75 percent of child sexual abuse.[59]

Expecting a child to say no makes no sense. A preschooler taking those first tentative steps toward acquiring what adults know as "conscience" judges right and wrong solely on the basis of adult definitions. There are various contemporary theories regarding the development of moral and social behavior; all agree that preschoolers lack moral sophistication. The most influential theorist in the area of moral development, Lawrence Kohlberg, extends and refines the thought of Jean Piaget.[60] Kohlberg explains that typical preschoolers exhibit "conventional morality." They tend to judge acts as "good" or "bad," not because they understand and adhere to abstract moral rules, but because they will receive praise for being "good" and will avoid the punishment that comes from being "bad." Only by age five can some children begin to evaluate actions in terms of their moral labels rather than in terms of their potential for reinforcement or punishment, and even then few have clear labels for many of the acts perpetrators perform.

Some theorists contend that children possess somewhat greater moral sophistication than Piaget or Kohlberg recognize, and others note that moral "reasoning" may differ from moral "behavior." Nevertheless, most tend to agree with Kohlberg's assessment of the early stages of human development. His theory suggests that unless a significant adult provides a preschooler with sophisticated sexual information, the child will have no frame of reference and no cognitive capacity to resist when a powerful adult issues orders to engage in even the most disgusting sexual behavior.

2. If abuse really occurred, why didn't the child tell an adult?

Children do try to tell adults about sexual abuse, but they don't always do so in ways that most adults understand. They tell in their drawings and stories, in their relations with peers and adults, in their physical symptoms, in their daydreams and nightmares, in their sudden mood swings, and sometimes most of all, in their silence and withdrawal. So urgent are their attempts to tell that researchers like the University of Vermont's Pamela Langelier have observed more than a hundred clusters of symptoms or complaints characterizing sexually abused children. One of the instruments she relied on is the Child Behavior Checklist (CBCL) that can help to describe and measure the symptoms and effects of sexual abuse.[61]

It is true, of course, that children often do not attempt to tell adults directly. Roland Summit, the psychiatrist who defined the child sexual abuse accommodation syndrome, explains this secrecy:

> Virtually no child is prepared for the possibility of molestation by a trusted adult; that possibility is a well-kept secret even among adults. The child is, therefore, entirely dependent on the intruder for whatever reality is assigned to the experience. Of all the inadequate, illogical, self-serving, or self-protective explanations provided by the adult, the only consistent and meaningful impression gained by the child is one of danger and fearful outcome based on secrecy. . . . "This is our secret; nobody else will understand." "Don't tell anybody." "Nobody will believe you." "Don't tell your mother; (a) she will hate you, (b) she will hate me, (c) she will kill you, (d) she will kill me, (e) it will kill her, (f) she will send you away, (g) she will send me away, or (h) it will break up the family and you'll end up in an orphanage." "If you tell anyone (a) I won't

love you anymore, (b) I'll spank you, (c) I'll kill your dog, or (d) I'll kill you." However gentle or menacing the intimidation may be, the secrecy makes it clear to the child that this is something bad and dangerous. The secrecy is both the source of fear and the promise of safety: "Everything will be all right if you just don't tell."[62]

Here again it is easy for the adult to ignore the child's reality. Threats that appear absurd from the adult perspective are very real and very possible to preschoolers and thus act as an almost insurmountable barrier to direct verbal communication about abuse. Child development experts agree that preschoolers' growing self-awareness is accompanied by an increased sense of personal vulnerability and great susceptibility to fears of both real and imaginary dangers.

Children are particularly concerned about body intactness, separation or alienation from parents, and death. As Erikson points out, the four- or five-year-old, having only recently acquired a sense of mastery over his or her body, is well aware of that body's physical limitations. Thus an adult can easily force a preschooler to secrecy by threatening physical as well as sexual abuse. Because their parents are still the central realities of their lives, preschoolers' fears of pain, mutilation, and death are focused primarily on their parents and secondarily on themselves. So strong is the parental bond and the need for parental love that even the threat of a parent's disapproval will intimidate a child. But adults sitting in judgment over child witnesses in courtrooms rarely understand the intensity of those needs and fears. Thus they may reach the uninformed conclusion that if a child did not tell right away the child, for that reason alone, should not be believed.

3. Several times this child denied that an assault occurred. Isn't that proof there was no sexual abuse?

Any recantation demands attention, but denial is predictable in child sexual abuse cases and does not mean that assault did not occur. Once a child has disclosed an account of abuse, denials almost inevitably follow. Frequently, a victim represses the experience to protect against the intense pain and fear she or he has suffered. Repression is the ego's way of defending itself by screening painful material from the conscious mind. The pain nevertheless finds expression through derivative mechanisms or behaviors that are somehow related to the original source of trauma. When a child's body is violated by an act of fellatio, for example, she or he may refuse to eat or may complain of problems with the mouth or throat. Evidence of such behavior is essential to the jury's full understanding when it learns of a child's recantation.

Once an assault is known, of course, the victim feels at great risk. Recantation is the child's way of regaining at least some control, of protecting herself or himself and others threatened by a perpetrator. If a child is terrified of an abuser, denial is a way of saying, "I kept my promise. I didn't tell, not really." If disclosure has disrupted a child's life and created pain, anger, or chaos in the home, denial is a means of banishing the trouble. Children's denial is also a tempting way for adults to make the problem appear to go away, but they can never trust it as proof that nothing happened. Once a child risks an account of sexual abuse, the inevitable recantation must be judged in the total context of the child's statements and actions. Adults charged with protecting and providing justice for children must anticipate recantation and be prepared to ask why it occurred and what it means to the search for truth. Unfortunately, this seldom occurs. In case after case, recantations capture headlines and adversely affect jurors' decisions.

4. Don't children lie? Aren't false accusations about sexual abuse common?
Children do not commonly make false claims of being sexually abused. Underreporting and denial are far more common. In their article "The Testimony of the Child Victim of Sexual Assault," Lucy Berliner and Mary Kay Barbieri establish that

> while adults are often skeptical when children report sexual abuse . . . there is little or no evidence indicating that children's reports are unreliable, and none at all to support the fear that children often make false accusations of sexual assault or misunderstand innocent behavior by adults. The general veracity of children's reports is supported by relatively high rates of admission by the offenders. . . . Not a single study has ever found false accusations of sexual assault a plausible interpretation of a substantial portion of cases."[63]

The veracity of sexually abused children has been analyzed by researchers, all of whom report that false accusations are extremely rare. A study by Jonathan Horowitz, professor of clinical psychiatry at Boston University Medical School, found a 5 percent invalidity rate among reports by Boston children.[64] In Denver, David Jones, a psychiatrist at the Kempe Center, reported the fabrication rate to be 2 percent or less.[65] In another survey of Child Protection Services social workers in North Carolina, M. D. Everson and B. W. Boat differentiated children according to age groups and found among children under the age of three a 1.6 percent false allegation rate; among three- to six-year-olds 1.7 percent, among six- to twelve-year-olds, 4.3 percent; and among adolescents, 8 percent. Everson and Boat also analyzed the social workers' expectations and found that they "may have difficulty believing that children tell the truth when they report sexual abuse. . . . The workers seem to view the child, and especially the adolescent, with a great deal of suspicion. A retraction is then accepted, not as a predictable phase of the disclosure process, but as evidence that the child is lying."[66]

The adult notion that children lie about sexual abuse is illogical to those who have studied them closely. Few three-year-olds have the will or capacity to process a lie, and the ability of children of four or five to formulate an untruth is offset by their inability to sustain the falsehood. The reasons are obvious. Preschoolers view adults as omniscient. Certain that they will eventually be discovered by the all-knowing, all-powerful authority figures in their lives, they seldom lie with enough ease or confidence to be believed. Concerned with pleasing adults, they are reluctant to engage in any deception that threatens to create trouble with them. Thus many who work with preschoolers contend that they might lie to get out of, but never into, trouble with grownups. And in a child's eyes, "trouble with grownups"—unknown authority figures like social workers, police, and lawyers—is what results from confessing to being sexually abused.

Another reason for preschoolers' inability to sustain a falsehood is their need to share their experience and knowledge with others. They have difficulty maintaining untruths for extended periods because their desire to communicate with others, especially their parents, is so great. When a sexual abuser intimidates a child into silence, the child usually finds ways to communicate beyond the lie of omission and to reveal the guilty secret they share.

Preschoolers' characteristic motivations for lying are simple to discern. They may lie to express very intense desires. A child desperately wishing to travel to Disney World might tell a friend, "This morning my mom and I went to Disney World, and then we came home and ate lunch." Children may also lie to avoid punishment. Confronted with his parent's discovery of a broken vase, a four-year-old boy may argue that his sister was the culprit; when that story is unsuccessful, he may persist: "Well, she made me do it." But the motivation to avoid punishment usually leads to silence, not false allegations. The fear of punishment allows an abuser to convince a child that punishment will follow if the truth is told.

The third major motivation for preschoolers to lie is to please their parents. This is the most frequent cause of false allegations. In a study by David Jones and Mary McQuiston, for example, only 45 of 309 allegations were found to be fictitious, and 36 of these were adult-initiated.[67] While the significance and potential danger of false allegations must be acknowledged, it is clear that educated professionals can develop awareness of these motives.

Jones and McQuiston identify certain "clues" or "leads" to children's veracity. They assert that a child's allegation should be scrutinized for explicit details. Although young children are incapable of relating numerous details, "the more detail that is recalled, the more likely it is that the account is truthful, especially as it is considered unlikely that an individual child could have gained such detailed knowledge unless they had had personal experience of the event in question."[68] Idiosyncratic details such as descriptions of the smell or taste of semen are also important. In addition to recollections of the sexual encounter itself, abused children may have seemingly unrelated recollections of events surrounding the incident. Children who are telling the truth sometimes mention details not typically associated with sexual abuse. In the last few years, descriptions of pornographic involvement, sadism, and ritualism have increased. Jones and McQuiston note that "these elements are probably underrecognized at present because we do not routinely inquire about them."[69]

A child's statements about sexual abuse must be analyzed for age-appropriate words and sentence structure and for what Jones and McQuiston term a "child's eye view" of the incident as opposed to an adult perspective. The child's expressed emotion in delivering an account of sexual abuse is also significant. A seemingly rehearsed or hollow presentation that is given in an unemotional tone without hesitation or reserve may, for example, be suspect. Jones and McQuiston also stress the importance of searching for clues that indicate that the child is experiencing some sort of psychological response to the abuse. Both interviews with the child and assessments of his or her behavior should demonstrate features characteristically associated with victims of sexual abuse. Children's use of toys and drawing materials may be revealing in this respect. A child's description of the pattern of the abuse over time may also help to establish veracity; in intrafamilial cases, for instance, children typically describe a progression of sexual advances by perpetrators.

The manner of disclosure should generally be similar to confirmed cases. Since children do not usually demonstrate promptness of disclosure, their motivations for doing so and the recipients of their confidence are significant in determining their veracity. Abusers frequently attempt to ensure secrecy by intimidating children, so details about the methods perpetrators used to elicit such secrecy emerge gradually in truthful accounts. Because sexual abuse and the trauma of disclosure involve complex dynamics, consistency is limited in most allegations. Thus Jones and McQuiston note that

> there is usually, in truthful accounts, a consistency of the core elements of the child's exploitation, but there may be some variation in the more peripheral aspects of the child's story. . . . The more violent elements of coercion and threatening behavior by a perpetrator may be very frightening for the child, and consequently, these elements may be suppressed by the child for a longer period than the sexual aspects of the abuse. This may give an air of apparent inconsistency to a child's account . . . over a period of weeks or months; however, running through the account will be a consistent thread.[70]

Sensitive to the possibility of false allegations, social workers, police, and prosecutors can intercept them before they produce criminal cases, but professionals must acquaint themselves with the dynamics of false allegations not only to prevent prosecution of the innocent but also to ensure that these same professionals learn when to trust the assertions of children who have no motive to lie.

5. But even if this child believes the account she or he gave, how do I know an adult didn't create the story? Aren't children very open to suggestion by others?

How likely is the possibility that an adult will be able to deceive a child into believing that he or she was sexually abused? While much more needs to be known before we achieve full understanding of children's suggestibility, certain points are clear. Adults are not, as many assume, immune to suggestive influences; and children are not as easily or as often manipulated as some suppose. An important advance in researchers' studies of suggestibility is the recognition that age is not the only or even the most salient variable affecting an individual's suggestibility. As Elizabeth Loftus and Graham Davies conclude in "Distortions in the Memory of Children,"

> Perhaps age alone is the wrong focus. . . . Whether children are more susceptible to suggestive information than adults probably depends on the interaction of age with other factors. If an event is understandable and interesting to both children and adults, and if their memory for it is still equally strong, age differences in suggestibility may not be found. But if the event is not encoded well to begin with, or if a delay weakens the child's memory relative to an adult's, then age differences may emerge. In this case, the fragments of the event that remain in the child's memory may not be sufficient to serve as a barrier against suggestion, especially from authoritative others. Of course, if the child's grasp of the language is so weak as to make him or her oblivious to the subtle implications in the suggestive information, then the child may be immune to the manipulation regardless of the interest value or memorability of the stimuli, or the loss of an accurate memory record.[71]

The bulk of current research suggests that children may be more open to external influence if an event is less personally interesting, significant, or memorable or if it did not actually occur. On the other hand, there may be instances in which they are less susceptible to suggestion than adults. Because of their greater experience, adults may draw inaccurate inferences when processing information, while children will be less likely to do so and will thus be less likely to respond to suggestive influence by others.[72] For example, precisely because of their more limited knowledge of sexuality, preschoolers might be far more difficult to manipulate into giving repeated and complex false descriptions of a sexual act than an adolescent or adult.

The issue of children's suggestibility requires more extensive research. We suspect that in children's minds significant events remain fixed and resistant to external suggestion; but this educated guess needs to be supported by careful observation and analysis of children in real life rather than in laboratory situations. Researchers do agree that suggestibility relates, in part, to children's memories, about which some of the most disturbing misconceptions exist.

6. *How can I accept this story when everyone knows that children have poor memories?*

Before examining the contention that children are incapable of accurate recall, it is necessary to review the critical role that memory plays in the American courtroom. As Gail Goodman, one of the nation's foremost researchers on child witnesses, points out, memory is "often viewed as the sine qua non of testimony."[73] To be considered reliable, a witness must demonstrate an accurate memory. If the memory appears flawed, the testimony is seriously, often hopelessly, damaged. In the courtroom a demonstration of good memory requires more than simple recall of an event that occurred months or years earlier. A witness is asked to remember details concerning the crime, and the jury's belief often will depend on whether the witness can vividly describe events before, during, and after the crime.

This is only the beginning. A victim who made previous statements to friends, relatives, police, attorneys, judges, grand jurics, and a variety of social workers, psychologists, psychiatrists, and physicians can be asked about any of those statements. Children may face a barrage of incomprehensible queries from defense attorneys: "Isn't it a fact that two months ago you told a social worker that the assault lasted fifteen minutes, and now you say you're not sure?" or "But when you testified at the preliminary hearing, you never mentioned that threat, did you?" or "But of course when the police first interviewed you, you claimed his shirt was blue, but now you don't know?" To be believed by a jury, the child may have to remember numerous interviews and court appearances. Each one generates a report or transcript, which is eventually scrutinized by defense attorneys. In each interview or appearance questions are framed in a different context. Yet one contradiction, one confusion, may doom the testimony.

Given these demands, the memories of even adult witnesses prove fallible. Numerous studies have confirmed that adult memory is quite malleable.[74] The difference in the fates of adults and children in court begins not with distinctions in their memory capacities but with their perceptions of the investigative process and courtrooms. Adults tend to assume that other adults are, if they choose, capable of clear recall; but as Yearney and Jones demonstrate, an overwhelming percentage believe that children are incapable of providing accurate testimony. Thus, while an adult crime victim usually is interviewed only once or twice by police, the child is interviewed again and again by a variety of family members and professionals. Some of the interviews are motivated by valid legal concerns, some by genuine consideration for the child, some by insensitive skepticism about the child's allegations. All combine, however, to produce anxiety and confusion and the potential for seemingly inconsistent trial testimony. The final irony is that often the child's testimony is not inconsistent but may appear so because the written report of the adult interviewer was inaccurate or incomplete.

How much truth is there in the belief that children's memories are inferior? One way to approach that question is to review the process by which individuals store and retrieve information. Most memory theory reveals that the process occurs in three stages. In the first, acquisition, fragments of information about an event are recorded or "encoded" into the memory. Then there is a second stage, retention, during which information is simply stored until it is called into consciousness in the third stage, retrieval.

Researchers have conducted various experiments to determine whether children's performance is different from that of adults at any of these stages. Two recent articles, "Distortions in the Memory of Children" by Elizabeth Loftus and Graham Davies and "Differentiating Fact from Fantasy: The Reliability of Children's Memory" by Marcia Johnson and Mary Ann Foley, survey the current literature on this subject. Loftus and Davies conclude:

> Nearly all laboratory studies report that children are less efficient than adults in recalling events they have witnessed. It seems possible to attribute such failings to two main factors: (a) a combination of encoding and retrieval inefficiencies caused by a dearth of mnemonic skills, and (b) lower levels of comprehension springing from the child's more limited knowledge base.[75]

Johnson and Foley's review of the literature and their own research bear this out:

> Younger children typically recall fewer items than do older children. This relationship between age and recall seems to be associated with a developmental trend in the acquisition both of enriched knowledge structures (e.g., an apple is a fruit) and of memory strategies (e.g., organizing or generating images).

But these authors go on to observe that although their findings suggest that children produce less detailed testimony in the courtroom, this is not necessarily true for all aspects of an event:

> For example, it is not clear whether children should be expected to be any worse than adults in recalling spatial arrangements of objects and people, or the temporal order and frequency of events. Our own work suggests that even young children may be able to recognize who did what.[76]

What are we to make of the similarities and subtle differences in these findings, and what are we to conclude about the reliability of children's memories? The most obvious point that emerges if one examines the literature in depth is that, taken collectively, developmental psychology's studies have yielded extremely limited and sometimes contradictory results. Thus in courtrooms one "expert" on memory may testify from one point of view and then be countered by another with similar or equivalent expertise and experience.

Nevertheless, the reasons for our limited and often biased appraisal of children and memory are becoming increasingly clear. Adults assume that adults have accurate memories and that children do not. In "The Limits of Childhood: Conceptions of Child Development and Social Context," Arlene Skolnick observes that both the law and developmental psychology, while having little interaction with each other, share the assumption that "the distinguishing feature of all of childhood is incompetence."[77] Asserting that the behaviors and abilities of children are more complex than Freud, Erikson, Piaget, Skinner, and others believed, Skolnick contends:

> [Their] theories set up a polar opposition between child and adult nature. If the adult end of the scale is defined as logical and rational, then the child is, by definition, autistic, irrational, emotional, and lacking in perceptual and cognitive structures. . . . In [traditional] models of development, . . . the adult has been taken as the measure of the child. . . . The overemphasis on the differences between children and adults in developmental psychology results from not only an underestimate of children's abilities, but an overestimate of that of adults.[78]

This is precisely the case in studies of children's memories and in actual courtroom experiences. Adults are the measure. Acquisition, retention, and recall are defined by adult standards; and if the child's memories cannot be called out or verbalized with the tools used by adults for adults, then the assumption is that the child is incapable of remembering accurately.

This same approach separates preschoolers from older children. In "Preschool Thought," an article in the *American Psychologist*, Rochel Gelman observes that in her work on preschool thought evidence is accumulating to dispute the theory that very young children lack memory and other cognitive skills. She argues that they have "considerable cognitive abilities," which have been disregarded for two reasons:

> First, we simply did not look. Indeed, we seemed to choose to ignore facts that were staring us in the face. . . . The failure to recognize facts that contradict existing theories is not unique to those who study cognitive development. It seems as if we have a general tendency to resist new facts if their recognition means giving up a theory without being able to come up with another that will account for the new as well as the old facts. [There is a] second reason for our failure, until recently, to acknowledge the cognitive capacities of preschoolers. Many of the young child's cognitive abilities are well concealed and require the modification of old tasks or the development of new tasks for their revelation.[79]

There is significant support for Gelman's position. Those who assume that children have terribly inferior memories ignore, for example, one of the most startling facts "staring us in the face": a child's vocabulary. The average child's vocabulary accelerates from 50 words at age two to between 8,000 and 14,000 words by age six. Such progress obviously cannot occur if children are incapable of remembering. Children frequently astound parents with their recall of minute details from events long forgotten. Adults' laboratory experiments often overlook these obvious facts. Loftus and Davies's discussion of children's memories was based on laboratory studies; but as Skolnick argues, we must design new tasks and look places other than the laboratory to achieve understanding of children's memory processes and abilities. Researchers generally test children's memories with slides, films, pictures, and stories that may or may not seize their interest and elicit reliable responses from them. Goodman maintains,

> One of the areas most in need of research is children's memory for real-life events. Relatively few modern studies have examined long-term memory for realistic, live events similar to those about which a child might testify. [Stimuli used in most memory studies] may not capture children's attention in the same way that actual events do and may not be retained as well as actual events, particularly events that are personally significant. Many developmental psychologists now recognize that an accurate picture of cognitive development must include children's memory for real-life, meaningfully involving events.[80]

Studies of child memory are themselves in their infancy. At present it is difficult to make definitive statements about the memory skills of children. We do know that children are capable of accurate recall of an event, especially a traumatic event; but we do not know how many details surrounding that event they are typically able to remember or articulate. Experts now suspect that they themselves know far less about children than they assumed and that children remember far more than the artificial world of the laboratory has revealed. What is certain is that the research process itself may encourage the biases that lead adults to doubt children's recall of sexual abuse.

7. This may be a case where the child believes his or her own fantasy. After all, don't children tend to confuse fact and fantasy?

The assumption that children cannot distinguish their fantasies from reality derives from everyday experience. Children tell of imaginary playmates and impossible personal feats and are often convinced they can alter reality with their own wishes. Piaget described this as the "preoperational" stage of cognitive development (ages two to seven), during which children tend to attribute lifelike qualities to inanimate objects (animism) and to engage in magical thinking, becoming the person, animal, or thing they imagine.

At the same time that they profess belief in Santa Claus and the Tooth Fairy, preschool children are also extremely concrete and literal. The child who looks forward to the Easter Bunny's spring visit is the same child who can become annoyed when a parent tells a neighbor she or he is four instead of four-and-a-half. Preschoolers are people who ask questions like "What would happen if my doll was really real?" and "Could this pretend boat really float on water?"

Perhaps the salient issue is not whether or not children fantasize. Of course they do. The crucial question is whether their normal fantasizing process has an impact on their perceptions and descriptions of sexual abuse. While the research is limited, one conclusion is certain: children sometimes do not distinguish between what they actually have done and what they have fantasized doing; but they do readily differentiate what they've done and fantasized doing from what they have perceived. Johnson and Foley explain:

> The belief is pervasive that children have more difficulty than adults in discriminating what they perceive from what they imagine, but it has little direct experimental support. Children in our studies did not appear to be more likely to confuse what they had imagined or done with what they had perceived. On the other hand, young children did have particular difficulty discriminating what they had done from what they had only thought of doing.[81]

Thus a young child might be expected to say, "I want to be a teacher" and "I am a teacher" with equal belief. However, this child would not confuse either assertion with "The teacher touched me between my legs." To say that children fantasize is to acknowledge the obvious, but fantasizing is part of a normal developmental stage with relatively clear boundaries. Fantasizing does not deprive children of the ability to perceive and tell about conduct outside their realm of reality or fantasy.

In the future, the questions that arise around fantasy, memory, suggestibility, and deception must be answered by discarding old biases and by recognizing the flaws in previous studies of children. Our knowledge and understanding have been severely limited by the conditions under which we have tested and observed them. Too often adults' perceptions and preferences are the basis for the instruments they construct to assess children's behavior and development. Like cultural bias, age bias may contaminate the results of tests administered to children. Another problem is the laboratory setting in which children are typically tested:

> American developmental psychology . . . has tended to emphasize laboratory studies in which the child performs an unfamiliar task in a strange situation with a strange adult. It has tended to neglect the study of social settings in which children live and the persons who are central to them emotionally. As a result of the emphasis on laboratory studies, developmental psychology tends to deal with bits and pieces of the child. The rationale for this approach is that eventually all the bits and pieces can be added together to give a comprehensive picture. It is rare, however, for anyone to try to construct the comprehensive picture. More often, there is a tendency for the bits and pieces to be taken for the real things they represent.[82]

Children suffer in the legal system because there are too many things adults take for granted, too much about children they do not know. The following are questions that should be asked—and answered—by juries, judges, and lawyers if children are to receive fair treatment in the courts. Once again the questions require insight into the complex world of child development if they are to be answered adequately. Yet most of the answers are not at all tentative. They derive from an established body of scientific research proving that the demands of the legal system do not meet the needs of children.

8. Does a preschooler have the ability to meet the legal system's expectations about proper and credible witness demeanor?

Most people tend to equate honesty with the ability to look a person directly in the eye while making a statement, but they also recognize that a distinguishing feature of the habitual liar is the ability to convince the listener of an untruth while maintaining eye contact and revealing no hesitation or discomfort. In courtrooms witnesses are judged on the basis of juries' perceptions of qualities like truthfulness, trustworthiness, certainty, and confidence. It seldom occurs to most people that some hardened criminals or pathological liars may be more likely than innocent people to appear honest, trustworthy, and self-confident. Children are not likely to look directly or long at a strange judge or a hostile attorney because they are frightened and because they have been instructed from infancy to avoid strangers. Yet few jurors consider that children's avoidance reactions may not be dishonesty but rather shyness, fear, and other predictable qualities that are heightened by their inexperience and impotence in the legal system.

Courtrooms are designed for grownups who can sit for long periods and engage in verbal combat without betraying fatigue or hesitation. This simply is not possible with children. They fidget after relatively short periods. They grow hungry and tired and disoriented long before adults. Thus children are at an enormous disadvantage if their testimony is judged by individuals employing unexamined assumptions about the physical demeanor of "honest" witnesses.

9. Since children do have rich fantasy lives, do they experience fears that might influence their behaviors in court?

The legal system, judges, and jurors often fail to understand the fears that guide children's responses and behaviors in courtrooms. Although educator Maria Montessori attempted to awaken adults to the predicament of children who must survive in what appears to them a world designed for giants, her message did not reach those who control the environments of courtrooms.[83] Thus four-year-olds who have yet to see the inside of their neighborhood kindergartens are expected to function with equanimity and confidence in courtrooms designed and administered with intentional formality. The chairs, like the other courtroom furniture, are much too large to accommodate them comfortably. Even the courtroom construction materials and art work may be unfamiliar and intimidating from a child's perspective, and few adults are sensitive or knowledgeable enough to correlate children's testimonies with the environmental conditions under which they testify.

Courtrooms filled with staring strangers can terrify children. Seemingly neutral objects like judges' black robes can be frightening for those to whom witches and goblins are very real. Unlike some legal authorities charged with the responsibility of protecting children, many perpetrators take advantage of their vulnerabilities. Warned by an abuser that "the man in the black robe is my friend and will be mad if you tell," a preschooler may, without warning, retract his or her story when these worst fears seem realized.

10. Do preschool children have the cognitive ability to participate in a trial? Are there limitations to what they should be asked to do in testifying?

Very young children know when they have been sexually abused, and they are clearly capable of processing that information and communicating it to juries. Their testimonies will, however, be different from those of adults and may appear less truthful and acceptable in meeting the demands of the legal system as it currently exists.

The most intensive study of children's cognitive development thus far is that of Jean Piaget, who theorized that roughly between the ages of two and seven children enter the developmental stage he classified as "preoperational." During this period, children progress from development of sensorimotor skills to that of symbolic functioning, learning to use words or actions that stand for something else. Piaget focused on the limitations in children's thinking in early childhood and thus took a "bits and pieces" approach that sometimes underestimated their cognitive abilities. Nevertheless, his basic observations are valid and can provide considerable insight into the dilemmas children face when attorneys insist they perform as adults in court.

Piaget explained that one cognitive skill preschool children either cannot or do not employ easily is reversibility in thinking. In his experiments, children appeared incapable of reconstructing events in reverse order, of undoing problems mentally by retracing their origins. While children are now considered more adept than Piaget assumed, it is clear that preschoolers have great difficulty retracing past actions in order to reconstruct an event. The result is that their thought often seems disjointed and fragmented to adults. In the courtroom, reverse thinking usually is imperative if a witness is to be believed. Adult perpetrators usually have the cognitive ability, experience, and motivation to construct seemingly flawless versions of past events. Children are not so adept. Thus when judges and juries evaluate their stories on their abilities to provide coherent descriptions of events surrounding assaults, children suffer enormous disadvantages.

Another difficulty for child witnesses is the tendency toward "egocentrism." The term does not imply selfishness but rather children's difficulty in distinguishing between their own points of view and those of others. Although Piaget may have overstated the case for egocentrism, it does exist in early childhood even though it does not occur in all situations and interactions. In the courtroom, egocentrism poses problems because it influences children's responses to questions by attorneys. For example, a four-year-old boy may perceive events only in reference to himself. Because he cannot comprehend differing perspectives, he does not realize that leaving out details or providing too much irrelevant information will confuse the listener. Hence he may fail to recognize and relate information that is critical to understanding and believing his allegation.

Egocentrism is related to "centration," a child's tendency to focus on a single aspect of an object or situation and to exclude or ignore all others. Because young children have difficulty "decentering" their thought, they will at times appear to answer a different question from the one asked. When faced with complex or unexpected questions, children may give attorneys the benefit of the doubt and respond to what they think their questioners meant to ask. In the courtroom this often proves disastrous, of course, because it makes children appear irrational, incompetent, or worst of all—deceitful.

Animism, children's tendency to attribute lifelike qualities to inanimate objects, also causes them difficulties in court. As more and more child sexual abuse cases have gone to trial, defense attorneys have learned to capitalize on this characteristic and undermine children's credibility. By pointing out to a judge and jury that a child believes that a teddy bear has feelings, a clever defense attorney can suggest that the child is really incapable of recognizing truth. Not only can animism be used to denigrate children and to make them appear absurd as witnesses, it also can be manipulated by abusers to intimidate their victims. A perpetrator may, for example, frighten a child into submission and silence by threatening that she or he will be swallowed by monsters in the television set if the abuse is revealed.

For most developmental experts, the ability to form concepts is one of the most important achievements of early childhood. Some concepts are easily acquired; it does not take long for children to recognize houses or cats or cars. Others are harder to comprehend; and the more abstract the concept, the greater the child's difficulty in handling it. Nevertheless, it is not unusual for judges and juries to expect too much and to stop believing children when they become confused. "How long did the assault last? How many days passed before you reported it? Did you make that statement last month or last year? How far from home were you when the abuse occurred?" a defense attorney will ask. What few understand is that children cannot locate events in time or comprehend distance as adults can.

Piaget contended that the essential steps in developing understanding of time, distance, and speed are the abilities (1) to represent and recall the order of events, (2) to conceptualize intervals between events, and (3) to avoid confusing concepts of time and space. Preschoolers, who have difficulty with all three, find it virtually impossible to understand and explain time, distance, or speed. Because young children have little remembered past and only vague comprehension of the future, time is an abstraction that cannot be measured against any conventional realities of their lives. When asked if two weeks elapsed between one event and another, most preschool witnesses find it impossible to reply to adults' satisfaction. Nevertheless, since they are beginning to conceptualize time and wish to comply, many child witnesses try to respond. The results are often negative. Since so much depends upon witnesses' being able to place events in time, defense lawyers can easily and unfairly destroy children's credibility by exposing inaccuracies in their attempts to place events in proper sequence.

Children's problems with distance and speed are similar but seemed irrelevant to sexual abuse cases until recent alleged victims around the country began relating what appeared to be outlandish fantasies about traveling from nursery schools and day-care centers to other locations. Their stories seem less unlikely, however, when considered within the context of the child's perspective. Preschoolers do not comprehend, for instance, that long time intervals may not involve long distances. Hence a child who is taken somewhere for a period that seems lengthy will assume that he or she has traveled a far distance.

Any abstract concepts, not simply time, distance, and speed, are difficult for preschool children to comprehend. The competency hearing is the most obvious example of a special barrier the legal system has historically imposed on child witnesses too young to manage abstractions. Underlying the competency test is a two-hundred-year-old theory from a British ruling that witnesses under a certain age must be able to prove their ability to discriminate truth from falsehood. The result in American courtrooms has been that five-year-olds have been required to explain to judges the meaning of truth, oaths, right and wrong, reality and unreality when adult thinkers throughout time have struggled unsuccessfully to do so.

11. In order to be believed, witnesses must not only possess certain cognitive skills but also the linguistic abilities to understand attorneys and communicate effectively. What are children's language abilities, how do they differ from those of adults, and how do these differences affect jurors' perceptions of their credibility?

During the investigation and trial of a sexual abuse case, a child must be able to communicate in language understandable to adults. No matter how horrible the offense, an abused child who lacks the requisite vocabulary or communication skills may have no legal recourse in American criminal courts. Children as young as four can use language to communicate their experience, but the legal system too frequently limits their opportunity by demanding that they do so in adult terms. Because so few judges or jurors understand the differences in the linguistic capacities of children and adults, attorneys are seldom required to accommodate questioning of children to their unique capacities.

Language development has been extensively analyzed during the twentieth century. Most theorists agree that children in general and preschoolers in particular differ from adults in several ways. It is obvious that children have smaller vocabularies and rely on much shorter and simpler sentence constructions. Between the ages of three and five, children typically add fifty words a month to their vocabularies and extend sentence length from two to six or eight words. The rapidity with which such development occurs is startling; but it is not adequate in courtrooms where attorneys seldom, unless instructed by judges, ask questions that contain six or eight words or use simple, concrete terms that children can readily understand. "Did you see a cat or a dog?" is a normal question for most people; but a lawyer is likely to ask, "At the time under consideration when you contend you accompanied John to the place of his residence, did you observe that he was the owner of a cat, or was it possibly a dog that you saw?"

Unable to comprehend unfamiliar or abstract terms, children use language that is simple, concrete, and literal. This poses problems because a child's testimony, while literally accurate, may strike adults as evasive, contradictory, or confusing. An attorney may ask a kindergartner, "Are you in school?" and the child will reply, "No." The point, of course, is that the child does not see himself or herself to be "in" school at the moment; rather the child is "in" a courtroom. To a jury, such a response may simply convey incompetence or immaturity that will undermine the child's testimony.

Berliner and Barbieri offer an example of the linguistic confusion that occurred in a case when a defense attorney cross-examined a five-year-old about an incident involving her father.

> DEFENSE ATTORNEY: And then you said you put your mouth on his penis?
>
> CHILD: No.
>
> DEFENSE ATTORNEY: You didn't say that?
>
> CHILD: No.
>
> DEFENSE ATTORNEY: Did you ever put your mouth on his penis?
>
> CHILD: No.
>
> DEFENSE ATTORNEY: Well, why did you tell your mother that your dad put his penis in your mouth?
>
> CHILD: My brother told me to.

The authors here observe, "At this point, it looked as if the child had completely recanted her earlier testimony about the sexual abuse and had only fabricated the story because her brother told her to. However, the experienced prosecuting attorney recognized the problem and clarified the situation":

PROSECUTING ATTORNEY: Jennie, you said that you didn't put your mouth on daddy's penis. Is that right?

CHILD: Yes.

PROSECUTING ATTORNEY: Did daddy put his penis in your mouth?

CHILD: Yes.

PROSECUTING ATTORNEY: What made you decide to tell?

CHILD: My brother and I talked about it, and he said I better tell or dad would just keep doing it.[84]

Syntax is another problematic area for preschool witnesses who have difficulty with complicated sentence constructions. Nevertheless, attorneys rely heavily on complex sentences and questions that confuse them. It takes time and practice to master difficult sentence constructions; and while four- and five-year-olds can generally use subordinate clauses beginning with "that" ("He's the man that did bad things to me"), they are less adept at dealing with clauses that imply coordination or temporal sequence. This means that questions or concepts introduced by "if," "so," "before," "while," "when," "after," and "until" are likely to create confusion; and yet these are the kinds of questions most frequently posed in courtrooms. Required to process a complicated construction, the preschooler's typical way of managing is to process selectively only part of the communication and then either ignore the other segments or reply to the last words she or he hears. This, of course, increases the possibilities for confusion in testimony. To their credit, some judges have developed strategies for coping with the differences in children's and adults' language. For instance, one uses a method called the "age plus one" rule that requires attorneys to limit the length of questions to the number of words in a child's age plus one.[85]

Another problem for preschool witnesses is that they tend to focus on the sequence of words and assume that events occur in the order in which they are spoken in a sentence. This is the reason that very young children do not use and often will misinterpret the passive voice. A three-year-old will understand the sentence "John lied to the policemen"; but the same child may become very confused about the source of the falsehood if told, "The policeman was lied to by John." Carol Chomsky, author of *The Acquisition of Syntax in Children from Five to Ten*, observes that until children reach nine or ten, they use the "minimum distance" principle to interpret language.[86] This means that they concentrate on the order of subjects in a sentence and assume that a phrase that follows a subject is related to it. Thus it is relatively easy for attorneys to confuse children and undermine their credibility.

Children's courtroom woes go beyond problems with vocabulary and syntax to issues of context. Preschoolers, just learning to consider relationships and make comparisons, need precise contextual terminology to provide accurate responses. Stressing the importance of context in understanding children's speech, S. I. Hayakawa offers a personal example: "Once when our little girl was three years old, she found the bath too hot and she said 'make it warmer.' It took me a moment to figure out that she meant, 'Bring the water more nearly to the condition we call warm.' It makes perfectly good sense if you look at it that way."[87] If an attorney asks a child, "Was the man who hurt you big?" the reply may be affirmative or negative, depending on the child's interpretation of "big." "Big" might refer to age, weight, or height; and the response might even be affected by the child's own or parents' stature.

To some it may appear too frustrating, perhaps even impossible, for the courts to respond adequately to the rapidly growing body of knowledge about children. It took centuries for civilization to acknowledge their humanity, and it has been only in the last hundred or so years that adults have attempted to probe their separate realities and to understand the mystery of who children are and what they can and cannot do. America's courts have been slow in learning and applying even the most certain advances in child development knowledge. Because some of that information is inconclusive or obscure, the courts have not had to consider sweeping changes in the ways in which child witnesses are treated. There is, as Skolnick observes, "a tension between the tentativeness with which scientific findings should be regarded and the needs of policy-makers for clear-cut principles upon which to make decisions."[88] What this means for the thousands of American children who are victims of sexual abuse is that recourse in the courts remains an uncertain prospect.

Child psychology will probably never yield "clear-cut principles"; but without the insight it can offer, intelligent and fair decisions are very difficult to achieve. However imperfect, developmental psychology has provided us a wealth of information about children. When that information is juxtaposed against the demands made on child witnesses, the injustice is clear. If the courts are to provide justice for children as well as defendants, they must seek greater understanding and accommodation of the realities of childhood.

4

There Ought to Be a Book: A Case Study

"It's rather curious, you know, this sort of life! I do wonder what can have happened to me! . . . There ought to be a book written about me, that there ought! And when I grow up, I'll write one—but I'm grown up now," she added in a sorrowful tone: "at least there's no room to grow up any more here."

—Lewis Carroll,
Alice's Adventures in Wonderland

ATTORNEYS and judges see the justice system succeed day after day under the most difficult and depressing conditions, so when a frustrated, despairing parent tells of a child victimized by the legal system, many would respond, "It wasn't the fault of the system. Your situation wouldn't have happened if you had had a better judge or prosecutor and the system had worked as it should." But to a parent whose child has been raped and has then been traumatized in a courtroom, the point is not how the system should work but how it did work. Theory and reality are vastly different, and it doesn't matter to that parent or child that a perpetrator "shouldn't" have gone unpunished. It matters that he or she did. To victims, such comments convey that the legal system is a toss of the dice. Those who are lucky enough to be in a state where laws protect children in and out of court, those who are fortunate enough to stumble upon a skilled prosecutor and a knowledgeable judge can afford to feel reassured. For the rest, the justice system promises uncertainty and danger.

It is hard for many, particularly those who have been through a court battle and lost, to regard the verbal combat of the adversarial system as a search for truth. In their minds, there is a vast difference between "truth" and "winning." It isn't enough to say that everyone deserves the best defense possible when that defense obscures the truth about sexual assaults of children and sometimes helps dangerous criminals to go free. Deep down, many of us worry that our legal system is—at its very roots—unable to grapple with this horror for which it was not designed. In many respects, the system is like the little girl in the nursery rhyme—when it is good, it is very, very good; but when it's bad, it's horrid.

There are by now thousands of parents and children who can relate what happens when the system goes awry. According to VOCAL, there are equally disturbing accounts on the defendants' side. The "good" cases are easy to analyze and understand, but what happens in the "horrid" ones? Some trials are flagrant travesties of justice—a divorced father is convicted when his ten-year-old fabricates a sexual abuse story to please her mother, or a wealthy defendant is rescued from punishment because of his position and an expensive attorney. Equally disturbing are those cases in which few facts emerge and where there always remains doubt on both sides. Children, families, defendants, and juries then must live with a verdict called "not guilty" that does not necessarily mean "innocent" and certainly does not mean that a community concerned about its children can afford to feel safe.

The trial we examine in this chapter is one such case. It never attracted the national notoriety of the Jordan, Minnesota, McMartin Preschool, or Country Walk cases; but it offers yet another example of the criminal justice system's inability to come to grips with the problem of how to handle child sexual abuse. It will be instructive to review reports about these cases before turning to the case study because these helped draw national attention to the complexities of dealing with child sexual abuse in the courts.

The McMartin Preschool case, still unresolved, has been since its inception a testament to the ineptness of the criminal justice system.[1] The first complaints came from parents who approached Peggy McMartin Buckey, manager of the prestigious Manhattan Beach, California, preschool. They questioned the behavior of her son Raymond, a college dropout who worked at the school. The problems escalated when a mother picked her son up from school one day and discovered blood in the area of his rectum. She took him to UCLA, where physicians diagnosed him as having been sodomized. Local police responded to the mother's complaint by asking that the boy and another suspected victim be interviewed at Children's Institute International, a nonprofit agency specializing in child sexual abuse.

The police then sent a letter to all McMartin parents, requesting them to report any unusual behavior from their children. Lacking adequate evidence, police dropped charges against Buckey. For more than a year the investigation continued; this was a matter of contention among parents since Manhattan Beach police refused to request help from more specialized, knowledgeable resources.

Although there were reportedly medical records documenting signs of sexual abuse, the primary evidence was, as in most such cases, the word of the children. An additional problem arose as parents of past and present McMartin students grew increasingly dissatisfied with the quality of the police investigation and began taking their children directly to the Children's Institute International, where therapists attempted both to counsel the children and to piece together evidence. The therapists' assumption of this dual role was to provide defense attorneys with a stronger argument when they advanced the theory that "brainwashing" had encouraged the children to say they had been molested. Indeed, to substantiate their claims at the preliminary hearing, the defense team used selected minutes out of the thousands of hours of videotape recording the diagnostic process. As time wore on, therapists and investigators interviewed an astounding number of children—more than four hundred. In what has become frighteningly familiar in such cases, the preschoolers told of being forced to participate in pornography, rape, sodomy, eating feces, sex acts with animals, animal mutilation, satanic rites, and corpse viewing. Some of the children told of being drugged and others of traveling in planes, boats, and balloons.

Sixteen months after the suspicions first arose, local police finally were joined by representatives of the sheriff's office. This addition of personnel came about primarily because therapists from the Children's Institute International, along with other interested parties, had demanded that California's attorney general order additional investigative support. More time passed as the sheriff formed a task force and began another investigative phase. The case became increasingly mired in politics. First assigned to the district attorney's child abuse section, which spent several months interviewing witnesses, it was later reassigned to three prosecutors in another unit.

The defense maintained that the defendants were the victims of a horrifying witch hunt by fanciful children and malicious adults. Cars on California highways reminded the doubtful that nothing had really happened in Manhattan Beach. "Salem 1692–Manhattan Beach 1984," their bumperstickers read. For months the pictures of plump, kindly grandmother Virginia McMartin and her daughter Peggy filled the pages of newspapers and television screens, seeming to remind the American public of the absurdity of the children's claims.

The media appeared to emphasize the children's "exaggerations" and questioned how and why these adults would or could engage in the behaviors of which they had been accused. Defense attorneys' fees and the financial burden to the state in prosecuting the case were frequently mentioned; the psychological and financial costs to the children and their parents appeared to be less important.

The legal system moved slowly, with delays at every turn once the investigation was finally completed. The problem for the prosecution, as the defense knew, was that with every day the memory, especially that of a child, grows less exact, more susceptible to charges of inconsistency and contradiction. And parents, watching their children struggle with the harassment of the legal system, drop away, believing it better to cope in private. The preliminary hearing in the McMartin case continued for eighteen months. Some children testified to the prosecutors and defense attorneys for more than a week; one ten-year-old, for sixteen days. The hearing cost the state $4 million, but it cost the defendants, the children, and their parents far more.

Ultimately five of the defendants were freed. The fate of two remains undetermined. Raymond Buckey and his mother Peggy McMartin Buckey face ninety-nine counts of molestation and one of conspiracy. He has spent three years in jail without bond; she was released on bond after two years. Jury selection took three months. The case has now cost more than $6 million, and there is no end in sight. The prosecution plans to call as many as two hundred witnesses; but out of all the children, only fourteen will be able or permitted to testify. No matter what the outcome, the defendants, the children, and their families will all have suffered through months of anguish, and the flaws and inability of our legal system to cope with child sexual abuse cases will have been demonstrated once again.

A second case that received extensive national coverage occurred in the small town of Jordan, Minnesota.[2] In 1983 Jordan was shocked when two dozen predominantly middle-class adults, many of them parents, were formally charged with abusing as many as fifty children.

The case began when two mothers accused a twenty-seven-year-old trash collector, James Rud, of sexually assaulting their daughters. One of the mothers was his former fiancée, and he was formally charged with ten counts of criminal sexual abuse. When police began interviewing playmates of the children, many not only corroborated the girls' accusations but said they too had been victimized. They implicated additional adults, in some cases their own parents. Then the mother of five-year-old twins approached police to offer information, further confusing the situation. She accused Rud of photographing her daughters in the nude and possibly molesting them, but she also stated she had been present in another room while these activities were occurring. She named three other victims whom she said Rud had abused and also stated that the first two mothers to complain had been present when some of the abuses occurred. In less than a week, all three women were arrested (charges were later dropped). Police discovered that Rud had two previous convictions for child sexual abuse; and as the weeks wore on and the number of alleged victims and perpetrators escalated, the children gave accounts of increasingly bizarre activities, including the torture and murders of other children.

The children's claims of being photographed nude and seeing scrapbooks containing pornography could not be corroborated because police waited nine days after Rud's arrest to search the trailer where he lived. The officer conducting the search took with him none of the materials he found. They included a box of pornographic magazines, two garbage bags of pornographic material, and various items of children's clothing including underwear. The investigator did not complete the search because the parents of the accused arrived and interrupted him; and to avoid an altercation, he left. He reported seeing the couple remove items from the trailer. When police returned the next day, the pornography and clothes were gone.

Corroborating medical evidence was ambiguous. Records indicate that ten of twenty-nine children examined by three doctors showed evidence of sexual abuse, four demonstrated signs of possible abuse, and fifteen revealed no signs. The bulk of the exams were performed by a family practitioner whose methods were questioned by the other doctors. One said his methods could not produce conclusive evidence, but the family doctor cautioned that sexual abuse often leaves no physical symptoms and that children's testimony is more essential. A third doctor also cast doubt on the methodology of the first but observed, after examining one of the alleged victims, that the girl had suffered such severe emotional and physical abuse that she had become incontinent.

The town was polarized not only over the charges but also over the conduct of the investigation. Advocates for the defense described it as a witch hunt. Those sympathetic to the children were concerned that they were forced to repeat their stories as many as twenty times beyond their accounts to prosecutors and therapists, that only twenty-four of the forty-five suspects were arrested even though some of those not charged had failed polygraph tests, that there were no experts on child sexual abuse investigating the case, and that officials sought no help from other agencies.

By the time the first trial, that of a husband and wife, was about to begin, James Rud had agreed to testify against them. Offered a plea-bargain, he implicated fifteen of the twenty-four defendants and described ten instances in which he and others had abused children. On the witness stand, however, he appeared unable to identify the male defendant. An eleven-year-old prosecution witness recanted on the stand; and even though several other children, including the couple's own son, testified against them, they were acquitted. Not long afterward, another girl recanted her account of seeing a child murdered. The county prosecutor dropped charges against subsequent defendants, and Rud later recanted part of his statement implicating others. He was sentenced to forty years in prison on ten counts of first-degree sexual misconduct. The judge also chastised him for discussing his case with the press while awaiting sentencing because he had warned him against doing so and had maintained that this would compromise his testimony in subsequent cases.

The case did not end, however, with the sentencing of Rud. A commission was appointed by the governor of Minnesota to investigate allegations that Kathleen Morris, the prosecutor, had mishandled the case and should thus be removed from office. The commission heard two weeks of testimony and examined five thousand pages of documents before issuing strong criticism about Morris's decision to drop the remaining charges in the case. By dropping the charges, the commission reported, no one really knew whether the innocent were truly innocent or the guilty truly guilty. The report continued, "Those children who were victims became victims once again, abandoned by the system and by the system's representative, Kathleen Morris."[3] Dropping the charges did not constitute malfeasance, however, and thus there was not sufficient proof to recommend that Morris be removed from office.

Jordan remains divided over the case that brought it national notoriety it neither wanted nor wishes to remember. Except for the children and the accused, in time this wish may be granted. After a four-month investigation, the attorney general of Minnesota ruled that none of the cases could be re-tried because the case had been so severely mishandled that the children no longer would be viewed as credible witnesses.

While the McMartin and Jordan cases had sent chills up the spines of parents contemplating exposing their children to the legal system, the 1985 verdict in the Country Walk, Florida, case became a ray of hope for those whose children have been victimized in child-care settings. The subject of the best-selling book *Unspeakable Acts*, Country Walk was the first case of its kind in which convictions were won. How it became a model is in some respects the most compelling aspect of the story. The charges were brought against thirty-six-year-old Frank Fuster and his seventeen-year-old wife, Iliana, who operated a babysitting service in a prosperous suburb of Miami. The victims, predominantly infants, toddlers, and preschoolers, were subjected to sexual abuse and pornography; to being drugged and terrorized by sadistic games, disguises, and animal slaughter; and to having to drink urine and consume excrement. Authorities estimated the couple had access to as many as fifty children; but by the time the case reached court, only eight were able or permitted by parents to testify.

Although some refused to become involved, a core parent group soon formed; and it was their unity and perseverance that inspired greater understanding of the plight of child victims. Defense attorneys and skeptics claimed as evidence of an unprovoked witch hunt the curious parallels between the children's charges here and those in other cases across the country, but the Country Walk parents were not satisfied with easy explanations. They had witnessed the horror first-hand, and they wanted to know how and why their children, too young to understand their own accounts of perversion, had developed such strange similarities to peers they had never met who lived thousands of miles away. One explanation, of which most Americans are ignorant, is that pedophiles are linked through both their informal networks and a profitable child pornography industry that offers not only monetary opportunities and sexual gratification but also detailed suggestions for dealing with children.

The details of Country Walk's well-publicized predecessors in other parts of the country were as accessible as the addresses of organizations that catered to the mutual interests of people consumed with children the way a dieter is consumed with thoughts of chocolate mousse. . . .

Society's last sexual outcasts were forming (and legally incorporating) their own clubs. Thus released from secretive sexual isolation, they found reassurance in their numbers and the appearance of normalcy that led them to the collective conclusion that they weren't sick—society was. For society was imposing "unnatural" inhibitions on their "natural" sexual bent. Why should they be denied broccoli simply because the "ruling mentality" liked carrots? . . .

Kid porn. A three-billion-dollar per year U.S. industry that grossed twice that worldwide. It was bigger than Disney. Much bigger.

Either 30,000 Americans were spending $100,000 apiece each year to purchase pictures of children being raped, or a hundred times more were willing to allot $1,000 of their annual budgets to support their recreational viewing habits. Kid porn provided them with the vital link through which they found each other and commiserated on the "unfairness of an intolerant society" and the "normalcy" of their deeds.[4]

The physical evidence Country Walk's prosecutor possessed was at least as limited as that of the Jordan and McMartin cases. Under American law, there was no way to convey to the jury what the prosecution had learned early in its investigation—that Frank Fuster had been previously convicted of murder and child molestation. The prosecution's case depended on the testimony of eight children, most of them younger and thus less articulate than witnesses in the Jordan and McMartin cases. However, to meet the specious arguments of the defense, contemporary principles of child development were employed in the interviewing process and the trial in Country Walk.

The defense tried many tactics to support its contention that nothing had happened to the children. It sought the legal delays that so often doom child sexual abuse cases, and objected to the use of exceptions to hearsay rules and of videotaped and closed circuit television interviews. To support its contention that the children had been brainwashed, the defense engaged Ralph Underwager, a Lutheran minister deeply involved in VOCAL. Underwager, who claimed to be an expert on Communist interrogation techniques, had appeared on shows like "Donahue" to warn people of the national witch hunt for child molesters. Many believed that he was the decisive figure in the acquittal of the husband and wife tried in the Jordan case. He did not fare so well in Florida. In *Unspeakable Acts*, Jan Hollingsworth records portions of the sworn deposition that she maintains proves Underwager to be an expert in neither child development nor brainwashing. Underwager did not return for the trial.

The task of providing expert testimony for the defense passed instead to a well-known witness, who had testified before for those accused of child molestation. This witness maintained on the stand that the use of anatomically correct dolls causes children to fantasize about abuse and that Country Walk interviewers were unreliable because their bias caused them to look for crimes where there were none. But the prosecution exposed the fact that the witness's expertise had developed over a period of only nine months, and the limited understanding of critical issues in child development that the witness displayed ultimately proved unconvincing to the jury.

Drs. Laurie and Joseph Braga, the husband and wife team who were in-house consultants to the State Attorney's office, had been professors at major universities for decades and were experts in child development. Their interviewing techniques were credited with being the decisive factor in enabling the children to tell their stories. However, the Bragas endured harassment and humiliation for their contribution. Early on, the defense began an investigation into their private lives and submitted motions stating the "real" Joe Braga was dead and therefore "this" Joseph Braga was a fraud. The defense demanded a special investigation be conducted on the Bragas and sought an injunction against their continuing to interview the children. The error, humiliating to the defense, was exposed when a court-appointed investigator cleared the Bragas.

The prosecution's other expert witness was Roland Summit, a child psychiatrist known nationally for his research and experience with sexually abused children. Whereas the Bragas were able to educate the jury about child development, Summit explained the complexities of the behaviors manifested by molested children. These testimonies, combined with those of the eight victims and some of their parents, were the heart of the case.

Convinced that, after five arduous weeks of trial, the jury had already formed an opinion, the prosecution hesitated to risk its case on the testimony of Iliana, Frank Fuster's wife, who in admitting to their crimes had described herself as a victim of Fuster's abuse. But the decision to take the risk was made, and Iliana Fuster testified against her husband. Not long afterward the jury returned a verdict of guilty on all counts. Frank Fuster will be eligible for parole in 2150. Classified as a "youthful offender," his wife Iliana was sentenced, over the protests of parents, to ten years. She will be eligible for parole in 1990.

Several points emerge from reading press accounts of the McMartin, Jordan, and Country Walk cases. Each demonstrates the inordinate complexity of evaluating charges and successfully prosecuting cases when witnesses are very young and when physical evidence is limited or nonexistent. They also exhibit the enormous confusion and frustration that result as investigations, interviews, trials, and press coverage drag on. All three cases reveal the potential for extraneous political forces or public feelings to influence legal proceedings and the extreme dissension created within communities when charges of child sexual abuse occur. Most of all, they communicate to the public the need for a better way to deal with cases of this kind, the need to employ contemporary knowledge of child development in courtrooms so that children have an opportunity to be heard.

While the details of these three cases or others like them appear exact in media accounts, they cannot be fully understood by any who have not participated directly in the legal process or followed it by reading records and transcripts of individual cases. Child sexual abuse cases, especially those with many victims and perpetrators, are so complex in human and legal terms that it is difficult to compare one to another or to make definitive judgments on the basis of second-hand accounts and press reports.

The following case study goes beyond press accounts and is based on analysis of transcript materials and court proceedings and on interviews with the families of a group of children who claimed to be abused and with some of the professionals who worked with them. It is not intended to retry the case or to suggest that the defendants, who were acquitted, were guilty. Neither the defendants nor their families and attorneys were interviewed. This was not because their problems in facing the charges were insignificant but rather because the focus here is on the experience of children and their families in dealing with the ordeals of the legal system, and on the restrictions that often deny juries access to information that might allow them to evaluate children's accusations with greater insight. Names and certain other characteristics have been changed.

The Parents' and Children's Story

Laurie Chapman was four years old when her parents enrolled her in Greenbrook Preschool, a prestigious school for upper-middle-class children housed in a former country estate in the northeast. Laurie attended the school for only two weeks. She missed one day the first week and one the second because she refused to go, and her parents allowed her to stay home.

On September 10, Laurie and her brother were playing in the kitchen while their mother, Patti, prepared dinner. Her mother had just told her that she didn't like the word "poopy," which Laurie had chanted over and over since entering school. Suddenly, she looked up at Patti and asked, "Mom, do you know 'dick' is another word for 'penis'?"

Startled, Patti replied, "As a matter of fact, I do. Did you learn that at school too?"

Laurie nodded. "Today at school we saw this video, and there was this man and he pulled down his pants and took his penis out." Becoming animated, she jumped out of her chair and continued, "He put it on her head and it went up in the air. Then Mike [the preschool director] said, 'Uh-oh,' and we saw the other movies."

Patti wasn't convinced. "Laurie, did you really see a video like that?"

"Yes, Mom, we really did," the four-year-old answered.

When her mother said that children shouldn't see such movies and that she was going to call the school, Laurie grew panicky and cried.

"No, Mommy, you can't tell. You really can't. Arnie [one of the teachers] said Mike has a knife." As Laurie spoke, she continually pointed into her mouth and cried, "Look, Mom!"

Unable to comprehend all of what the four-year-old was trying to tell her, Patti was worried that her daughter was genuinely confused and had misunderstood something that had happened at school. "That's ridiculous, Laurie. I'm calling tomorrow," she said.

The child's reaction was so violent that her parents decided to contact their pediatrician. When they did so, the doctor on call said that one of his associates had a child in the school and that he would call her and have her find out "who was who." Patti protested that confronting the school's staff directly would not be the option she and her husband would take. Whether or not Laurie's story *was* true, those involved would deny it. The doctor replied that he would call the other pediatrician to see what she could find out, but Patti reiterated that she was not sure if she and her husband wanted to do that. He said he understood.

Turning to Laurie, Patti asked, "Are you upset because you told a lie or because you were afraid I would tell?"

The little girl began to cry again. "You really can't tell, Mom. Mike really does have a knife."

At 8:30 A.M. the following day Mike Herbst, the school's director, called the Chapmans and said that he had spoken with the pediatrician and wanted to assure them that Laurie's story was false. Patti replied that she was open to the possibility that it was a fabrication but that Laurie had gone into some sexual detail and had said that Mike had a knife. She told him that the child had again refused to go to school and that she would not return until she and her husband had contacted a few other sources.

Patti then called the pediatrician who had informed the institution about the incident and told her that she felt it was inappropriate for her to have given information without permission. Patti was particularly upset that the pediatrician had identified Laurie, but the doctor maintained it was necessary to do so in order to find out who Laurie's teacher was. She went on to say that she felt nothing had happened, that four is "the story-telling age," and that Laurie had probably picked up comments from other children. Patti countered that her daughter's reaction was severe and that her fear seemed real. The doctor advised that she would be concerned only if the child were having nightmares or showing other symptoms.

That night Laurie woke up screaming and refused to tell what bothered her. Her mother recalls, "She hadn't had a nightmare for as long as I can remember. The last I remember was when she was three. [The other thing that bothered me was that] she will either tell me what a dream was about or that she didn't remember—never 'I can't tell you.'"

Patti called a parent group that had shown Laurie's class a prevention film about sexual abuse and a therapist that she herself had seen for a year. Both felt the story was unusual for a preschooler and supported the decision not to send Laurie back to school until her fear was resolved.

"The therapist, who knew the history of my relationship with Laurie, said she had always been independent and her fear should be respected. I was sure if I could solve Laurie's 'problem,' she would go back to school. If there was more to tell, she would eventually tell it," Patti asserted.

The Chapmans decided to call Mike and ask to meet with Laurie's teacher, Arnie Hart. Mike refused, contending that it was against policy, that he needed to protect teachers from harassment by parents. Patti remembers "telling him I was concerned about anything that might have frightened Laurie. Had the children been making sexual comments during the movies? Had Arnie reprimanded her severely? Had one of the other children frightened her?"

Mike still insisted there was no reason for the meeting. Arnie had noticed nothing, he said. When Patti called again the next day to insist that she be allowed to see Arnie, she told Mike she wanted to go over Laurie's day with him. "I said I could pick up on a fear they missed, and I needed to meet with the person who cared for her four hours a day. I said I had no objection to Mike's being present. He asked me if I wanted my pediatrician to attend. I said it would not be necessary."

Laurie refused to discuss or attend school and denied seeing the video she had described. The meeting with Mike and Arnie wasn't particularly helpful. Mike offered to refund Laurie's tuition, but Patti replied that she believed in teaching her child to solve problems. "If there's a problem, we solve it. We don't run away. If they could make her feel safe, I was sure she'd be back, I told Mike."

Returning home, Patti assured Laurie that Mike and Arnie were "very sorry that she was frightened and they would do everything they could to make her feel safe." Once again Laurie refused to go back to school and refused to talk about the problem. Patti remembers being at wit's end: "This was so unlike her. We have always solved problems. She'd never been forced to go anywhere. If she didn't like something, she could tell me why and we would solve it. There was never a thing she couldn't tell me. I called my mother. My mother said, 'If she said she saw a video, she saw a video. She doesn't need to make it up to quit school' . . . Later I talked with my college roommate, whose daughter was an assault victim. She told me to try telling Laurie that I believed her about the video. Through my questioning and exploring other options, I may have given her the message that I didn't believe her."

After the call, Patti attempted to convince her daughter she believed the incident with the video had actually occurred. When Laurie vehemently denied her own story, her mother responded, "It's okay. I know you're afraid. I'm not afraid of Mike or Arnie . . . You don't have to tell me, but I don't want you to be afraid or confused about what you saw. You can talk to me about it. I won't ask you any more questions. Tell me when you're ready. You don't ever have to go back to that school if you don't want to. You don't have to tell me why."

That night Laurie interrupted her mother while her brother was being put to bed. She told her that she saw a video, that a man pulled down his pants and took his penis out, that he put it in a girl's mouth. She said her teachers were in the film and that at one point Mike said, "Uh-oh, we'd better close this door."

Patti asked if this was when she was told not to tell her parents. "She said yes. I asked her what they said would happen if she told. They said they would be fired. I asked her if she knew what that meant. She said she didn't. I explained it to her and said that they knew they were in big trouble. She said Arnie really said Mike had a knife . . . She was very frightened."

That night the Chapmans called a second community support group to ask for advice; they were told to call the police. That call began the legal ordeal from which they and three other families will never recover. They expected that the coming months, possibly years, would be difficult for Laurie; but they had no idea that the legal system itself would become a source of trauma.

Laurie's disclosures, denials, and symptoms continued. She drew bizarre pictures, had violent temper tantrums, wet the bed, and awakened screaming from nightmares. She refused to play with other children or to leave the house. The Chapmans were unable to use babysitters because Laurie grew hysterical whenever they tried to leave her. She complained that her throat and jaw hurt and developed a curious habit of scratching her face. She talked constantly of being afraid that Mike and Arnie would kill her mother and father with Mike's knife. She made what Patti and Tom considered at the time "goofy" and "nonsensical" statements about animals and food. She kept talking about eating "weiners." In public and private, there was no predicting her behavior. Once when her mother returned after leaving her with a babysitter, she was wearing a diaper. Other times she removed her clothing and masturbated or fingered her anus.

The record of Laurie Chapman's experience appears in a notebook her mother kept after Laurie's nightmares began:

She started to talk about school, then she began shoving her fingers in her vagina, taking her fingers out, putting them in her mouth and pretending she was eating. Then she did it with her anus. I asked her what she was doing. She giggled. I told her to stop. She kept doing it and giggling. I asked her if it was a clue. She nodded . . .

She went to the Smiths' Wednesday. Sandy had to bring her home because she and Kellie were so out of control. Thursday she refused to go outside and play. She gets so obnoxious . . . so defiant. I am so tired . . . so frustrated . . . I am adding to [her problem]. I walked out of church today . . . I became angry because she was difficult in the shoe store yesterday . . . and earlier because she was wild while we were shopping. My patience is just running so thin. She is so wild, and I am beginning to feel trapped. Everyone needs so much attention, and I don't see any movement toward normalcy.

The notebook is a record of frustration and despair, of the push and pull between parent and child as the mother hesitates between denial and belief. Finally, having accepted the child's story, she tries to help Laurie free herself by telling what happened. The child offers a little and then retreats, denies what she's said the day before, and then returns a few days later with more. It is a painfully slow, tormenting process, and the mother suffers: "I feel so inadequate . . . I couldn't [help] her. She was so angry with me. Dr. Stephens [Laurie's therapist] kept telling me to tell her I did the best I could. I didn't know they were bad. I can't know everything. Children give us this magical power. We are supposed to *know*. Didn't we know they were hungry or wet or bored before they could talk? They expect us to *know*. The hard part is I expected myself to know."

Gradually, Laurie began to tell her story. She described being raped on five different occasions by Mike and Arnie. She said they had "put their penises" in hers and other children's mouths and anuses. She said that she and other children watched teachers act in and then were themselves photographed in "bad" movies. Laurie told of being taken during rest period to a "camera room" where she and another little girl were told to "go up on the thing—the big penis" and stand up and take their clothes off. She explained how she and other children were then forced to fondle each other. She described oral intercourse between the children and told of being made to suck on a friend's penis. She talked of being made to smell "poo-poo" and of being threatened with having to eat it as she said Arnie had done. She said "the penis [in her anus] didn't hurt too much. It was like a popsicle stick going in." She worried about what happens "if you drink . . . something [that] comes out of a penis." She went on to describe Mike holding a knife to her mouth, vagina, chest and eye; she connected the knife with black-and-white checked floor tile. Later, after the trial, Laurie would tell even more; but even these revelations seemed more than the Chapmans could bear: "I think about Laurie. She was not yet five. He held a knife to her head and told her he would kill her. I didn't even know about it until [seven months later]. The fear, my God."

Late in September Patti Chapman talked to Brenda Sanders for the first time. They did not live in the same neighborhood; they had never met. The only link was that both their daughters attended Greenbrook Preschool. When Laurie identified the Sanderses' daughter Tina as being involved in the school's activities, the police visited their home. According to the trial transcript, Tina's testimony corroborated that of Laurie. Today her parents will not discuss the trial and have requested that the details of their experience remain private. The parents of Mark Dunham, the fourth child, have also refused to speak about the case.

Like the other three families, Hillary and Jeff Young, parents of four-year-old Allison, learned to live with pain and confusion as they came to believe their daughter's accounts of abuse. During the second week of school Allison began wetting the bed and adamantly refusing to attend school. The bed wetting continued in an almost unbroken pattern of Sunday through Thursday nights; it never occurred on Friday or Saturday nights. Allison also began having headaches so severe that a doctor suspected sinus or inner ear problems and then suggested that the Youngs take her to a pediatric neurologist, who found nothing wrong. Worse than the headaches were the nightmares. For almost a year she awakened screaming in the middle of the night, often crying, "Get away, don't touch me." Her sister, who was ten at the time, recalls, "It hurt my school work because I'd be up all night listening to her screaming. Before that, when she was in school, she never wanted to go. She'd tell me that if she didn't walk fast enough, they'd kick her. Then sometimes she'd say weird stuff out of nowhere like about people dancing naked and animals getting killed and stuff."

The Youngs took their three children to the beach one weekend after the third week of school. While there, they left them with a sitter one night and were called back because Allison had become so hysterical and violent. They found her soaked from head to toe with urine. Hillary says, "Her face was so white and drawn I almost didn't recognize her. I had never seen a child so completely soaked from wetting the bed. It really scared me."

Eventually, Hillary called the school to inquire why Allison was so unhappy; Mike Herbst replied that they knew of no problem, that she was a "fine student." Soon afterwards the Youngs learned of the investigation. They had witnessed so much bizarre behavior from their daughter that they were inclined to believe the complaints, but there was no verbal indication from Allison that she had been involved. In October, she was subjected to a urinalysis because her urination was so excessive.

Two incidents finally convinced the Youngs that Allison was in trouble. During a game of tag, she hurt her hand and was bleeding so profusely that she had to be taken to the hospital, where she refused to allow anyone to touch it. Nevertheless, covered in blood and obviously in pain, she at no time shed a tear. Not long after that while at an amusement park, she again injured the hand and again refused to show it to anyone. This time she huddled screaming in the back of her mother's car, asserting that her hand was her "private property and [that] nobody [was] going to touch [her]."

It was about that time, her mother says, that Allison turned to her one night at bedtime and said, "A little boy in line at school said he was going to kill me, and Arnie said he was going to kill me." Suspecting the worst for months, Hillary Young now recalls, "I thought I was going to die when she said that. I felt so out of control because now I knew it was true, and I knew there was no way to get it all out of her. That's when I made an appointment at the hospital. What else could I do? I was desperate. You feel like here is this child I gave birth to and fed and took care of all these years. We investigated this school and the people there, and then this happened anyway. The worst part for me was that I was completely blinded for so long by my own child's behavior. I couldn't even figure out what was going on in my own home. We thought of everything else— maybe she had sinus problems or she didn't like the car pool she was in or maybe she was upset with her brother and sister. Everything. But not this."

Allison's disclosures, like those of Laurie, came sporadically and unpredictably. She told of a skit in which Sarah, a teacher, and Mike fondled each other and danced around naked while Arnie took pictures. She described a room where "there was a big penis and we sat around it like Indians without any clothes on and Sarah and Arnie took pictures." She said that the "big penis" was brought into the room during rest period and that Mike and Arnie told her that they would kill her and her mother if she told, and that even if they went to jail, they would come back and kill them someday. She complained constantly of problems with her throat and talked about having dirt put into her vagina and anus. Finally, in January she told her mother that Arnie took her hand and made her touch a knife and whispered in her ear that he would kill her if she told anyone. That was when Hillary and Jeff Young remembered the bizarre picture she had drawn months earlier of a knife lying on a tile floor patterned exactly like that at the school. It was the same black-and-white floor Laurie had described.

Before the Trial

In the year that followed Patti Chapman's call to the police, the children related their charges to approximately two dozen doctors, psychologists, psychiatrists, social workers, police, prosecutors, and grand jurors. They occasionally displayed confusion about minor details, but their basic assertions did not change. Nevertheless, the children faced great difficulty. Their charges were heard in a state with limited legal protections and services for sexually abused children. Bewildered about how to proceed and where to go for help, they and their parents were subjected to multiple interviews that created frustration, stress, and confusion. After the seemingly endless turmoil of the investigation, they were forced to face a series of legal hearings that produced extensive testimonies upon which the defense would later focus.

More than a year after the alleged assaults, three defendants from the Greenbrook Preschool appeared in criminal court to be tried on charges of engaging in fellatio and furnishing minors with an obscene movie. No physical evidence, such as the knife or movie, was ever located to support the children's allegations. Any proof of that kind would long since have disappeared if the teachers were alerted by the pediatrician's telephone call. Furthermore, no medical evidence supported the children because they were given only routine medical examinations. Colposcopy, a medical procedure used to identify trauma not obvious in regular physical examinations, was either unknown or unavailable.[5] There were only the children, their parents, and a handful of experts to convince a judge and jury with little knowledge of child development or sexual abuse.

But before the children were permitted to tell the jury what they believed had happened to them, they were subjected to still another ordeal—the competency hearing in which the judge determined whether they should be allowed to testify. Had the children been in federal court or in many other states, they would have been spared this indignity, which is widely regarded as archaic and unfair; but for Laurie, Allison, Tina, and Mark, it was mandatory.

Laurie's experience was revealing. The Chapman family was told that competency hearings usually take five minutes and involve only a few questions from the judge. They were not told that, without warning or preparation, the child would be required to identify the defendants outside the presence of the jury. "It scared her to death," her father recalls.

Not yet six years old, Laurie Chapman sat for more than one hour through hundreds of questions by six defense attorneys, the prosecutors, and the judge. Reading the transcript gives a sense of the difficulties the courtroom logistics posed for a little girl. The judge told her to "take [her] finger and go like this on that little microphone there. You want to talk in there so your voice comes through." A defense attorney asked, "Are you falling out of your chair again? . . . Looks like you're slippery up there." But no one did anything about the discomfort, and she went on responding to questions that were either impossible for a young child to answer or irrelevant to the issue of whether she was capable of telling the truth: "Do you have one doggie or more than one doggie?" "You have a pink pen?" "What's Bugs Bunny look like?" "Do you know who the president of the United States is?" "What kind of car does your daddy drive?" Some of the questions were incomprehensible even to an adult: "Did the prosecutor tell you anything there that was incorrect when you talked to the judge over there?" Laurie was pressed to remember how many times she had talked with the prosecutor during the month of October and whether, four months later, she "told some things that were not correct, isn't that true?"

When tested with questions of substance and relevance to the issue of her competency, Laurie did very well. Asked, "Do you know what an oath is?" she replied, "No." Asked "Do you know what your duty is in this court-room?" she answered, "Tell the truth." When she was asked "what it is to tell a lie," she said, "Not the truth." Perhaps her best moment, the moment that demonstrated an essential difference between a five-year-old and most adults, occurred when she was asked, "Do you always tell the truth?" Laurie Chapman replied, "Not always." The defense attorney pressed on. "You tell lies at times, isn't that correct?" "Yeah," replied the child.

In all four cases, the defense attorneys urged the judge to disqualify the children and prevent them from testifying. They contended that Laurie, for example, was incompetent because she couldn't remember the number of children in her class and couldn't describe the rooms in the school. No matter that a year had passed and the questions required Laurie to muster cognitive and linguistic abilities beyond the capacity of a five-year-old. No matter that most of the questions were irrelevant to Laurie's memory of whether or not someone placed his penis in her mouth. No matter that after a year, most adults would have trouble with the same questions.

Perhaps the most significant point of the competency hearing came when the defense tried to prohibit Laurie's testimony on the grounds that she had no "understanding of the compulsion of the law." This was because she re-plied no when asked, "If you don't tell the truth in here, you don't know what's going to happen in here, do you?" Even the lawyers appeared to struggle with that question. After several minutes of repeating that intimi-dating query and trying to determine the penalty if Laurie lied, the judge finally acknowledged the absurdity of the situation:

JUDGE: What is the penalty for a five-year-old who lies on the stand?

FIRST DEFENSE ATTORNEY: Obviously nothing.

JUDGE: If she says she doesn't know the penalty, I've just asked six law-yers and not one has told me. If you people don't know, how is a five-year-old—

FIRST DEFENSE ATTORNEY: Penalty is perjury.

SECOND DEFENSE ATTORNEY: Two to five years, your Honor.

JUDGE: I'm asking you a serious question, so I can't feel she's deficient for not knowing what you don't know.

Somehow out of the confusion and posturing came the judge's decision that Laurie and eventually the other children could testify: "She's clearly stated what happened. She clearly showed it with the dolls. Now, whether the jury will believe it or not and so forth is up to them, but she was clear as to several essential facts in this case. If she was unclear as to others, that's something you can take up with the jury."

The Trial

By the time the Greenbrook Preschool case went to trial, the community was polarized, and the members of the school's board of trustees had moved to the side of the defendants. Perhaps this was inevitable. In almost every multi-victim, multi-offender case, institutions have tended to view their survival and welfare as linked to those of defendants. It is a stance that will probably be altered only when it becomes possible to separate the financial liabilities of institutions from the behaviors of the people they employ.

There was from the beginning of the trial the aura of a three-ring circus—too many victims, too many defendants, too many attorneys for the jurors and everyone else to keep straight. Defense attorneys frequently confused the children's names, the charges, and sometimes even the defendants, a mistake that caused the parents to wonder how these same attorneys could be taken seriously when they attacked the children for not having precise recall of minute details from their grand jury testimonies months earlier. In closing arguments one of the prosecutors would comment to the jury:

> You've heard a lot of numbers thrown about in this case. You've heard a child didn't talk about a rape for six weeks or two months or, God forbid, 241 days. Well, I've got numbers for you too. That's the number of times that Ms. Kirby [a defense lawyer] called Laurie Tina and Tina Laurie, and called Laurie Mary [one of the prosecutors] and Mary Laurie, and called Mrs. Chapman Mrs. Sanders and Mrs. Sanders Mrs. Chapman; and I know that you are convinced beyond a reasonable doubt that Ms. Kirby knew who was the prosecutor and who was the five-year-old, and she mixed up names. And she had reams of notes in front of her, . . . but the five-year-olds were expected to remember.

Defense Strategies

It is not difficult to establish reasonable doubt in a child sexual abuse case. Encumbered by myths and ignorance about children and the dynamics of child sexual abuse, jurors are reluctant to believe a crime so perverse and personally threatening. In her analysis of the Country Walk case, Hollingsworth captures the very essence of the offense when she describes it as "an invisible crime of illogical motive."[6] Invisible, illogical, impossible. A crime without understandable motivation, without witnesses, a crime seemingly impossible to carry out. The setting and characters may change, but the crime and the structure and theme of the defense seldom vary. The defense attorneys in the Greenbrook case employed common legal histrionics.

If my client is found guilty in this case, we in effect are going to amputate
. . . part of his life from him . . . We're going to shut off and crimp that
aspect of his life.

The reasonable doubt standard is a profoundly important thing. The
law imposes this standard because Blackstone, a distinguished British
philosopher from whom we borrowed this, said it is better to let ten
guilty men go free than to have one innocent man be convicted.

Now it is your responsibility as the jury to pump life and meaning
into that. You see, proof beyond a reasonable doubt . . . that can be
merely empty words that have no meaning unless you put meaning into
it, unless you feel a fire in your belly for that phrase. You must give it
life in this case so that when it is struck, it will bruise; so when it is cut,
it will bleed; so when you put your ear up to its heart, you can hear the
beat—and that's your responsibility.

The defense also predictably advanced the witch-hunt argument:

Back in 1692, some girls who were kids started saying that various
people in the village of Salem, Massachusetts, were witches, and they
would throw themselves on the floor, and nineteen people were hung for
being witches . . .

Now, our country has gone through various times of hysteria. It's
found various causes which have made hysteria, and it has behaved in
irrational ways. One of the favorite ones right now is child sexual abuse
. . . I submit that if we do not temper our concern about child sexual
abuse with good common sense, we're going to convert that concern into
a suicide pact; and . . . unless a message is sent in this case, some other
people will be in that chair with [Arnie, the defendant] with this kind of
junk.

The Greenbrook defense attorneys knew that the best defense is a good
offense, and they proceeded to discredit the allegations by challenging the
techniques used to obtain evidence from the children. This strategy places
the prosecution in an almost impossible position. Years of research and study,
corroborated by surveys of adults who were child victims, contend that children will not risk disclosure unless they sense they will be believed and supported. But by expressing this essential belief in the child, an adult opens
the way to charges of contaminating the child's thinking and reinforcing fantasy. Child development experts maintain that children's life experiences are
mirrored in their play. This understanding influenced the evolution of the
anatomically correct dolls and other methods used in play therapy to help
abused children overcome their fears and describe the horrors they have suffered. Yet to most adults, dolls and games are not reality; and it is easy for
defense attorneys to convince a jury that a child was "just playing" when
disclosure was achieved through the use of specialized techniques developed

to help children communicate. Thus the Greenbrook defense attacked one of the prosecution's experts:

> Her clinical manuals, her protocol says you must believe a child. She comes into court, testifies that she has never seen a five-year-old child lie about sexual abuse. Anytime any expert or anybody tells me the word "never," I have a hard time swallowing it. . . . Is she saying this because she's head of the child abuse team, wants to go the extra yard?

During the investigation, therapists had used a game to reach one of the children. The child was asked to pretend she was someone else ("Pretend you are a little girl who is afraid to tell something bad that happened to you. Why can't you tell?"). The theory is that in responding through an imaginary child, the victim will feel free to reveal details she would otherwise refuse to communicate. The technique sometimes works with children, but it jeopardized the Greenbrook prosecution when it confronted adult biases about children's fantasy. The defense wisely capitalized on the prosecution's predicament: "Isn't that a terrific thing for a jury to rely upon, that procedure, that contamination, in determining my client's future?"

The only hope for successfully eliciting testimony from many child witnesses is to prepare them for court, support them during the process, and then reinforce them when they testify. Unfortunately, this process can play into the hands of a defense attorney. In the Greenbrook trial the defense implied that the children had been bribed to lie with gifts and that they had been told what to say by prosecutors and parents. They protested when a child was allowed to sit on the lap of Carol Miller, a child advocate: "Carol Miller, Tina's in-court prompter, her in-court prompter! You think she's going to change her story sitting on the lap of her in-court prompter? No way."

Another predictable defense strategy used in the Greenbrook trial was denigration of the children's abilities and minimizing of their symptoms. Although researchers have identified symptoms that characterize sexually abused children, a defense attorney can easily attribute them to other causes. What child doesn't wet the bed or have nightmares from time to time? What child doesn't occasionally fight with siblings and hesitate to leave his or her mother? What child doesn't draw gruesome pictures in an age when television and VCRs bring sex and violence into preschoolers' homes? In this case Laurie's unusual behaviors became, according to the defense, "bits and pieces thrown into one composite"; and after all, she had had nightmares before, they maintained.

Children's fear, impotence, and reluctance to report abuse create substantial time lapses between the events and the disclosures, which come in fragments. It is easy to suggest to a jury that the time lapses and fragmentation are evidence of deception or brainwashing. Proceeding gingerly to avoid arousing sympathy for the child, a smart defense attorney will make it appear that the child fantasizes, confuses, distorts, and lies. The attorney can maintain that other children, adults, and the media have planted sexual images in the minds of alleged victims so that, somehow, a child witness is unable to differentiate between the pain of anal intercourse and a stolen glimpse of someone else's genitals.

Thus the Greenbrook defense attorneys argued that the children concocted intricate descriptions from pornographic movies they may have watched at home and from misunderstanding movies they saw at school. Although most of the movies were once shown to millions of children who did not go home and talk about having oral sex forced upon them, the defense argued that the films might frighten and confuse a young child. One film probably appeared pornographic to preschoolers, asserted the defense, because it used a visual technique that "had things stretching out which are pinkish in color which had a certain erotic aspect."

The defense also introduced the brainwashing and the "true perpetrator" arguments. Defense attorneys frequently employ "experts" to make analogies between the techniques used to elicit testimony from children and the brainwashing practices of the North Koreans, Chinese Communists, and North Vietnamese. After introducing the brainwashing or programming argument, a defense lawyer tries to establish that someone other than the accused set events in motion. The "true" perpetrators in child abuse cases can be parents, physicians, social workers, psychologists, psychiatrists—anyone who believes that normal children do not suddenly begin talking about swallowing semen. Defense attorneys can suggest more than one "true" perpetrator and suppose a variety of motivations, a relatively simple task because the reasonable doubt standard does not require proof of any of their insinuations.

During Florida's Country Walk case, child advocates Joseph and Laurie Braga warned authorities they would become the defense's "perpetrators." Jan Hollingsworth quotes both Bragas at length. Laurie Braga began:

"The defense will build its case around us. We will be the targets. . . . This is the posture being taken in mass abuse cases all over the country. The attorneys for the abusers are crucifying the people who talk to children."

"Jurors are uncomfortable with the whole idea of children being raped," said Joe. "They would rather believe that it didn't happen, so anybody that gives them an excuse—they'll accept that."

"Because people's initial reaction," interjected Laurie, "when all the publicity started coming out about the amount of sexual abuse that existed . . . was, 'It can't possibly be that widespread.' Especially when the accused can't be picked out of a crowd. If the accused is a policeman or banker or teacher, that's very upsetting, because that puts them in the uncomfortable position of not knowing who to trust."

Amid that kind of inner conflict, they pointed out, reasonable doubt is not difficult to cultivate.[7]

In the Greenbrook case, the defense labeled Patti Chapman the "true perpetrator": "This isn't a case of sexual child abuse. . . . For reasons known only to Mrs. Chapman . . . she has . . . pressured her child into saying these things. In a strange sort of way, either inadvertent or purposeful, Mrs. Chapman is the perpetrator." The defense scenario was that Patti Chapman had initiated the programming process; and that having brainwashed her own daughter, she then convinced her husband, Allison, Hillary, and Jeff Young, Tina and her parents, and Mark Dunham and his parents that the children had seen and participated in pornographic movies and been sexually assaulted in various ways.

In broad strokes, the defense wove the programming theory, always cognizant that it had to prove nothing: "We've denied the charges, and that's all we have to do. We don't have to demonstrate . . . and this is critical, that the little girl was programmed. We don't have to demonstrate that she was manipulated. We don't have to demonstrate that she wasn't telling the truth. You know whose job that is. It's their job."

The unpredictable element in this, as in any child sexual abuse case, is the possibility of recantation. It is what every defendant and defense attorney hope for and frequently get. The unique dynamics of child sexual abuse often aid the defense, which can always exploit evidence of recantation. Children who have been molested are ashamed, frightened, and confused; so they make their disclosures in ambiguous and sporadic ways. When their revelations threaten relationships or the equilibrium of their lives, they retreat, they recant, they shrug their shoulders and say nothing happened, because denial makes life easier than the truth. Although experts know that denial and recanting are standard behavior for abused children, most jurors do not and thus can be convinced that they are evidence of deception. A smart defense attorney will probe for evidence of recantation and will return to it again and again as proof that the child is lying or has been programmed. The Greenbrook defense had only to hope and wait.

This is not meant to imply that the defendants were guilty or that defense strategies were unethical, but it does suggest that the strategies employed were, as in similar cases, often antithetical to a genuine search for truth. An innocent defendant, no less than a true victim, may have a great stake in hearing and probing all that a child and experts can offer because only through accurate and critical questioning can the full truth emerge.

The Judge
In order to move beyond polemics and strategizing to an analysis of the children's veracity, the legal process in the Greenbrook case should have probed exactly what the children said had been done to them. That never happened.

The jury never heard the substance of the children's accusations. In part this occurred because the case was tried before a judge who appeared to have limited knowledge of child sexual abuse and a very narrow interpretation of the law of hearsay.

"Hearsay," testimony from one person about what someone else has said, is not usually allowed in a trial. The reason is obvious. The Constitution guarantees a defendant the right to confront prosecution witnesses; in-person testimony helps produce a full and fair trial because the witness knows the subject best, can answer follow-up questions, and the jury is thus enabled to assess the witness's demeanor and weigh the witness's credibility. The evidence laws of every state do, however, recognize that there must be exceptions to allow essential hearsay to be presented to a jury. The exceptions that apply in child sexual abuse cases will be discussed in detail in chapter 5, but for now it can be said that hearsay is permitted when it is the best evidence available and when it is reliable enough for a jury to analyze and assess. Judges who apply incorrect or narrow hearsay interpretations to such cases effectively deprive both children and defendants of an honest search for truth.

In the Greenbrook Preschool case, the judge's rulings on hearsay evidence prevented the jury from hearing what would have been the most critical testimony of the trial. Again and again, the judge refused to allow testimony about the children's disclosures. Because their knowledge of them was so limited, the jurors could not fairly assess the credibility of the accusations.

It was essential that Patti Chapman be allowed to tell the jury of her daughter's first disclosure about the assault. The theory of the defense was, after all, that Patti had conspired to build a case against the defendants, using her daughter, other children, and their parents to do so. If the substance of Laurie's disclosures and the circumstances around them were not known to the jurors, they had no way of making an informed judgment about either her accusations or the defense theory. But the court repeatedly prevented the jury from hearing anything of significance. At one point, Patti was trying to describe Laurie's initial disclosure.

PROSECUTOR: Was that the extent of what she said at that particular time?

PATTI: No, sir. She said, "Today we saw a video at school and a man pulled down his pants."

DEFENSE: Objection.

JUDGE: Wait. The agreement was, I think, that you [the prosecutor] only go so far as to say that they saw a video.

The absurdity is apparent. The jury could not render an intelligent and fair verdict about whether the child saw a pornographic movie unless it knew everything the child originally said about the movie and the circumstances in which she said it. Laurie's mother could have told that, but to demand that five-year-old Laurie recall the exact details of the event and her subsequent disclosure after a year was to ask the impossible. Without crucial information about the substance of Laurie's disclosure, vital portions of the remaining testimony were stilted and misleading. For example, at one point Patti described her confrontation with Mike and Arnie about Laurie's allegations:

PATTI: I asked if they had any explanation for the sexual detail that Laurie had gone into. [Note: the jury had no knowledge of the sexual detail because the court's rulings had prevented it.]

DEFENSE: Objection.

JUDGE: Wait a minute. The jury will not assume that she went into sexual detail because that would be hearsay.

Deprived of information essential to understanding the charges against the defendants, the jury could easily assume that "it didn't happen." The judge's rulings on hearsay pervaded the trial, distorting and confusing even expert testimony on behalf of the children. Explaining how she used play therapy with the children, their psychiatrist was asked how they reacted when they discussed some of the alleged sexual activity. The defense objected. It was hearsay. The judge intervened, "We don't want you to tell us what they said." Perhaps the judge himself summarized best how his rulings prevented essential evidence from reaching the jury when the prosecutor asked the psychiatrist to give her professional opinion on whether the children displayed signs of being traumatized: "An expert witness has to be subjected to cross-examination for the basis of her opinion [on the children's statements to her], and if you [the prosecutor] are going to talk just generally about the information given her, then there's been no basis for the opinion; and I don't know how you are going to get the basis since you agreed that you couldn't bring in any hearsay."

The prosecutor's acquiesence to the judge's interpretations of hearsay law exacerbated the problem. At one point the prosecutor had the chance, through the defense's own questions, to demonstrate to the jury the innocence of Tina's disclosure and her mother's response; but, incredibly, he objected on hearsay grounds and missed the opportunity.

TINA: [Arnie] followed us into the bathroom and he peed in our mouth.

DEFENSE: Okay now, what did your mommy say when you told her that?

PROSECUTOR: Objection. It's hearsay.

JUDGE: Sustained.

DEFENSE: I'm questioning credibility here, your Honor. I would like to have the opportunity to question the witness about this.

PROSECUTOR: Object.

JUDGE: Sustained.

To complete the absurdity, the judge allowed the child to describe what her mother *did* rather than what she *said*.

DEFENSE: What did your mommy do when you told her that?

TINA: Nothing.

Because the prosecution did not effectively resist the judge's faulty notion of hearsay, the web of ambiguity and confusion grew. When the prosecutor continued to make counterproductive objections to hearsay elicited by the defense, he compounded the chaos. For example, a defense attorney asked Laurie's therapist, "You do know, don't you, that Laurie Chapman on numerous occasions told her mother that the stories that led to the trial were not true?" This question was a perfect opening for the therapist to explain the dynamics of recantation by child victims, but the prosecutor objected, thus preventing critically important testimony. The judge sustained the objection and left the jury with only the unanswered question and the impression that Laurie was lying. Thus the case became an exercise in futility. The jury knew little about what the children believed had happened to them and how they had responded, and the judge did little to facilitate the search for truth.

The judge's demeanor was also problematic. Much of the time he seemed inattentive. For example, when he was asked to rule on various objections during the testimony of experts for the prosecution, he appeared not to be following the testimony. The transcript is replete with his assertions of "I don't know." At times his observations reveal much about both his own and the attorneys' limitations: "The question was so long. Can you ask it again, maybe more simply so I can understand it?" His inattention not only appeared to confuse the proceedings and limit his control of the eight attorneys; it also may have suggested to the jury that he considered the charges and the trial insignificant. One observer commented that the judge "acted like the whole thing was boring him to death. You would have thought he was trying a dispute between two neighbors over their backyard property lines."

The Children

It was to this courtroom that the children, five and barely six years old, came to testify. The prosecution opened its case with the children and their parents. After that, the prosecution experts were scheduled to appear. An argument could be made that this was a tactical error by the prosecution. It might have been preferable to inform the jury first about the dynamics of child sexual abuse, its victims, and children's abilities to handle courtroom procedures—and then have them hear the children's charges.

The children's words were all that they and the prosecution had. If there had been physical evidence at the school, it had been removed. Physical examinations might have provided important evidence, but the proper diagnostic methods had not been used. The children's parents were to be effectively silenced by the court's rulings on hearsay, so the prosecution could rely only on what four exhausted and terrified children would tell the jury. The defense never let the jury forget that: "The next thing we have to look at is the total absence of support for what they say. No movies, no fingerprints, no semen. We got to believe these kids or there ain't no case." The children had talked to too many people in too many different environments under circumstances too dissimilar to allow even an adult to have clear recall; yet it was upon such recall that the defense built its questioning.

Analysis of some of the children's testimony impresses one with the attention that was devoted, not to what they said had happened to them, but rather to their numerous statements to parents, social workers, psychiatrists, physicians, police, judges, attorneys, and grand jurors over the course of a year. Once the trial was in motion and they were testifying, they were also forced to recall what they had said in previous testimony to two prosecutors and six defense attorneys. At times the discrepancy between the standards imposed on the five- and six-year-olds as opposed to those the lawyers applied to themselves was almost amusing.

JUDGE: That's been asked and answered, hasn't it?

DEFENSE: I don't recall.

PROSECUTION: I do. He just asked it.

DEFENSE: I want to find out what she says happened.

JUDGE: I can't remember every question that is asked and answered . . . Has she testified she told her mommy that?

DEFENSE: She testified—I'm embarrassed to say I forgot.

The first substantive question one defense attorney asked Tina, for example, had nothing to do with what she remembered about the assault; rather it focused on what she remembered she had said about it in the grand jury: "First of all, do you remember telling Judge Black about Greenbrook and something that happened there?" Although the little girl replied "No," in the series of questions that followed the defense insisted that the child comment on her prior testimony.

DEFENSE: Do you remember telling this in front of another man that has a black robe on like Judge White. . . . Do you remember doing it in an office, telling it to another man? . . . Do you know what a preliminary hearing is? Do you know what a grand jury is? . . . Did you appear before a grand jury two times? . . . How many times did you appear before a grand jury? . . . Now, before you went before the grand jury, remember telling your story to another man in his office where he had a lady like that taking things down as to what you said? . . . Who have you told it to besides the grand jury and these nice people here on the jury? . . . Do you remember anybody else you've told this sort of thing to? . . . How about Miss Zornes? Do you remember telling it to Miss Zornes?

Despite the fact that developmental experts have repeatedly established that five- and six-year-old children are incapable of dealing well with sequential concepts, the defense demanded that the children recall temporal sequences. It was an easy and effective means of confusing them and making them appear inconsistent and untruthful:

DEFENSE: After these things happened, did you go home and tell your mommy right away about it?

LAURIE: Not right away, but—

DEFENSE: Well, yesterday you said you told your mommy the same day when Mike did it. Do you remember that?

LAURIE: Yeah.

DEFENSE: Do you remember also testifying yesterday that you told your mommy the same day—

LAURIE: Uh-huh.

DEFENSE: —about this when Arnie was supposed to have done it. Do you remember that?

DEFENSE: Do you remember yesterday saying—strike that. Did you go home and tell your mommy that same day that Sarah did that?

LAURIE: No.

DEFENSE ATTORNEY: You didn't tell her that?

LAURIE: No.

DEFENSE: Which one of these happened first?

LAURIE: I don't—

PROSECUTOR: Objection. Which one what?

DEFENSE: Which one of these stories or acts of putting a penis in your mouth occurred first, which was first?

JUDGE: I don't know if she knows what "occurred" means.

DEFENSE: Happened first.

LAURIE: I don't know. I don't remember.

DEFENSE: I beg your pardon?

LAURIE: I don't remember.

DEFENSE: Did the one with Arnie happen first?

PROSECUTOR: Objection. She stated she doesn't remember.

DEFENSE: Your Honor, I have a right to test the memory.

PROSECUTOR: I object.

JUDGE: She just said she doesn't remember.

DEFENSE: Which one happened second?

PROSECUTION: Objection.

JUDGE: Do you understand the question?

LAURIE: No.

DEFENSE: All right. Which times or which persons put his penis in your mouth the second time?

LAURIE: I don't remember.

DEFENSE: Which person put his penis in your mouth the third time?

PROSECUTION: Objection.

JUDGE: Overruled. You can tell us if you remember.

LAURIE: I don't remember.

Running through the trial was a vague sense that modified procedures could assist child witnesses. The children were permitted to have a silent advocate present; they were offered breaks and refreshments; and occasionally when the confusion became pronounced, an attorney was asked to modify his language so that they could understand his questions. But these allowances were limited and were problematic, in that they contributed to a general sense of disparagement of the children. Constantly referred to as "hon" or "honey," they were asked almost too often if they were hungry or thirsty or tired, reinforcing the overall impression the defense attorneys may have hoped to create—that the children were incompetent and too pliable to provide accurate testimony in court.

Throughout the trial confusion occurred because the children could not understand lawyers' vocabulary or sentence constructions. Usually when the language was modified, they could respond effectively. Sometimes, of course, there were questions to which there could be no effective reply:

DEFENSE: Do you remember being asked over there during the preliminary hearing "How about this young lady, do you play with dolls for her?" and she referred to somebody from the Women's Service Organization?

LAURIE: I don't understand.

———————

DEFENSE: Do you remember being asked about the play when you told those lines, was that the truth you were telling, or was that a lie because they were made up?

MARK: I don't understand.

———————

DEFENSE: Tina, remember anything that you didn't understand when you were answering my questions last Friday?

TINA: I don't understand.

DEFENSE: You don't understand?

TINA: Huh-uh.

DEFENSE: You don't understand my question right now?

TINA: Yeah.

What the defense regarded as the high point in its cross-examination of the children was a low point for those familiar with child development, child sexual abuse, and child witnesses in the legal system. Tina Sanders had testified to the prosecutor the previous afternoon and to two defense attorneys during the morning. Despite the fact that the attorney could not keep the name straight—the prosecutor or the judge constantly had to remind him that the child was Tina, not Laurie—he pressed Tina to recall what she had said in preliminary hearings and grand jury proceedings months earlier.

DEFENSE: Now, did Arnie—when you were in front of the grand jury, you remember this question and this answer? Okay now, did Arnie touch you with his penis? And you answered no. Do you remember that?

TINA: No.

DEFENSE: And then the question was, "Okay, who touched you with his penis?" And you answered, "No one." Do you remember answering that way, honey?

TINA: No.

DEFENSE: Honey, when—see, somebody took this down like—somebody like Brenda, and typed it up, and said that's what you said to the grand jury. Now, did you make that up when you told the grand jury that?

PROSECUTION: Objection. She said she didn't remember.

DEFENSE: I want an answer to my question, your Honor.

JUDGE: Well, she says she doesn't remember.

DEFENSE: I want to ask her if she said that then.

JUDGE: She already says she doesn't remember. If she doesn't remember, how can she say she made something up she doesn't remember?

DEFENSE: Did you say that to the grand jury? [Note: By now the proceedings had reached the point where the judge had lost control, and the defense attorneys ignored his ruling and did as they pleased.]

DEFENSE: Did you say that to the grand jury?

PROSECUTION: Objection.

JUDGE: Sustained.

DEFENSE: Did you tell the grand jury those particular things, honey?

PROSECUTION: Objection.

JUDGE: Sustained.

TINA: I don't remember.

Tina asked for a break. It was the second one she'd had, the first was five minutes long, and the second lasted not quite three minutes. She was returned to the courtroom where a second defense attorney took over. When he was finished, a third defense lawyer declined to ask questions. Then a fourth defense lawyer indicated he had "a few" questions. Tina asked for a break. She had by now answered hundreds of questions. She had had fewer than ten minutes in all for breaks; she had testified for almost three hours.

JUDGE: Well, how few questions do you have?

DEFENSE: It depends on your definition of a few.

JUDGE: Do we need a break?

DEFENSE: The child seems to be the one controlling it. If she wants a break, give her one.

JUDGE: I'm not saying she's controlling it. If you're going to take three or four minutes, do it . . .

DEFENSE: I don't think I'll be that long.

JUDGE: Tina, do you think you can go for a few more minutes?

TINA: Okay.

JUDGE: All right. Go ahead and then it will all be over.

Before it was "all over," the attorney's "three or four minutes" had expanded to more than ninety questions. Tina was pressed for temporal understanding, recall, and detail she was incapable of possessing. She believed she had seen a "bad" movie or, as Laurie had testified, more than one "bad" movie. After a year, only a few essential images from the experience remained. There was no way for her to retrieve what she had said to the grand jury; but if what she remembered now didn't correspond with what the lawyer said she had testified months ago, then it just might seem better to acquiesce to the adult. Obviously tired, confused, and frightened, she eventually shrugged her shoulders and said what the attorney wanted.

DEFENSE: Well, you also—you were asked up in grand jury, who was in the movie, the bad movie, weren't you?

TINA: Yeah.

DEFENSE: And you said Mike and Arnie, didn't you?

TINA: Yeah.

DEFENSE: Okay. Now, today you've said it was Arnie and Sarah right?

TINA: Mike and Arnie were in a different movie, I think.

DEFENSE: You think. Do you know?

TINA: I think that was a different movie.

DEFENSE: You think. Well, you only saw one bad movie, that's what you told us. Right, Tina?

TINA: Yeah.

DEFENSE: Well, in the bad movie, you told the grand jury that Mike and Arnie were in that movie, didn't you?

TINA: Yeah.

DEFENSE: Well—And here you've said that Arnie and Sarah were in that movie, didn't you?

TINA: Yeah.

DEFENSE: Now, are you making up a story about Mike? Did you make up a story about Mike?

TINA: I guess.

DEFENSE: You guess. Well, you told the grand jury that Sarah wasn't in the movie, didn't you?

TINA: Not this time.

DEFENSE: Not this time, in here, but when you were up in grand jury they asked you, was Sarah in the movie, and you said, "No." Do you remember that?

TINA: No.

DEFENSE: Okay. Mr. Prosecutor, I'll call your attention to the transcript, page 95. Remember being asked, "Was there somebody named Sarah in the movie?" And your answer was, "No."

TINA: I don't remember it.

DEFENSE: You don't remember it. Well, you told the grand jury, didn't you, up there, that you saw Mike and Arnie naked in the movie, didn't you?

TINA: I don't know.

DEFENSE: Well, did you make up a story about Mike?

TINA: I don't know.

DEFENSE: Okay. Well, did you tell the grand jury that Sarah was not in the movie?

TINA: I don't know.

DEFENSE: You could have made up a story about Sarah right? . . . And when you were up in grand jury, you swore to tell the truth, didn't you?

TINA: Yeah.

DEFENSE: Okay. And you told the grand jury that Sarah wasn't in that movie, didn't you?

PROSECUTOR: Objection, repetitious.

JUDGE: I think she's answered that. Sustained.

DEFENSE: Well, was that the truth?

TINA: No.

DEFENSE: So you told the grand jury a lie, right?

TINA: Right.

DEFENSE: Okay. And Mike wasn't—You're saying in here today Mike wasn't in that movie, aren't you?

TINA: Yeah.

DEFENSE: But in grand jury you told them he was, didn't you?

TINA: Yeah.

DEFENSE: That was a lie, wasn't it, Tina?

TINA: Yeah.

DEFENSE: Okay. You also told the grand jury that you saw Mike and Arnie naked in the movie, didn't you?

TINA: I don't remember telling that.

DEFENSE: Well, Mr. Prosecutor, I'll call your attention to the same page 95. Tina, they asked you this question. "You saw Mike and Arnie naked in the movie?" and your answer was, "Yep." Do you remember that?

TINA: No.

DEFENSE: You don't remember that. Well, if you said that, that would have been a lie, wouldn't it have, Tina.

TINA: I guess.

DEFENSE: You guess. Well, if you said that, you would have made it up, wouldn't you have, right?

TINA: Yeah.

DEFENSE: Well, if you made it up then, that's a lie, isn't that correct, Tina?

TINA: Yeah.

DEFENSE: Okay. Now, you told the grand jury that Mike and Arnie were looking at each other while they were naked, didn't you?

TINA: I don't remember.

DEFENSE: Well, I'll refer you to page 96, Mr. Prosecutor. Question to you, "Tina, were they licking each other?" And you said, "Yes." Do you remember that?

TINA: No.

DEFENSE: Okay. And then the question was, "Who was licking who?" And your answer was, "They"—meaning Mike and Arnie—"were looking at each other." Do you remember saying that?

TINA: No.

DEFENSE: Well, if you said that, that wouldn't have been true either, would it have, Tina?

TINA: [Shrugs shoulders.]

DEFENSE: Could we have the record indicate she shrugged her shoulders?

DEFENSE: Now, Tina, if you told the grand jury that, that wasn't true, was it?

TINA: No.

DEFENSE: You made up stories, didn't you?

TINA: Yeah.

DEFENSE: And then they asked, somebody—"Was anybody licking?" And you said, "No." Do you remember saying that?

TINA: No.

DEFENSE: You don't remember that either. You didn't say that? Are you—huh?

TINA: I don't remember saying it.

DEFENSE: Now, you never saw a movie with naked ladies in it, did you?

TINA: No.

DEFENSE: Remember, you told the grand jury that there was nobody in the movie besides Mike and Arnie that you knew, didn't you?

TINA: I don't remember.

DEFENSE: Well, Mr. Prosecutor, I'll refer you to page 97, about a third of the way down the page. Tina, you were asked this question. "Was there anybody in the movie besides Mike and Arnie that you knew?" And you answered, "No." Do you remember that now?

TINA: No.

DEFENSE: Well, if you told the ladies and gentlemen of the grand jury that, did you make that up?

TINA: Yes.

DEFENSE: I see. So you didn't tell the grand jury the truth, did you?

TINA: No.

DEFENSE: I see. And you were under oath, weren't you? Do you remember that?

TINA: No.

DEFENSE: Well, didn't they tell you to tell the truth so help you God? Didn't they, Tina?

TINA: Yeah.

DEFENSE: You raised your right hand and said that, right?

TINA: Yeah.

DEFENSE: And you've made up stories about at least one person here, haven't you?

TINA: Yeah.

DEFENSE: And you've made up some other stories too, haven't you, Tina?

TINA: I don't know.

It was a complex dynamic. The child reiterated continuously that she could not remember what she said in the grand jury, but the defense insisted she answer questions about her former statements. The judge had already asked one attorney, "If she doesn't remember, how can she say she made up something she doesn't remember?" but he and the prosecution allowed the defense to press on. The child was pressured to respond to several levels of questions: what she remembered about the events themselves (ironically, a minor concern to the defense), what she remembered she had said to the police about the events, and what she remembered she had said at the grand jury. She tried again and again to clarify, to mesh the recollections and non-recollections, to tell the truth about what was happening in her mind and memory. "I guess," "I think," "I don't remember," "I don't know," she told the court. But the attorney persisted; and finally after more than a year of responding articulately and consistently to thousands of questions by more people than she could count, Tina started saying, "Yeah" when asked if her stories were fabrications. "It was," one of the spectators observed, "as if she was telling the attorney, 'Okay, so what? If this is what it takes to make you let me alone, to stop yelling at me, it's what I'll do.'"

Some believed the incident was not only an illustration of inappropriate questioning but also a demonstration of classic recantation. To those knowledgeable about child sexual abuse, Tina acted predictably, offering a perfect illustration of the urgent need for courts to accommodate new techniques and new sources of evidence in the criminal justice system. But to most people, she was just a six-year-old who had lied. In closing arguments a defense lawyer would tell the jury, "Tina Sanders, filled with inconsistencies, she's an admitted liar." The judge accepted it. In the middle of the trial, he dismissed the charges about the movie. Laurie Chapman had not recanted; it was the jury's function to assess Tina's veracity. But the judge dismissed the charges, thereby sending a message to both the jury and the public.

For Allison Young, the trial ended even sooner. Her situation was another example of the maddening ambiguity that characterizes such cases. Allison was calm and articulate before the grand jury; the prosecution was convinced that she would have no problem testifying. But the courtroom setting was different from the other offices and rooms she had seen. The transcript catalogs the inappropriateness of the environment in which she found herself. The lawyers repeatedly protested they couldn't hear or see her. The judge had similar difficulty, and at one point it was impossible for the jury to see a critical gesture she made.

Allison would not answer questions pertaining directly to the defendants. The prosecutor repeatedly urged, "You have to give me an answer. You have to speak, Allison"; but she would usually only nod, to avoid having to say aloud anything of substance. Frustrated by her reticence, the prosecutor tried desperately to get her to communicate. Finally, she asked, "Do you see the person in this room—can you point to anybody in this room that had a knife at your school? . . . Instead of answering the question, can you point?" The little girl nodded and pointed. The courtroom erupted into still more chaos.

FIRST DEFENSE ATTORNEY: Judge, let the record reflect she's pointing at Mrs. Miller [child advocate].

JUDGE: I can't tell.

FIRST PROSECUTOR: She hasn't pointed yet.

SECOND DEFENSE ATTORNEY: I would like to have the record reflect that I object to this line of questioning. It's inflammatory and prejudicial and makes it impossible to have a fair trial with this kind of thing thrown into the case.

JUDGE: Overruled. I don't see who she pointed to. I'm sure the jury did.

SECOND PROSECUTOR: Your Honor, I don't think she pointed yet.

JUDGE: I don't know whether she did or not. I didn't see her hand.

SECOND PROSECUTOR: Allison, can you point to someone for us, if there's somebody in the room, in the courtroom?

In the midst of dissension and chaos enough to terrify any child, whether or not her life had been threatened, the little girl gave her most revealing testimony: "I don't want everybody to see." To half the courtroom, it meant she had nothing of substance to say; to the other half, it meant that trauma had followed trauma and she was too threatened by the presence of the defendants to speak. A few minutes later she was taken from the room and did not return.

Days afterward, when the possibility of her resuming testimony was still being debated, the judge concluded:

JUDGE: Well, I'm only going so far to accommodate a witness who doesn't want to testify. . . . If she's not competent this day, that's the end of it. . . . I only go so far to accommodate the witness. I'm trying to accommodate everybody, but I can't just run the whole trial on the schedule of the child. . . . Tomorrow is the last chance. If she isn't going to testify, that's fine with me.

In another court, Allison might not have been so traumatized. In a court with better understanding of hearsay law, Allison's story could have been told even if she was "unavailable" to tell it. Her therapist or one of the physicians or social workers familiar with her allegations could have presented them to the jury. In this courtroom that was not allowed.

Meanwhile beyond the observation of judge and jury, the children were living out yet another drama in response to their ordeals in court. Laurie testified for ten hours over five days. The worst time was a late afternoon when she was severely intimidated by a defense lawyer who demanded "full latitude to cross-examine." As Laurie would later say, that meant having him "yell" at her, "try to trick" her and "saying it really didn't happen but it really did."

Tricking Laurie meant asking her to place in sequence events that had occurred over the course of hundreds of days when she could barely count to fifty, to recall minute details that would escape even an adult. Tricking Laurie meant pitting her against her mother by telling her that her mother's statements contained different details from hers. Tricking her involved implying that she was lying because she couldn't remember the clothes the defendants removed or what she had testified about them at an earlier hearing.

DEFENSE: Now, Laurie, after Arnie—you told us yesterday about Arnie. Do you remember that?

LAURIE: Yeah.

DEFENSE: Now, what part of Arnie's clothes did he remove, Laurie.

JUDGE: Do you understand that?

LAURIE: No.

JUDGE: Take off.

DEFENSE: What clothes did Arnie take off?

LAURIE: His pants.

DEFENSE: Took off his pants?

LAURIE: Yeah.

DEFENSE: Nothing else?

LAURIE: No.

DEFENSE: You sure of that?

LAURIE: Uh-huh.

DEFENSE: Now, Laurie, do you remember telling the judge months before that Arnie removed all of his—took off all his clothes?

LAURIE: No.

DEFENSE: Laurie, do you remember this sequence—

PROSECUTOR: Objection. She doesn't know what sequence is.

Tricking her meant asking a kindergartner, who had not yet been taught addition and subtraction, about time concepts she could not possibly comprehend:

DEFENSE: Now, Laurie, I want to ask you about when you talked to the judge about this. . . . Now, Laurie, that was . . . last year. . . . So that was, I guess, about five months after this thing is supposed to have happened. . . . Now, Laurie, we're now about fifteen months away from when that happened, aren't we?

"Yelling" at her meant harassing and confusing Laurie about what she told her parents on the day an event occurred or what she told another judge or what she was presently saying about minor details.

DEFENSE: Did you tell the other judge that?

LAURIE: Yeah.

DEFENSE: That was wrong when you told the judge that?

LAURIE: Uh-huh.

DEFENSE: It was wrong?

LAURIE: Uh-huh.

DEFENSE: So sometimes you tell things that are wrong to a judge, don't you?

LAURIE: Yeah.

DEFENSE: And you could be telling these good people something wrong too, couldn't you?

PROSECUTION: Objection.

LAURIE: No.

JUDGE: Overruled. Go ahead.

DEFENSE: No? . . . You can't be telling them something that's not right?

LAURIE: I can tell them what's right.

DEFENSE: Will you always tell them what's accurate. You know what accurate is, by the way?

After three hours, Laurie's parents refused to let her continue that day. While they stayed behind to talk with the prosecutor, her aunt and uncle took her home. They reported that in the car Laurie rocked back and forth repeating some incoherent phrase. At home she sat in a chair and continued rocking until she suddenly grew wild and ran to her room where she attempted to destroy her furniture and all her possessions. Her aunt had seen behavior like this before. Months earlier, on the day the Chapmans testified in pretrial hearings, Laurie became uncontrollable; she ran screaming through the house and locked her aunt out. Her aunt called Laurie's therapist, who explained that the outburst was related to the fear that her parents would be hurt. She was finally reassured when her mother called her to tell her that they were well.

After Laurie's trauma in the courtroom, her parents refused to allow her to return unless it was cleared of spectators and she was permitted to sit on the lap of her advocate. Later the advocate would say,

> The case has absolutely haunted me. I felt as if I were a witness to children getting beaten up by the system. I don't think I'll ever forget Laurie after finishing her testimony. She was sitting on the end of a couch with a vacant look in her eye. It was as if somebody had taken her heart. She was empty, just a shell. I don't think I'll ever get over it. I saw families in anguish. It would break your heart to see it. They wanted to get at the truth, and the children were so terrified.

The Experts

Even the "experts" could not help "get at the whole truth." Like many others of its kind, this trial included testimonies by professionals who supposedly were to educate the jury about the dynamics of child sexual abuse and the relevant characteristics of preschool children. As in similar cases, however, this trial included experts whose reputations were identifiable with one side or the other. The prosecution experts tried, within the limits imposed by the judge's hearsay rulings, to establish that their examinations of the children revealed the presence of symptoms consistent with sexual abuse. Defense experts, who had not worked directly with the Greenbrook children, testified about children's suggestibility and memory implantation. One expert even maintained that "an exhaustive battery of tests" she administered to one of the defendants caused her to conclude that she did not fit the "profile" of an abuser. This testimony was allowed despite the fact that the most distinguished experts in the country have established that it is impossible to develop accurate profiles of sexual abusers, and appellate courts have consistently rejected such testimony.

Limited by the hearsay rulings, the experts who followed the children and their parents were able to provide only fragmented information about the children and their verbal and behavioral responses to sexual abuse. As is customary, the lawyers pitted prosecution and defense experts against one another, and their collective knowledge and experience were never used to provide the jury with a coherent foundation for assessing its already limited information about the children's complaints. The conduct of the Greenbrook case emphasizes the need for a more appropriate approach to expert testimony. If juries are to engage in serious pursuits of truth, they must have more than inconsistent information from adversarial experts.

One of the people most disturbed by the process was the therapist who treated three of the children. Unlike the other experts, he was unaccustomed to serving as a witness at trials and was not prepared for the "unprofessional" behavior of the defense attorneys. He thought his "function in the courtroom was to provide a professional opinion based upon his education and experience." Instead of being asked to give insight and information, he found himself under attack.

The notes from his interactions with the children and their parents were one point of contention. Subpoenaed by the defense, they were, he felt, constantly taken out of context. He tried to clarify that point: "What you have to understand about my notes is they're my notes, and I take them for various reasons, and I sometimes write down things and sometimes write down very little, so if you take something out of context, you are not going to understand what it meant."

The attorneys' disputes over the legal complexities of expert testimony frequently diverted attention from the real issues and on more than one occasion overwhelmed the judge:

JUDGE: Just calm down. I can't remember everything that was said in this case . . . The eight attorneys even argue over what was presented. Now, I'll leave it to the jury to decide whether in fact this evidence was presented or not.

Frequently, the defense initiated disputes with the witness:

THERAPIST: I cannot answer that question as you have stated it.

FIRST DEFENSE ATTORNEY: Is this because you don't believe that's what happened like we got into the other day or you don't understand my question?

THERAPIST: You are talking about something so hypothetical with one child that it's not something I feel anyone could answer.

FIRST DEFENSE ATTORNEY: When you were answering the State's questions, you were willing to talk about the world of five-year-olds, but now you can't get into this hypothetical?

While attorneys' sarcasm and argumentativeness may not bother members of the legal profession, they can be extremely disconcerting to those unfamiliar with such strategies. To minimize such adversarial sparring and broaden the search for truth in child sexual abuse trials, some suggest that judges appoint neutral expert witnesses. Certainly in this trial an expert's techniques and opinions would have been far more important to both sides than the defense attempt to convince the jury that the psychologist was keeping the children in therapy and participating in the trial to make money.

THIRD DEFENSE ATTORNEY: How many meetings did you say, Doctor, that you had with Laurie Chapman?

PSYCHOLOGIST: About twenty-six at the last count.

THIRD DEFENSE ATTORNEY: That's twenty-six billable hours at least?

PSYCHOLOGIST: Yes.

THIRD DEFENSE ATTORNEY: And Mark Dunham would be fourteen billable hours?

PSYCHOLOGIST: Yes.

THIRD DEFENSE ATTORNEY: We're not talking about billable hours today, are we?

PSYCHOLOGIST: No, we're not.

THIRD DEFENSE ATTORNEY: I understand. That I understand.

PROSECUTION: I object at this time and ask to approach the bench.

THIRD DEFENSE ATTORNEY: I'm done. I just wanted to make sure everything was billable.

Throughout the testimony, the psychologist struggled with his impotence in a system that did not allow for sustained, intelligent discourse. Later he would comment on the trial:

I was appalled at the way I was treated. The experience shocked me—not simply for Laurie and Mark, but for my own children and children in general. The defense wasn't interested in the truth; they didn't want my knowledge or even my opinion. They wouldn't let me testify as an expert. While I was on the stand, I kept feeling myself slipping into despair because there was no accurate or truthful way to respond to verbal sequences that began with assumptions; and I knew they were trying to prevent me from telling the truth.

Perhaps the most devastating blow to the psychologist's testimony came when the defense employed one strategy that occurs in almost every case in which a child brings sexual abuse allegations against an adult:

DEFENSE: Doctor, it is your opinion that if Mark Dunham were to say something was real, it really happened, that he would be accurate in making that statement?

PSYCHOLOGIST: Most of the time.

DEFENSE: Are you aware that Mark Dunham believes in Santa Claus, the tooth fairy, and Easter Bunny?

PSYCHOLOGIST: Didn't you?

DEFENSE: I wasn't testifying in a case where I was making allegations such as were made in this case.

The Parents

The parents experienced the same sense of shock and disbelief that haunted the psychiatrist. Upper-middle-class college graduates, they assumed that the justice system was designed to protect them and their children, and they turned to it with hope when trouble occurred. They no longer have that faith. Perhaps the best illustration of the reason for their loss of faith is the court-room experience of Laurie's mother, Patti Chapman, the woman the defense described as "the perpetrator."

The defense argument was that Patti had manipulated her child and husband, three other children, six parents, and approximately two dozen professionals into believing that the children had been abused. Aware that under the "reasonable doubt" standard they had no legal obligation to prove or demonstrate that Laurie had been programmed and manipulated, defense lawyers simply made innuendos about Patti and her motives and methods. The defense suggested that Patti was emotionally unstable because she had once seen a therapist. Indeed, they returned again and again to that point.

DEFENSE: You were undergoing treatment with Dr. Stephens for approximately one year before bringing Laurie to him, were you not? . . .

PATTI: No, I was not undergoing therapy when I brought Laurie to see Dr. Stephens . . .

DEFENSE: Did you have occasion to go into Dr. Stephens's office prior to the time you just told us about relative to Laurie? . . . I'm asking if there was any time you were there before that.

PATTI: I was in Dr. Stephens's office—I was in therapy with Dr. Stephens from October of 19—no, August, to I believe it was the next October. Maybe it was September . . .

DEFENSE: Were you undergoing family therapy with Dr. Stephens between August and September or October of the following year?

PATTI: No . . .

DEFENSE: Was your problem in general terms a problem dealing with your family? . . . Were you seeing Dr. Stephens with regard to difficulties in the relationship between yourself and your husband? . . . Have you seen Dr. Stephens in any way with regard to sexuality? . . . Were you seeing Dr. Stephens with regard to your relationship with your children?

PATTI: No. [Patti's responses to all of these questions were negative.] I can make this easy. [Turning to the judge.] Would you like me to tell you why I was seeing Dr. Stephens?

JUDGE: It's up to counsel and you.

PROSECUTOR: Judge, I object to anything that isn't relevant to these proceedings. Counsel knows it isn't relevant.

Although the defense knew it wasn't relevant, a defense attorney would finally argue to the jury:

DEFENSE: Now first of all in evaluating Mrs. Chapman, we got to keep something in mind . . . I don't know the whole story. I'm not a master of abnormal psychology. It's not my field, but there are some distinctive and peculiar things about Mrs. Chapman. First, she was under psychiatric care before these—this thing erupted.

A second motivation the defense attributed to Patti was an obsession with the issue of child sexual abuse. Her best friend's child was a sexual assault victim, and the defense repeatedly argued that this was proof of the "mind set" she formed about the "innocuous statements or bizarre statements of [her] little girl."

Once they had implied—without needing proof—that Patti was emotionally unstable and obsessed with child sexual abuse, the defense attorneys had little difficulty converting normal parental responses into sinister motives and behaviors. First there was the matter of her attitude toward the defendants:

DEFENSE: Mrs. Chapman, isn't it fair for us and these people on the jury to infer that you are what is called a hostile witness against these three people over here in this case? . . .

PATTI: I don't understand what you're getting at.

DEFENSE: You feel hostility towards my client Arnie Hart, isn't that correct?

PATTI: I do.

DEFENSE: In fact, you in effect have been heavily involved in setting up this entire prosecution against my client, isn't that correct? . . . And you remember, Mrs. Chapman, your being upset about the fact . . . that the only thing that had happened to Arnie and Mike was that so far they had suffered public humiliation, but that's small consolation.

PATTI: It is small consolation.

DEFENSE: Is that what your religion teaches you, Mrs. Chapman? Is it fair to say, Mrs. Chapman, that you have a hate for my client? You want to commit acts of physical violence against him? . . . You remember what you wrote in your notebook—

PATTI: I know precisely what you are referring to.

DEFENSE: "[I] couldn't sleep again last night. I couldn't stop thinking about Arnie. I just wanted to run off of the stand and strangle him." Is that what you wrote?

PATTI: That is what I wrote.

Patti was attacked for dismissing the pediatrician she and her husband believe violated their confidentiality and his own professional ethics by contacting his colleague who phoned the school. The defense contended the Chapmans "shopped around" until they found a pediatrician who would agree that Laurie had been abused. Patti was attacked because she and her husband took Laurie to a psychologist; that, argued the defense, was a tactic they concocted at the advice of social workers and prosecutors in order to "have an expert witness available to testify at trial." She was attacked because she attempted to organize the parents involved into a support group; the defense maintained that this was a strategy to create "an effective prosecution." She was attacked because she and her husband had consulted legal counsel about their options. Like other parents, the Chapmans maintain they pursued the criminal court recourse first, rather than instituting a civil law suit, because it was the only means of removing the defendants from society; and, justifiably or not, they believed the defendants were a threat to other children. But the defense implied that the Chapmans were using the sexual abuse charge as a money-making scheme and that they sought a criminal conviction first to support a civil law suit later.

Patti was attacked about having written in her notes, "The main issue is getting some testimony in that they are now calling hearsay, specifically what Laurie told me." Patti's entry was logical and legally accurate, but the defense would argue that she had intended all along to try "to get in as much hearsay as she possibly could." To the judge and jury, "hearsay" thus appeared analogous to "falsehood," even though most "hearsay" in this case was vital information.

The defense's most credible charge was that Patti's interactions with Laurie had "contaminated" the disclosure process. She had recorded summaries of detailed conversations with Laurie; when these were taken out of context by the defense, they supported the contention that Patti's intervention had influenced Laurie's responses. The Chapmans, like all the parents, had no centralized resource specializing in child sexual abuse to which they could go for diagnosis, advice, and treatment when their child first began to act so strangely. While considering a variety of recourses, they also were trying to cope with Laurie's bizarre behavior. She continued acting out and giving additional verbal "clues" that could not be ignored. They could either tell Laurie that they believed her and encourage her to continue talking, or they could ignore her convoluted attempts at communication and push her further into denial.

It was a no-win situation; they could not tell their daughter, "Wait to talk about pornographic movies and oral sex until we've hit on the right course of action because you may be susceptible to suggestion, and we don't want to be accused of programming you." Instead they did what normal parents faced with a horror would do: they listened to their child, they asked questions, and they tried to support her. But they paid heavily for that in court. Like most parents who are hesitant to believe the almost unbelievable, the Chapmans cast about for other explanations; they questioned and probed until they felt they had no choice but to admit that their worst fears had been realized. By then, it was too late; the "contamination" had occurred:

> DEFENSE: Don't you think, Mrs. Chapman, that the procedure of continuing to question the child after she denied seeing the video was a message to her, "Laurie, I don't believe you when you say you didn't see it?"
>
> PATTI: That was not the message.
>
> DEFENSE: Certainly your attitude during that time, however, was, "I believe you, Laurie, when you say you saw the bad video"; that was the message you were giving her?
>
> PATTI: My attitude was that I believed that something bad had happened, and I wanted her to be able to tell me what it was. I wanted her to know no matter what anyone else believed, that I believed her and she could tell me when she was ready.

In this case the "contamination" theory was given support by the notebook Patti Chapman began when she became worried about Laurie's strange behavior. Only portions of it were put in evidence. The prosecution tried to enter the entire notebook but the judge denied the request. Taken as a whole, Patti's notes provide invaluable and sympathetic illustrations of the daily frustration and despair confronting a family that believes a child has suffered abuse. Since only portions of her notes were introduced, Patti struggled continuously, within the restrictions of the adversarial system, to explain them and put them in context:

> DEFENSE: You know, I can't find that in your notes, can I?
>
> PATTI: Because I didn't put it in them because I didn't know you were going to read it, Ms. Kirby.
>
> DEFENSE: In other words, if you knew that we were going to read them, your notes would be different?

DEFENSE: Isn't that what you wrote?

PATTI: Again, that is taken completely out of context.

DEFENSE: Can you answer my question—

PATTI: If you are going to refer to my notes, then I think I have the right to put them in the context in which they were written.

The defense contended that Patti had harassed her child for months into believing a lie. The notes actually record more than two dozen conversations or brief verbal interactions between mother and daughter. Of these, only six were initiated by Patti and generally followed Laurie's acting out. The notes dealt only partially with such exchanges, however. Most of them centered on private material unrelated to Laurie's situation, on intimate reflections and experiences that Patti did not want "placed on display for all the world to know about." During the trial she told a defense attorney, "I did not think you had any right to my personal notes. I did attempt to keep them from you and I'm not ashamed of that."

The notes explained why Patti had been "in therapy for more than a year," as the defense proclaimed. The Chapmans claim defense attorneys knew the reason but nevertheless persuaded the judge to keep those portions of her notes from the jury in order to portray Patti Chapman as emotionally unstable, a woman with "distinctive and peculiar things" about her. They maintain the defense preferred to let the jury speculate rather than provide the truth about Patti's reason for seeking therapy—to cope with the death of their premature baby girl. Their baby lived for only a few months, never leaving the hospital where she was born. Her mother speaks of her in the journal, but the jurors never heard those entries. They would never know that today she believes the "strength and courage" her baby taught her helped carry her through the abuse and indignity she suffered in the courtroom.

I was always in awe of that child. In human terms, she was little more than a vegetable. But she taught me more about strength and courage than I will ever know again. When she left me, I knew where she was going. In a moment, I was connected to what comes next. Never have I been closer to God than at the moment he took my child from me . . . and never have I been more horrified. To find God in the depths—it is just not what I expected.

It's been three years. I feel peace, but I will never stop feeling there is something missing. The scar on my belly doesn't hurt anymore, but it is always there. I keep telling myself part of me is with God. She is mine, and she is with God. I will never be afraid of losing again. I have already lost all that mattered. I survived. I understand there is a reason to keep living and trusting. Losing is part of it.

Invasion of privacy is only one element of the personal assault that parents in such situations must be prepared to endure. They are often subjected to sarcasm, verbal assault, and public humiliation by lawyers who assume—mistakenly—that such behavior is somehow appropriate and necessary to defend their clients. If anything, it discourages faith in the legal system and circumvents a genuine search for truth. The defense lawyers in this case were, as a spectator noted, "like wolves in winter on a piece of meat" when they cross-examined the parents.

PATTI: That's taken out of context.

DEFENSE: Did I ask you if it was taken out of context, Mrs. Chapman? Did I ask you that?

PATTI: No, sir you didn't.

DEFENSE: You think you can confine yourself to my questions, Mrs. Chapman.

PATTI: Yes, sir, I can.

DEFENSE: [Your son] started stuttering, isn't that correct?

PATTI: Yes, [he] developed a stuttering problem. Our whole family was in a crisis.

DEFENSE: Did I ask you about your whole family being in a crisis?

DEFENSE: Was there a question addressed to you, Mrs. Chapman, before you started the soliloquy for the last thirty seconds? Was there?

DEFENSE: Did you say, Laurie, for God's sake stop the nut stuff; did you ever tell her that?

PATTI: No.

DEFENSE: Ma'am, this is typical of your entire testimony in this case, isn't it?

PATTI: Please don't point your finger at me.

DEFENSE: I'll do what I feel like.

If this is the best way Americans can devise to search for truth when children say they've been raped, then children and their parents had better avoid courtrooms. The jury deliberated for hours and then returned the verdict of not guilty. One juror remarked to a reporter, "We knew they weren't guilty from the first day." Other observers were less certain. Some expressed confusion about who had been on trial in the first place. Without minimizing the impact of the charges themselves, it became clear that the defendants were protected by intricate, well-articulated constitutional guarantees and legal precedents. However, the children could be harassed, humiliated, and required to perform tasks beyond their ability, and the parents were forced to tolerate unsubstantiated accusations and character defamation. There were no protections for them.

It was trial by combat and trial by ordeal all over again, and in a sense the children and their parents were not the only losers. In the minds of many, the defendants were not exonerated but only found not guilty under the law. Equally disturbing, a clear message about the legal system was sent to those who sexually abuse children and to parents whose children are victims: For the young, the legal system offers no refuge and little hope for justice.

Beyond the Courtroom

Prosecutors face a range of problems beyond those readily apparent in multi-victim, multi-perpetrator child sexual abuse cases. The prosecutors of the Greenbrook case had more than their share of concerns hidden from the courtroom. First of all, there were other children who participated in the grand jury proceedings but who did not testify in the trial. A defense attorney pointed out to the jury in closing arguments that there were "no other witnesses to corroborate what these four children said." Under the law, he could make that statement because no other children had come forward in that courtroom. But in actuality, there were others who had information about the school.

Several children tried to testify at the grand jury hearings. Of these, some provided insufficient evidence; but others were not permitted by parents or therapists to participate in the trial. One child refused to participate after she accidentally saw a television news show that revealed the defendants would be in the courtroom with her.

Then there was Amy Henderson, the little girl whose therapist advised that she was making gradual but encouraging progress and that testifying in an open courtroom would be too traumatic for her. Torn between their concern for their daughter and their desire to ensure that the other children's accounts be corroborated, the Hendersons felt they had no choice but to protect their daughter. Sue Henderson described the nightmare that began that summer:

> As I think back to the time I first suspected something was wrong, two thoughts come to mind. My daughter had developed a sudden unexplainable fear of dogs which caused her great anxiety any time she came near a dog. Prior to this, she had been very comfortable around all kinds of animals. Secondly, I noticed an excessive preoccupation with breasts

and genitals. She used language that I had never heard her use before. She spoke repeatedly of "her wiener"—"my wiener is in my butt" . . . "my wiener is in my hair, etc." None of the other children nor my husband or I used this particular phrase. This excessive attention to genitals and breasts was revealed frequently in her daily speech. She repeatedly asked to see my breasts—she had never inquired about this before.

She also began to act out violently. At one point, she tried to strangle her older brother with a rope. She also threatened to kill her baby brother on two separate occasions. She repeatedly tied his ankles together with ropes, so tight that his circulation was being cut off. At one point, I needed to use scissors to unbind his ankles which she had tied together. I began to notice that the dolls lined up on her bed were all naked—some had been dismembered. Arms, legs, and heads were severed from several of the Barbie-type dolls.

As her violent and bizarre behavior increased, I began to believe that she had been sexually abused. The first time I asked her if anyone had touched her, it was because she had started masturbating and had rubbed herself raw. She also complained of intense itching . . . It wasn't until late autumn that she revealed for the first time that someone had scared her at school. She was extremely reluctant to discuss it with me. She said that she couldn't tell me about the bad touching because if she did, she would die. Also her baby brother, her big brother, and mommy and daddy would die. She looked at me and stated simply, "You will die, if you tell."

At this point we made arrangements for her to be evaluated by the hospital sexual abuse clinic. She was seen by two social workers trained in interviewing sexually abused children. She demonstrated with anatomically correct dolls what had happened to her. She acted out a scene in which the baby girl doll performed fellatio on the adult male doll—also the adult male doll performed oral sex on the baby girl doll—She also drew a picture of a baby with its arms and legs severed—only face and trunk present. This was her picture of herself. The therapist interpreted this as "the helpless baby." Her second picture consisted of a lady covered in blood, a picture entirely in red color. The lady is bleeding. When asked by the therapist if she was the lady in the picture, she replied no.

The two social workers felt that Amy should be seen by a child psychiatrist to help her with her fears, to help her articulate what had happened to her. She saw a psychiatrist for approximately seven months during which time she experienced bed-wetting episodes, night terrors. [A night terror resembles a nightmare although it occurs at a deeper level of R.E.M. sleep. The child cannot be wakened from this as in a nightmare; nor will she be able to recall the terror, unlike a nightmare.] She would get out of her bed—3 or 4 A.M.—run through the house [to the]

kitchen or hallway, urinate on herself and cry hysterically. She was not awake during these episodes. At one point she was so hysterical that my husband and I could not calm her. We called her doctor and were instructed to take her to the hospital emergency room.

We were both frightened. She appeared to be completely out of touch with her surroundings. I wondered if she could be having an acute psychotic episode. Her doctor explained to us that her feelings of terror were so intense that these feelings which had been repressed or kept at bay were just beginning to surface, and her fears were almost too intense for her to handle or process. . . .

During this course of treatment children were being prepared to testify. Amy was subpoenaed by the defense attorneys. At this point in her therapy she was just beginning to make some progress—the bedwetting was declining, as were the night terrors, and she was willing to play outside again—she seemed to be feeling safe again. But this was a slow gradual process, the result of [the] hours with her therapist. On the medical recommendation of her attending child psychiatrist, my husband and I decided not to let her testify. Her doctor's opinion was that she was making gradual but encouraging progress and that testifying in an open courtroom—before these defendants, jury, would be too traumatic for her—and would surely reenact the original psychic trauma. As we believed that this doctor was making progress with Amy and that he had her best interests at heart, we followed his recommendation.

Today Sue observes that "it has been an ongoing, slow process" but that Amy is beginning to act like a "normal" child again. She plays with other children, attends parties and school without protest, and is willing to go out without her mother. Sue is still shocked by what happened in the courtroom: "Sometimes I feel that out of the parents, it took me longer to face it, understand it, and realize it. I can't believe anyone would think we made something like this up and got our children to go along with it. I even have trouble getting my children to brush their teeth. Do people seriously believe a parent would be crazy enough to make something so horrible up and would then be able to convince a child to do all these crazy things? The trial was so terrible for the other parents and children. We wanted them to know about Amy, but we couldn't let her do it. She was so afraid."

Bret Bennet's mother, Molly, is less certain of her son's future and her relationship with him. The pain of abused children is so real that it communicates itself at every turn. It's in their bizarre drawings, in the fear on their faces when they're separated too suddenly or too long from their parents and in their aloneness when they're with other children who have not had t grow up so rapidly or so brutally. But the suffering of the children's paren is no less disturbing. Of all those involved in the Greenbrook case, Bre mother is the one whose despair is most apparent. Bret was another of t

children who did not testify—not because he was too frightened or too
along in therapy to testify safely, but because he has continued to deny th
anything happened. Whatever he knows is locked away in a place that neithe
his parents nor social workers and therapists have been able to reach.

Molly Bennet knows very little about what caused the change in her son.
She remembers only that he begged so hard not to go to school that she began
writing notes asking that the teachers be especially sensitive to his insecurity.
He insisted on wearing an extra set of underpants to school; and for months
after his parents withdrew him, he refused to be driven near the area where
the school was located.

The most observable change in the little boy came after his parents decided to remove him from the school. His mother recalls:

> For almost three months he got so hostile and nasty and impossible to
> handle that we didn't know what to do with him. He was especially awful
> to me. Every day he would go to the bathroom in his pants. He was six
> at the time. Then Patti called me and told me that there had been some
> trouble at the school. She said she didn't want to say much more but
> that Laurie had said Bret was her partner sometimes. She told me it
> might be a good idea to call the social worker who had seen some of the
> children. That night I said to Bret, "I understand some things happened
> at school that were pretty awful. Laurie told her mom about them and
> said you were her partner." Bret didn't say anything; he just cried and
> hugged me. He didn't say anything at all, just hugged me. I guess I
> felt—I had mixed emotions. At that point I was thrilled to know he
> responded to me, but I felt helpless. I had no idea what happened to
> him, and there was nothing I could do to change it.

After that conversation, Bret stopped going to the bathroom in his pants.
His mother says, "It was like he thought, 'Thank God, they know. Now the
pressure is off.'" But he would not answer questions about Greenbrook. The
Bennets took him to social workers, who told them his drawings and other
behaviors indicated that he had been traumatized somehow but that he had
verbally denied that anything had happened. They said that boys tend more
than girls to resort to denial and suggested that Bret see a therapist.

He went for nine months. His parents recall that he "hated every minute
of it, [that] it was like pulling teeth to get him to go." He did admit to the
therapist that something happened at the school, but he would not say what
it was. The Bennets thought the therapist would give him "the perfect opportunity to let loose because the most important thing was to get him to
talk; but he didn't, unfortunately. It was like he really needed to just be left
alone." The therapist is unable to predict what will happen with Bret; she
told his parents that male children have a much harder time coping and that
the fact that they "know may eventually help him to open up"; or, she contended, "He may just close out on it."

For a long while Bret had difficulty sleeping. His mother would stay on the floor in his room, or his parents would make a bed for him on the floor next to them. Eventually they decided to put his sister in the room with him, and "it really helped out." He went through a stage where he tried to educate his sister and the other children in the neighborhood about not allowing people to touch them where they didn't want to be touched.

According to his mother, Bret Bennet doesn't appear any different from other children, except perhaps that he's more "serious" now:

It's like he's hardened. He's very temperamental, and I don't know whether it's just his personality or that he's grown older or that it's because of what happened to him. The hardest part for me is trying not to live my life or let him live his in light of that one experience. It's a no-win situation. No matter what you do, it's not going to be right. Our relationship definitely isn't the same, has not been the same since Greenbrook because I'm the one who made the final decision. I'm the one who researched it and decided to send him. I feel like I've lost a part of him. I don't know what happened to him or what never got out that's eating him up. I feel like he really dislikes me alot.

Molly continues quietly:

He attributed everything to being bad. I think he won't admit what happened because he blamed himself for agreeing to whatever it was. It's locked inside him, and I'll tell you the truth—sometimes I hope it never comes out because when it does, I don't know what form it's going to take. He blamed himself. Then there's me making him go there every day. I feel guilty. I feel like I ruined his life.

In addition to the other children the Greenbrook prosecutor couldn't discuss in court, the parents related later disclosures that no one understood or that were too bizarre to take into a courtroom where even the most fundamental issues of child sexual abuse were suspect. They said that some of the strangest accounts by the children came early, and others occurred in the months that followed the trial. Some talked about black robes and weird ceremonies, about killing animals and babies. Amy Henderson, who had become so unexpectedly frightened of dogs, asked, "Why did the puppy fly apart into pieces when they shot it?" Allison Young kept asking her older sister to tell her "about how animals die." Amy began drawing crosses and chanting, "You will be punished for your sins." Laurie Chapman described having to "go up on a cross but it wasn't a cross like Jesus was on." No one knew what to make of it. Many of the parents began to believe that what their children had described was ritualized abuse.

Sexual abuse is only one facet of this "new" crime, which presents incredible dilemmas for experts and the criminal justice system. Until very recently, there was not even a name for ritualistic abuse; and only within the last few years have researchers attempted to define it and to describe its characteristics.[8] Cloaked in greater obscurity than sexual abuse alone, ritualistic or ritualized abuse is an even more unbelievable and ambiguous crime. Children who have been both ritualistically and sexually abused present a variety of symptoms, and some do not demonstrate behaviors consistent with sexual abuse alone. What happens when the ritualistically abused child is treated only as a sexual abuse victim? To children, experts say, sexual impositions are much less horrifying than witnessing or participating in actual or contrived animal and human sacrifices. Thus a new kind of victim has suddenly emerged; not talking or acting like typical sexual abuse victims, who are themselves still misunderstood, the ritualistically abused face even greater isolation and disparagement. In such cases, one phrase is all too frequently heard—"You don't understand, mommy; you don't understand."

Probably no one will ever know with certainty what happened at Greenbrook Preschool, but one thing is clear—the legal process damaged the children, their families, and the defendants. In a sense, everyone lost something. Jeff Young says today:

There are all kinds of costs. Financially, it was a tremendous drain on our family; but the intangible costs were greatest. It disrupted our family life as we knew it. My way of coping was probably different from everyone else's. I went through various stages of disbelief. Then when I finally admitted to myself it really did happen, my first concern was what to do to help Allison erase this thing. Obviously, it was a new thing for me. I didn't even know how I was supposed to act. I had never had any interplay with legal procedures. My only experience with those was being in traffic court.

I wanted everything to progress as quickly and efficiently as possible, but we couldn't get away from it. We couldn't go out to dinner even for a short time without discussing it. It was a tremendous cost to the other children because we had to spend so much time with Allison, especially in the beginning. My objective is just trying to keep my family together, but this is a sore that will always be with us. I don't think it will ever totally heal.

Tom Chapman doesn't believe his family will ever be totally "healed" either. His anger is directed as much at the legal system as at the defendants:

I was absolutely shocked at the way the judge allowed us to be treated. The defense attorneys were allowed to point at Laurie, raise their voices, bully her, and scream at her. On the stand was a child described by the school system as "gifted," and they were able to terrify and confuse her to the point that she forgot her own name. I knew she was in trouble and scared to death; but I had to sit there and watch it and know there was nothing I could do.

They tried to publicly humiliate my wife and destroy her credibility so that they could keep her from telling the truth. This is the way American courts protect citizens?

I'm angry as hell about what happened to us. There was no attempt to get at the truth. It was a game played by a set of rules, and the rules were what was important—not the truth.

There may not be much we can do to change people who abuse children, but we don't have to put up with a system that abuses the children. The judge and lawyers did their own abuse of our child; Laurie was traumatized as much if not more by what happened in the courtroom. It's hogwash for the legal system to say it can't help or doesn't know what's happening to children. Ignorance of what they did to my daughter is no excuse.

The legal system was concerned not about the truth but about innocence *under the law.* In my mind, that's a warped sense of justice. It's not what the founding fathers wanted or intended at all. I had never been in a criminal court before, but I'll tell you what—if every citizen of the United States were to spend one day in a criminal court proceeding, there would be such an outcry at how outrageous the system is that the whole thing would be dismantled in a year.

5

The Trial:
Conflicting Concepts
in a Crowded Jury Box

*"I always thought [children] were fabulous monsters!" said the Unicorn.
"Is it alive?"*

"It can talk," said Haigha solemnly. The Unicorn looked dreamily at Alice, and said, "Talk, child."

Alice could not help her lips curling up into a smile as she began: "Do you know, I always thought Unicorns were fabulous monsters, too? I never saw one alive before!"

"Well, now that we have seen each other," said the Unicorn, "if you'll believe in me I'll believe in you. Is that a bargain?"

—Lewis Carroll,
*Through the Looking Glass
and What Alice Found There*

THE legal system does not always appear as flawed as it did in the Greenbrook case. Children have gained justice in criminal courts when laws and trial techniques have enabled them to testify effectively. To evaluate the criminal justice system's ultimate ability to respond to sexually abused children, it is necessary to understand the criminal jury trial and its potential for accommodating child victims.

America's devotion to trial by jury is enshrined in its earliest documents—in the resolutions of the Stamp Act Congress, the First Continental Congress, and in the Declaration of Independence. Indeed, the states would not have ratified the Constitution without the Bill of Rights, including the

Sixth Amendment's guarantee that "the accused shall enjoy the right to . . . trial by jury."[1] Although many countries implemented the original jury concept, by the twentieth century trial by jury had fallen into substantial disfavor everywhere except the United States.[2] The jury trial's continued vitality in America seems to be closely connected to democratic ideals: (1) The relationship between citizens and government is enhanced when citizens are required to take an active role in society's most important decisions. (2) Lawyers and judges who practice and apply trial law are motivated to shape its substance and to adapt its complexities to the common sense of jurors. Hence, as Tocqueville concluded, "The jury, which is the most energetic means of making the people rule, is also the most efficacious means of teaching it how to rule well."[3]

Armed not with laws and technicalities, but with common sense, citizens become the jury and, according to the theory, the jury discovers truth. The prosecutor introduces evidence to prove the defendant's guilt. The defense attorney challenges that evidence through cross-examination and sometimes by introducing other evidence. The power of the adversaries' efforts should produce a friction that sparks the truth. The judge assures that the evidence presentation is full and fair—"the truth, the whole truth, and nothing but the truth." Then the jury sifts, analyzes, and returns a verdict. The concept sounds admirable. Historically, however, the search for truth has been compromised by another tradition, equally fundamental to the American criminal justice system.

Presumption of innocence, requiring proof beyond a reasonable doubt, is as sacred to Americans as trial by jury. The Supreme Court explained that the reasonable doubt standard forms "the foundation of our criminal law" because it "provides concrete substance for the presumption of innocence":

> The requirement of proof beyond a reasonable doubt has this vital role . . . for cogent reasons. The accused . . . has at stake interests of immense importance, both because of the possibility that he may lose his liberty upon conviction and because of the certainty that he would be stigmatized by the conviction. Accordingly, a society that values the good name and freedom of every individual should not condemn a man for commission of a crime when there is reasonable doubt about his guilt. . . .
>
> Moreover, use of the reasonable doubt standard is indispensable to command the respect and confidence of the community. . . . It is critical that the moral force of the criminal law not be diluted by a standard of proof that leaves people in doubt whether innocent men are being condemned.[4]

Most Americans learn very early what the Supreme Court termed a "fundamental value"—"that it is far worse to convict an innocent man than to let a guilty man go free."[5] Accordingly, while juries can decide civil cases by lesser standards—preponderance of the evidence, or clear and convincing evidence—they can only find a defendant guilty in a criminal case when evidence proves guilt beyond a reasonable doubt to all twelve jurors.[6]

Defense attorneys almost always emphasize the presumption of innocence and reasonable doubt standards during "voir doir," the jury selection process in which the lawyers ask questions of prospective jurors. Typically, an attorney might inquire, "Now ladies and gentlemen, before this jury is selected, before you have heard any evidence, does anyone have a view as to whether my client is guilty or not guilty?"

Prospective jurors seldom respond because they assume that it would be improper to have preconceived notions of a defendant's guilt or innocence. A perceptive defense attorney might then continue:

> Well, ladies and gentlemen, you should. You see, my client is presumed innocent. That legal presumption means that if you were to vote now, your verdict would have to be "not guilty" because no evidence has proved guilt. And do you understand that the defense is not required to prove innocence? We don't have to do or say a thing in this trial; the prosecution must prove its case.
>
> Is there anyone who would expect my client to take the stand, give his side of the story, or introduce any evidence of innocence?

Often, prospective jurors raise their hands because they assume they will hear from the defendant. But the defense attorney then cautions:

> I understand that we all have a natural tendency to want to hear both sides. But have you ever been in a situation where someone said you did something and you had no witnesses to show you did not? That can happen to anyone. Because of that, our laws say that it would be terribly unfair to require a defendant to prove innocence in order to remain free. So can each of you, right now, promise to follow the judge's instructions to presume my client innocent?

Thus the jury's conceptual box becomes cramped. On the one hand, the jury must search for truth. On the other, that search leads, not along an open path, but through a crowded street where "not guilty" does not necessarily mean "innocent." "Not guilty" means only "not proven beyond a reasonable doubt."

This is not to suggest that the presumption of innocence is wrong or the burden of proof unfair. Most Americans share the Supreme Court's conclusion that these standards are indispensable to justice. Consistent with American values, presumption of innocence and reasonable doubt have protected the innocent from reckless accusations, improper prosecutorial motivations, careless evidence, and inflamed citizens. They offer protection for citizens who are falsely accused.

But of course, the same protections exist for defendants who are truthfully accused, preventing convictions of guilty defendants in child sexual abuse cases, and discouraging other victims from reaching the courts. Prosecutors attempt to present evidence to prove guilt, but defense attorneys do everything possible to challenge that evidence—not necessarily to show innocence, but to suggest uncertainty. The prosecutor's legal and ethical obligation is to see that justice is done. The defense attorney, as the person standing between the defendant's freedom and the government's power, has a very different responsibility—to zealously represent the interests of the defendant. However indecent or immoral it may seem to some, the defense attorney's obligation is to represent the murderer, the arsonist, the rapist, and the child abuser; for to offer effective representation only to those who commit minor offenses would be to abandon the concept of justice cherished by citizens who want those same protections for themselves.

Some view the reasonable doubt and presumption of innocence standards as sources of a separate injustice. With the prosecutor seeking truth and justice and the defense attorney committed to protecting a client's interests, isn't the jury sometimes denied the chance to find truth? Aren't victims and witnesses subjected to defense tactics that are painful and unfair? These questions have bothered legal scholars throughout America's history. Long before anyone focused on the child witness, Jerome Frank explored the problem for all witnesses in *Courts on Trial—Myth and Reality in American Justice:*

> Many lawyers maintain that the "fight" theory and the "truth" theory coincide. They think that the best way for a court to discover the facts . . . is to have each side strive as hard as it can, in a keenly partisan spirit, to bring to the court's attention the evidence favorable to that side. . . .
>
> But frequently the partisanship of the opposing lawyers blocks the uncovering of vital evidence or leads to a presentation of vital testimony in a way that distorts it. . . .
>
> This is perhaps most obvious in the handling of witnesses. Suppose a trial were fundamentally a truth-inquiry. Then, recognizing the inherent fallibilities of witnesses, we would do all we could to remove the causes of their errors when testifying. Recognizing also the importance of witnesses' demeanor as clues to their reliability, we would do our best to make sure that they testify in circumstances most conducive to a revealing observation of that demeanor by the trial judge or jury. In our contentious trial practice, we do almost the exact opposite. . . . The novelty of the situation . . . the agitation and hurry which accompanies it, the cajolery or intimidation to which the witness may be subjected, the want of questions calculated to excite those recollections which might clear up every difficulty, and the confusion of cross-examination . . . may

give rise to important errors and omissions. . . . It is not strange that frequently truthful witnesses are . . . misunderstood, that they nervously react in such a way as to create the impression that they are either evading or intentionally falsifying.[7]

Just as the adversarial process can create false impressions about witnesses, the presumption of innocence can restrict evidence. Jury trials attempt to present evidence in a full and fair way so juries can decide whether the evidence proves the defendant guilty, but the presumption of innocence assures that certain things will not be presented. What is most troubling in some child sexual abuse cases is that the defendant may have a criminal record of child sexual abuse. While this is crucial information that a judge always receives before sentencing, it is almost never provided to a jury. State statutes or appellate decisions prohibit using such information in a trial because, in legal terms, its "prejudicial effect outweighs its probative value." That is, if the jury knew of a prior sexual abuse crime, it would almost certainly find the defendant guilty, no matter how uncertain the evidence. The prior conviction would have little "probative value" in the case, but its "prejudicial effect" would be overwhelming.

Exceptions do exist. If a defendant decides to testify at a trial, the prosecutor can cross-examine to expose the criminal record. However, such cross-examination may be limited to the number of convictions, not the nature of the crimes. Only if the defendant's alleged sexual assault followed a pattern of prior offenses—locations, age of victims, nature of sexual conduct—can the prosecutor sometimes introduce specific evidence of prior assaults. Then, although the prior offense evidence is highly prejudicial, it also has substantial probative value for the allegation at the trial.[8]

Other rules of evidence that derive from the presumption of innocence restrict the presentation of evidence to the jury. Before a trial, the prosecution must provide "discovery" to the defense—investigative reports as well as other evidence intended for the trial. The defense has to provide almost nothing. While the prosecution must "do justice" and give the defense information about evidence to be presented at the trial, the defense can "put the prosecution to its proof" without revealing its own strategy.

Protected by the Fifth Amendment right against self-incrimination, the defendant is not required to help the prosecution. The prosecutor is thus prohibited from calling the defendant to testify or from commenting to the jury that the defendant has invoked that right. Even a slight reference that the defendant has not testified or offered some explanation assures a mistrial.

Other evidence may be withheld from the jury because of what the law terms the "exclusionary rule." Often criticized and rarely understood outside courtrooms and classrooms, this rule provides that illegally obtained evidence cannot be used at a trial. The rationale for the rule is strong. Citizen authority over police is fundamental to the justice system of a nation that is a democracy rather than a police state. Police, even in the interest of public safety, must not break into homes, coerce confessions, or employ other unlawful means to obtain evidence. When they do, courts must not countenance such conduct by allowing the prosecution to use the evidence. Exclusion of such evidence is the only effective deterrent to such police conduct because exclusion removes the police incentive to obtain evidence by unlawful means.

Although exclusion of evidence is intended to discipline police conduct, it can also produce important results in a trial. For example, when a court excludes an involuntary confession because it was coerced by the police, the exclusion not only serves to deter police misconduct, but also to prevent introduction of unreliable evidence. However, when illegally seized child pornography materials are excluded, the rule reduces the jury's access to reliable evidence. Arguments over the merits and proper range of the exclusionary rule will continue. Whatever the outcome of those legal battles, it is important to recognize that the issue is problematic. Some rules of evidence deter police misconduct, some prevent presentation of unfair evidence, and some also restrict the reliable evidence offered to the jury.

When a prosecutor evaluates a child sexual abuse case, all these limitations must be part of the calculation. Most exist only in criminal cases. If a case is tried as a civil custody suit in juvenile court, the alleged child abuser may be required to testify, pretrial discovery may be the same for both sides, and even illegally seized evidence may be allowed. Nevertheless, the limitations imposed in criminal trials are based on constitutional principles that are not going to change. With that understanding in mind, a prosecutor must evaluate each case, knowing that after all the evidence has been presented, the judge will send the jury to deliberate with a final instruction: that the defendant is not required to prove innocence, that the law presumes innocence and requires a not-guilty verdict unless evidence proves guilt beyond a reasonable doubt.

The prosecutor's trial tactics must serve the primary purposes of the trial—discovering the truth while preserving the presumption of innocence. Guided by ethical requirements, the prosecutor must present the evidence fairly. Guided by the need to prove guilt beyond a reasonable doubt, the prosecutor must also make the evidence full.

How does one provide fair and full evidence to juries in child sexual abuse cases in which the only sources of evidence are (1) the testimony of the victim, (2) the corroborating testimonies of others usually not present at the assault, and (3) the statements or conduct of the defendant? Answering that question demonstrates why the testimony of child victims generally is so critical and at the same time so difficult to present to juries.

Without eyewitnesses to the assault or extraordinary circumstantial evidence, the prosecutor cannot prove a sexual abuse case unless the victim testifies. Someone has to tell the jury, "I was assaulted. He did it." This requirement relates to the most basic concept supporting fairness and the search for truth in a trial—the person who knows about an offense must come to court to tell the jury.

The idea that the victim should testify in court seems so obvious that people rarely pause to examine its rationale, but that rationale is critical to the analysis of almost every evidentiary question about a child's testimony. It is essential to understand why, at times, a judge should allow a child's testimony, and why, at other times, a judge should accept some kind of substitute for the child's testimony. The victim or witness who knows about an offense should tell the jury because that person actually heard the words, saw the behavior, or suffered the pain about which the jury needs to know. Furthermore, in a criminal case, the witness must be available for follow-up questions and cross-examination. After all, other evidence at trial may lead lawyers to ask questions that could not be explored if the witness is allowed merely to send in a deposition. In addition, jurors must be able to see the witness in order to evaluate credibility.

Accepted as fair and fundamental to justice, this concept is embodied in the Sixth Amendment to the Constitution: "In all criminal prosecutions, the accused shall enjoy the right . . . to be confronted with the witnesses against him." This "confrontation clause," the United States Supreme Court explained, "is to advance a practical concern for the accuracy of the truth-determining process in criminal trials."[9]

The confrontation clause implies disfavor for any testimony that is not in-person. Just as courts trust the process of searching for the truth when the person comes to testify, they distrust hearsay—one person relating what another person said. "Well if that's what that person said," a juror might assume, "then that person should walk into this courtroom and tell us. You can't answer follow-up questions. The person you heard isn't here for cross-examination. Don't tell me what you heard that person say. I can't trust it."

While the confrontation clause and corresponding disfavor for hearsay produce a fair and full search for truth in most criminal trials, their incorrect application causes injustice in many cases of child sexual abuse. Too often judges have applied simplistic interpretations that prevent witnesses from giving crucial testimony to substantiate children's accounts of sexual abuse. In some instances, judges have even ruled that children are not competent to be witnesses and then disallowed the testimony of adult witnesses who, in the absence of the children, would have been able to offer hearsay evidence about the children's experiences.

To prove sexual abuse, prosecutors must be able to present statements of victims so that a jury can determine whether a defendant is guilty. Prosecutors must resist arcane concepts of competency so that children will be permitted to testify, and they must open the court to presentation of reliable hearsay evidence when in-person testimony is not possible or sufficient.

Until recently, prosecutors usually accepted the premise that child victims couldn't provide evidence to juries. They accepted that young children would not be competent to testify in person and that testimony of others would be precluded by hearsay rules. Recently, however, many prosecutors and judges, motivated by new understanding of child sexual abuse, have reexamined these assumptions and discovered that incorrect application of these rules has interfered with the search for truth. Competency and hearsay rules, carelessly interpreted for years, have produced unfair trials and have denied justice to children.

Competency

Because the trial was intended to be a search for truth and because witnesses were to testify in person, rules evolved to assure that those testifying were able to do so. Judges assumed responsibility for the integrity of the trial by protecting the jury from those not "competent" to offer reliable testimony. Historically, the law's assessment of competency has reflected social assumptions and values. Thus for many years slaves and women, as well as children, were not allowed to testify.[10]

As social and legal reform eliminated the most obvious competency biases against women and minorities, some competency concepts remained. Judges retained responsibility for protecting juries from those they believed incapable of appreciating the seriousness of trials and the obligation to speak the truth. Because many young children could not understand the terms "oath," "testify," or "solemnly swear," they were denied the right to speak the truth in court. Believed to live in a world of fantasy, children were not trusted to testify.

Ironically, while that has been the prevalent assumption about child competency, it was never intended to be the law. In 1895, the Supreme Court considered child competency when a defendant appealed his conviction for murder, claiming that the five-year-old child of the victim should not have been allowed to testify. Affirming the conviction in *Wheeler v. United States,* the Supreme Court asserted:

> That the boy was not by reason of his youth, as a matter of law, absolutely disqualified as a witness, is clear. . . . There is no precise age which determines the question of competency. This depends on the capacity and intelligence of the child, his appreciation of the difference between truth and falsehood, as well as of his duty to tell the former. The decision of this question rests primarily with the trial judge, who sees the proposed witness, notices his manner, his apparent possession or lack of intelligence, and may resort to any examination which will

tend to disclose his capacity and intelligence as well as his understanding of the obligations of an oath. . . . To exclude [a child] from the witness stand . . . would sometimes result in staying the hand of justice.[11]

Instead of understanding the Supreme Court's commonsense support of the opportunity for children to testify, however, courts mechanically applied the *Wheeler* criteria and formalized competency requirements by asking, "Does the child have capacity and intelligence? Does the child appreciate the difference between truth and falsehood? Does the child accept the duty to tell the truth? Does the child know the obligations of an oath?"

Implementing this protective role, judges and lawyers would question a child witness, usually outside the presence of the jury. Some would do so skillfully, framing questions with words and concepts appropriate for the child. Others would ask questions such as, "Can you tell me the difference between truth and falsehood?" and quickly disqualify the child for not being able to answer questions that have stymied philosophers through the ages.

The classic tale told in many law classes relates a child's competency questioning by a judge:

"Billy, if I told you that grass is red, would you tell me that I am lying or telling the truth?"
"Telling the truth."
"And if I told you that ice cream is warm, would you tell me that I am lying or telling the truth?"
"Telling the truth."

In the anecdote, the judge rules the child incompetent, and shocked parents and prosecutor hurry him to the hallway and demand an explanation. The child softly answers, "I would never tell the judge he's a liar."

Stilted application of competency criteria excluded countless children who unquestionably would have been allowed to testify under correct application of the *Wheeler* standards. Ironically, while the Supreme Court allowed the testimony of that five-year-old child, most states developed laws that presumed competency only for those over age fourteen.[12] Applying those laws, judges excluded so many children that state competency laws came to be considered "the No. 1 legal rule preventing successful prosecution of child-molestation cases."[13] Precluding the most essential source of testimony, the rule absolutely prohibited prosecution in many cases. As the Supreme Court had warned, improper applications excluded child witnesses and thus "stayed the hand of justice."

The competency laws were illogical and discriminatory. Only children's truthfulness had to be reviewed in advance by judges; yet in many criminal trials, adults lied. Only children's appreciation of an oath had to be examined; yet few adult perjurers were inspired to truthfulness by raising their right hands. And while juries evaluated the credibility of every other witness, the competency rule refused to entrust them with evaluation of child witnesses. Thus the rule countered American trial traditions by elevating judges over juries and excluding one set of witnesses from the truth-seeking process.

In 1974, the revised Federal Rules of Evidence abolished the competency rule for trials in the federal courts. Acknowledging the absurdity of the old rule, the new version allowed for the testimony of virtually all witnesses. This gave juries the responsibility for assessing the credibility of child witnesses. Many states followed the federal lead so that by 1985, a United States Justice Department survey found that twenty state laws ruled every person competent.[14] Other states enacted laws that required courts to presume the competency of child witnesses.[15] In addition, appellate courts began to approve greater flexibility even where the old rules remained. For example, a child could "promise" to tell the truth, even without understanding how to "swear" to an "oath."[16] Such flexibility was consistent with the *Wheeler* ruling and with traditional legal principles. As John Henry Wigmore explained in his seminal treatise on evidence in 1904, the purpose of the oath "is not to exclude any competent witness, but merely to add a stimulus to truthfulness."[17]

The trend away from the old competency rule became so strong and the logic so compelling that by 1986, Marquette University law professor and former child sexual abuse prosecutor Daniel Blinka could write: "Anything resembling the old . . . procedure should be used sparingly and rarely, since jurors are readily capable of assessing the veracity of the child witness. The . . . evidence code is in favor of allowing the child to testify. All doubts should be resolved in favor of permitting the child to take the witness stand."[18]

Despite the trend, old and unfair practices persist. Even in states that have adopted the new rule, some prosecutors and judges remain oblivious to the change. The Arizona Court of Appeals, for example, recently had to reverse the decision of a trial judge who failed to follow new competency standards in a trial of child sexual abuse.[19] Yet even when a state has not revised its competency statute, a judge can apply the rule in a sensitive, commonsense way consistent with the modern trend. Satisfying the statutory requirement for a competency hearing, a judge can phrase questions in age-appropriate terms and help a child become familiar and comfortable with the court setting and procedures.

In 1987, the United States Supreme Court considered for the first time whether a judge could modify the procedures of a competency hearing to accommodate a child. In *Kentucky v. Stincer*, the defendant appealed his sexual assault conviction because the judge excluded him from the competency hearing when the seven- and eight-year-old victims became afraid to testify in his presence. In allowing the defendant's exclusion, the Supreme Court emphasized that its decision was not limited to pretrial hearings and that even during the trial the important question is whether the defendant's "presence would contribute to the fairness of the procedure."[20] Thus, for the first time, the Supreme Court declared that the constitutional rights of defendants must coexist with the opportunity for children to testify. "Fairness" is the standard, and fairness may even include trial proceedings without the intimidating presence of the defendant.[21]

The modernization of competency rules does not imply that a child's memory and communication are the same as those of adults. The contemporary view does convey that whatever the individual characteristics of each child or the overall differences of children from adults, juries should be allowed to see and hear child witnesses and to evaluate their credibility. At the conclusion of criminal trials, judges will instruct juries that they can evaluate the testimonies of witnesses based on many factors such as demeanor on the witness stand, clearness of recollections, intelligence and reasonableness of testimony, and bias or possible motives for falsifying.[22]

No one can guarantee that jurors will be able to assess the credibility of every child or, for that matter, every adult. What is certain, however, is that if judges adhere to illogical competency rules, juries will seldom have the chance to make such assessments because so few child sexual abuse cases will go to trial.

Confrontation and Hearsay

Just as the search for truth should assure children the chance to testify, it should also assure that in some cases their voices be heard through hearsay rather than in person. Evidence laws of every state are replete with exceptions that allow certain hearsay in trials. When all the distinctions from one state to another are stripped away, the reason becomes clear. Hearsay evidence often helps the jury find the truth; excluding hearsay testimony can deny the jury crucial evidence. A few examples make this clear.

1. With a last gasp, a murder victim tells paramedics, "Smith shot me." At Smith's murder trial, the paramedics offer the only evidence of the victim's accusation. The jury evaluates the victim's statement, and weighs the paramedics' ability to remember, the consistency of their testimony with other evidence, and the likelihood of their falsifying information. This hearsay would be allowed, under an exception known as the "dying declaration," which assures the potential for prosecution despite the victim's "unavailability." Moreover, the law considers such death-bed utterances as having particular reliability.

2. After a woman tells a hospital emergency room doctor that she has been beaten by her boyfriend, the police charge him with assault. Fearing the defendant, the woman leaves town and cannot be found for trial. The doctor testifies, repeating the victim's statements, and showing

the medical reports of her injuries. The medical reports are allowed as a common hearsay exception because there is no apparent reason to doubt their authenticity. Some of the victim's statements may also be allowed under another hearsay exception for statements "for purposes of diagnosis or treatment." In principle, this exception acknowledges that a jury can assess the reliability of such hearsay knowing that statements to medical personnel are motivated by a unique self-interest; the victim appreciates that the quality of medical treatment depends on the accuracy of information she provides.

3. A man abducts his ex-girlfriend, takes her to an apartment, tears off her clothes and beats her legs, arms, and breast with a dress iron. The police arrive at the door and hear the victim's screams. They pound at the door, the woman breaks away, throws open the door and cries, "Help me, help me! He burned me with an iron!" Months later the victim and defendant have reconciled, and she refuses to testify; but the police officer is allowed to tell the jury her statements. They fall within the "excited utterance" or "res gestae" hearsay exception because the victim's words were spontaneous, almost involuntary. She had no chance to consider or prepare a false account.

Legal scholars have written volumes analyzing the conceptual underpinnings of these and other hearsay exceptions. The subject is challenging and important because the hearsay exceptions provide instances when, despite the importance of in-person testimony and despite the constitutional right of confrontation, courts allow second-hand testimony of crucial statements.

In *Ohio v. Roberts* (1979), the Supreme Court summarized with two questions the basis for allowing hearsay: (1) Is the actual witness "unavailable?" (2) Does the hearsay statement of that unavailable witness have sufficient "indicia of reliability" to be given to the jury? If so, another person who heard the witness's prior statement can be allowed to repeat it to the jury.[23]

Unfortunately, just as judges have prevented children from testifying by misinterpreting competency requirements, they have also prevented prosecution of child sexual abuse by misinterpreting the *Ohio v. Roberts* standards. In the first place, judges often fail to distinguish physical from testimonial "unavailability"—that is, sometimes a witness is physically available but cannot testify for reasons such as fear or memory loss. In the second place, judges frequently fail to understand that "indicia of reliability" do not have to be absolute. To allow hearsay, a judge does not have to be certain that the hearsay is true—only that it has sufficient reliability that the jury will be able to assess whether it is true. By allowing hearsay, a judge is not telling the jury, "Believe this testimony," but rather, "Hear this testimony and decide whether to believe it."

How do these misinterpretations prevent prosecution of child sexual abuse? In countless cases, child victims have told trusted adults about abuse.

Months or even years later, when a case is ready for trial, many children have only faint recollections of their experiences. They fear the courtroom confrontation with the abuser and cannot testify. Logically, then, judges should allow adults to tell juries what the children have said, even though defense attorneys will argue that they have not had the chance to cross-examine the children. Judges with limited knowledge of the law frequently refuse such hearsay evidence from adults because, in the most simplistic sense, the child is "available" to testify. When this happens, the prosecution usually loses, even in cases in which there is overwhelming evidence of abuse.[24]

Whether or not a child victim can testify, prosecution of child sexual abuse should be possible, and the jury should receive crucial hearsay evidence of a child's earlier disclosures, allegations, and recantations. In 1986, the Supreme Court emphatically explained the basis for admission of such hearsay. In *United States v. Inadi*, the Court clarified that "unavailability" is not a prerequisite to the admission of hearsay. It explained that judges had been misinterpreting *Ohio v. Roberts* and excluding hearsay that should come before juries, that *Ohio v. Roberts* did not "stand for the radical proposition that no out-of-court statement can be introduced . . . without a showing that the declarant is unavailable." In the Court's analysis, such an interpretation adds nothing to the determination of the truth in a case, which is the object of the confrontation clause.[25]

This decision challenged the notion that a statement made earlier and out-of-court is less trustworthy than one made before the jury. In fact, the Court explained, some "statements derive much of their value from the fact they are made in a context very different from trial, and therefore are usually irreplaceable as substantive evidence."[26] With enormous implications for child sexual abuse cases, the decision asserted that hearsay evidence can have significant value for a jury precisely because it provides statements from a different time and context, statements made without regard to their usefulness in a trial. Such statements might, in fact, carry greater weight than those presented during a trial because they were spoken at times closer to the incident and were less affected by memory loss or memory enhancement in preparation for the trial. Although it did not deal with a child sexual abuse case, *Inadi* established a solid basis for admission of children's statements.

This, indeed, was the conclusion of the Arizona, Arkansas, Delaware, Vermont, and Washington supreme courts in recent decisions that applied the *Inadi* principles. Allowing the hearsay statements of a ten-year-old victim to a psychologist, the Arizona Supreme Court declared:

> An additional factor of great weight in this case is the unlikelihood that more trustworthy or probative evidence could have been produced by [the child's] in-court testimony. A young child's spontaneous statements about so unusual a *personal* experience, made soon after the event, are at

least as reliable as the child's in-court testimony, given months later, after innumerable interviews and interrogations may have distorted the child's memory. Indeed, [her] statements are valuable and trustworthy in part because they exude the naivete and curiosity of a small child, and were made in circumstances very different from interrogation or a criminal trial.[27]

In applying the *Inadi* ruling to a child sexual abuse case, the Arkansas Supreme Court was even more definitive in its finding that "the reason for the unavailability requirement disappears."[28]

It is not surprising that most citizens are confused by the legal subtleties inherent in discussions of the confrontation clause, hearsay rules, unavailability, and reliability. Legal scholars have debated them for years. In fact, from court to court, case to case, and state to state, very different analyses control the admission of hearsay. Some states have statutes specifying the hearsay that will be allowed in a child sexual abuse case. In others, where there are no statutory rules, appellate decisions have provided guidance. Elsewhere, statutes and appellate decisions are silent or vague on these issues. Most important, everywhere there are prosecutors and judges who do not know the laws of their own states, do not understand or probe the conceptual bases for hearsay, and do not analyze unavailability or reliability according to the purpose of "advancing the accuracy of the truth-determining process in criminal trials."[29]

Although these legal concepts may seem like an evidentiary swamp, they often will determine whether and how child sexual abuse can be prosecuted. Without statements from the victim, prosecution is almost impossible. With proper competency standards, courtrooms can be opened to child witnesses; but many are too young or too frightened to testify, or perhaps too much time has passed for them to remember. In some cases the family or a therapist may believe the trial would be harmful to the child's emotional recovery. Physically available to the court, the child is thus functionally unavailable to testify. Still, months earlier, perhaps right after the assault, the child told parents, police, teacher, doctor, or a counselor what occurred. The prosecutor then must depend on their hearsay accounts of the child's statements.

There are a number of different approaches to child hearsay, and it is helpful to know their conceptual subtleties in order to understand how they can lead to admission of evidence. Whatever the precise statutory or appellate court rules, child hearsay should be allowed in many cases. Even with such evidence, the verdict remains uncertain and in the jury's control; without it, there can be no trial. This realization underlay the Supreme Court's decision almost one hundred years ago in *Mattox v. United States:*

[Hearsay exceptions] are admitted not in conformity with any general rule regarding the admission of testimony, but as an exception to such rules, simply from the necessities of the case, and to prevent a manifest failure of justice.[30]

Recognizing that children often are functionally unavailable to testify, hearsay exception laws developed over the years to allow others to tell juries what children had said about being sexually abused. Realizing that without such evidence, trial is impossible, those traditional hearsay rules have expanded in recent years "to prevent a manifest failure of justice."

Hearsay Exceptions: An Expanding Tradition

The "Complaint of Sexual Conduct" Exception

In 1985, the Oregon Supreme Court applied "an ancient and firmly rooted hearsay exception" to allow testimony by a child's mother in a sexual assault trial. The court ruled that the mother could testify that "at my home while seated in the recliner chair in the front room my three-year-old told me that a person licked her tee-tee." Tracing the "complaint of sexual conduct" exception (sometimes called the "prompt complaint" or "complaint of rape" exception) to 1840, the court explained that the rationale for the rule is to allow evidence "to corroborate the testimony of . . . witnesses or to negate an inference of consent."[31] In other words, this exception derives from commonsense understanding that such hearsay could help prove that the child's allegation was not a recent fabrication and that she had not consented to the sex act. Evidence of a child's prompt complaint would enable the prosecution to counter defense claims that the child fabricated the incident or consented to the act.

Some legal commentators believe that the complaint of sexual conduct exception has limited value in child sexual abuse cases because where the victim is a young child, consent is not an issue (and cannot be a legal defense) and because many victims do not make prompt complaints. They "frequently endure ongoing abuse for long periods of time—even years—before their victimization is revealed."[32] Nevertheless, for several reasons, the complaint of sexual conduct exception is very important. First, it reminds lawyers and judges that hearsay exceptions that have been specifically articulated for child sexual abuse cases are not a new notion. They are based in traditional evidence law. Second, the complaint exception establishes that on the unique subject of child sexual abuse, the law has always considered a victim's statements to trusted persons to be important for the jury to consider—even when the statements are not made to a doctor for diagnosis or treatment. Third, and perhaps most important, since the unavailability requirement has receded under the *Inadi* decision, complaint hearsay may be allowed even when a child does testify simply because a child's initial complaint of sexual abuse has significant, independent value for the jury.

Finally, hearsay testimony about the victim's original disclosure may prove essential in a growing number of cases where charges of recent fabrication, persuasion, coercion, or subsequent recantation are at the heart of the defense. When, for example, a divorced father is accused of sexually abusing his child during visitation, the child later may recant; or the defense may assert that the mother, determined to cut off visitation, coerced the child to make up the allegation. Then perhaps the most important evidence might be the child's earlier complaint to a teacher, friend, or police officer.[33]

Thus the traditional complaint exception remains an active means to hear children's words in court in sexual abuse cases. In some states, it may provide the most clear statutory or appellate authority for courts to allow hearsay. Even in those states where such authority does not exist, its rationale should support the admission of hearsay in an increasing number of cases.[34]

The "Tender Years" Exception

More than one hundred years ago, on May 21, 1884, a man intending to commit rape assaulted a ten-year-old girl. According to the Michigan Supreme Court, "upon the trial the mother of the girl was permitted to testify to what her girl told her . . . in the month of August following." The victim also testified and explained that the defendant told her "that she must not tell her father about it; that, if she did, he would give her an awful whipping."[35]

The Michigan Supreme Court affirmed the conviction and the use of hearsay, even though the child's statement was not a prompt complaint or excited utterance and even though the child was not "unavailable" and did testify at the trial:

> We think the [excited utterance] rule not an inflexible one, and ought to yield where . . . the party outraged is of tender years, and her silence is the direct consequence of fears . . . induced by threats. . . . The lapse of time occurring after the injury, and before complaint made, is not the test of admissibility. . . . She appears to have been under a sort of duress, caused by fear of the whipping . . . and it was with great reluctance she finally disclosed the facts to her mother.[36]

The "tender years" exception traditionally has allowed juries to hear children's prior statements about sexual abuse. In states where it exists by statute, this exception may offer the best basis for presenting child hearsay. Regardless of whether a particular state has this exception, however, its rationale can have substantial impact.

Like the complaint exception, "tender years" demonstrates the traditional allowance for child sexual abuse hearsay. Moving beyond the complaint exception, it focuses not only on the subject (sexual abuse), but also on the source of the statement (a child). Whereas the complaint exception evolved from adult cases of rape, the tender years rule evolved from cases of child abuse. For more than a century this exception has acknowledged the special circumstances of child victims, the fact that their complaints can be deterred by threats, and the reliability of their disclosures even after much time has passed.

The "Diagnosis/Treatment" Exception

A third traditional hearsay exception allows juries to hear the statements a patient has made to a doctor for purposes of diagnosis or treatment. The law explains that because a patient has a compelling reason to tell the truth to a doctor, the statements are very reliable. Consequently, a jury should have the chance to consider them even when a patient does not testify at a trial. Until recently, the "diagnosis/treatment" exception had limited value in child sexual abuse cases. The exception could be applied only when the crime caused physical injuries that required a doctor's examination or treatment. Because sexual abuse frequently leaves no physical injuries and is not promptly reported, doctors often are not involved. In many such instances, diagnosis or treatment is provided by a psychologist, social worker, or counselor who, according to many state laws, does not enjoy a doctor's status for purposes of the hearsay exception.[37]

The exception also has had limited value because even in cases with physical injuries, it has allowed doctors to tell "what" but not "who." A doctor could thus tell a jury what the patient said about the nature of an injury, but not what the patient said about who caused the injury. Courts distinguished between allowing hearsay "reasonably pertinent to diagnosis and treatment" and disallowing hearsay that identified the offender. Thus the diagnosis/treatment exception could help confirm sexual abuse but could not substitute for a child's testimony identifying the offender.

These limitations may have been obliterated by the 1985 decision of the Federal Court of Appeals in *United States v. Renville*. Renville allegedly had abused his eleven-year-old stepdaughter, but during the trial she recanted her accusations. Her doctor, however, testified about the acts of anal intercourse and cunnilingus she had described during an examination a few weeks after the assault. The judge allowed the doctor to testify that she also identified Renville as her abuser. Carefully examining the rationale for the traditional limitations on diagnosis/treatment hearsay, the court departed from earlier decisions to explain why such hearsay should be allowed to include a child's identification of the offender.

> First, child abuse involves more than physical injury; the physician must be attentive to treating the emotional and psychological injuries which accompany this crime. . . . The exact nature and extent of the psychological problems which ensue from child abuse often depend on the identity of the abuser. . . . [In other] cases, the statement of fault is not rel-

evant to prevention of recurrence of the injury. Sexual abuse of children at home presents a wholly different situation.

Second, physicians have an obligation, imposed by state law, to prevent an abused child from being returned to an environment in which he or she cannot be adequately protected from recurrent abuse. . . . Information that the abuser is a member of the household is therefore "reasonably pertinent" to a course of treatment which includes removing the child from the home.[38]

Although the *Renville* decision involved a physician, it provided the basis to extend the diagnosis/treatment exception to psychologists, social workers, and counselors who might receive a child's disclosure and treat the emotional and psychological injuries which accompany [the] crime." And while *Renville* involved abuse within a family, the decision holds clear implications for cases of extrafamilial sexual abuse. Information identifying the abuser is pertinent to a child's treatment in every case—whether the perpetrator is a relative, teacher, childcare worker, member of the clergy, acquaintance, or stranger.

Recent state supreme court decisions have begun to follow the *Renville* rationale. In 1987, the Arizona Supreme Court affirmed a sexual abuse conviction and rejected the claim that a psychologist should not have been allowed to tell the jury that the ten-year-old victim named the defendant during treatment.[39] Also in 1987, the Wisconsin Supreme Court reached a similar conclusion and moved the diagnosis/treatment rationale a step further when it concluded that even a three-year-old child is aware that statements to a physician and to a psychologist are for medical purposes.[40] Thus the *Renville* decision, scholarly and compelling, has transformed "diagnosis/treatment" hearsay to provide justice for many children whose cases otherwise could not be prosecuted.[41]

The "Excited Utterance" Exception

"Excited utterance" or "res gestae" hearsay is testimony about a "statement relating to a startling event or condition made while . . . under the stress of excitement caused by the event or condition."[42] As we have discussed, the law allows juries to hear a witness's hearsay account of what a victim said when exclaiming in reaction, without any opportunity to contemplate or prepare a statement. Once the startling event passes, the statements lose their reliability because the victim gains time to reflect, prepare, and possibly lie. Narrow application of this exception would have virtually no use in child sexual abuse cases. No witnesses hear the child's immediate reaction to the assault; and unfamiliar with the behavior, children often do not perceive sexual abuse as shocking. Their reactions may be as matter-of-fact as that of the seven-year-old girl who casually said to her father, "Daddy, does milk come out of your wiener? It comes out of Uncle Bob's and it tastes yukky."[43]

For this reason, courts have expanded traditional excited utterance exceptions in child sexual abuse cases. Excited utterance no longer refers only to immediate statements in reaction to an assault but may also encompass the child's first disclosure, whenever it comes. Thus the Wisconsin Supreme Court explained:

> The fact that the assertions are not made within a few minutes or even hours of the alleged assault is not controlling, nor is the fact that they are not volunteered but made in response to questions. . . . A young child may be unable or unwilling to remember . . . all the specific details of the assault by the time the case is brought to trial; or be unwilling to testify, or at least inhibited in doing so from a feeling of fear or shame, or as a result of the strangeness of the courtroom surroundings, particularly with a jury and perhaps members of the general public present. . . . The trial court should consider the age of the child, the nature of the assault, relationship of the child to the defendant, contemporaneity and spontaneity of the assertions in relation to the alleged assault, reliability of the assertions themselves, and the reliability of the testifying witness.[44]

Years ago, most courts would not deviate from a narrow interpretation of the "contemporaneity" of the statement. In 1945, for example, a conviction was reversed when a defendant appealed the trial judge's decision to allow the excited utterance hearsay statement of a victim who, during normal dinner conversation, told his family of being sexually assaulted at school earlier that same day.[45] Now, however, an increasing number of courts allow statements made even months after the assault because of their growing awareness of a critical characteristic of a child's response to sexual abuse: a child's disclosure may be delayed *and* spontaneous. The temporal proximity of the assault and disclosure is less important than the circumstances under which a child discloses the crime. This temporal flexibility for excited utterance hearsay recognizes "the fact that children of tender years are generally not adept at reasoned reflection and at concoction of false stories under such circumstances."[46] That is, a child cannot falsify what he or she cannot imagine and has not experienced. The modern trend, then, is to examine not only the length of time between the assault and the statement, but also whether the time reduced spontaneity or somehow motivated fabrication.

In "A Comprehensive Approach to Child Hearsay Statements in Sex Abuse Cases," Judy Yun argues that this trend destroys "the integrity of the exception, stretching it far beyond its traditional bounds, and creating much uncertainty in its application."[47] She maintains that such expansion violates traditional evidence theory and demonstrates the need for a separate hearsay exception, designed specifically for child abuse and sexual assault. Perhaps a more compelling argument would be that these expanding interpretations reflect more critical analyses by judges and their increasing ability to apply traditional hearsay principles in the special context of child sexual abuse. After all, as Yun explains, many child victims "are traumatized more by the reactions of their family and society [than by] the incident itself. The younger the victim . . . and the closer the relationship . . . to the assailant, the more likely it is to be a longer period of time" before disclosure.[48] Hence an assault, the period between the assault and disclosure, and the disclosure itself are all parts of the traumatic event. From the child's perspective, they are, literally, "res gestae: words spoken, thoughts expressed, and gestures made . . . closely connected to [the] event in both time and substance."[49] When a child discloses a sexual assault to an adult days, weeks, or even months after it took place, his or her statement should be allowed under a true and traditional interpretation of the excited utterance hearsay exception.

The "Residual" Exception

After specifying twenty-three separate hearsay exceptions, the Federal Rules of Evidence provide for the admission of other hearsay evidence if it has "equivalent circumstantial guarantees of trustworthiness" and if "the interests of justice will best be served by admission of the statement."[50] Most states have either adopted this federal "residual" exception or developed a comparable one. The residual exception holds great potential for children precisely because it permits hearsay even when no other specific exception seems to apply.

In a recent case, a four-year-old girl was visiting her aunt and cousins. As the children were undressing for baths, the little girl spread her legs, faced her cousin and said, "Get me." Asked where she had learned that behavior, the child pointed to her genitals and told her aunt, "Uncle W. tickles me." A doctor with the Child Protection Team of the University of Colorado Medical Center examined the child and testified about his conversation with her:

> I asked: "What does Uncle W. do to you?" and she said: "He touches me here," and pointed to her genitals. I asked: "With his fingers?" and she said: "No . . . with his cock." I asked: "Does he hurt you with it?" She said: "Yes."

The trial judge allowed both the aunt and doctor to testify about the child's conversations with them; he ruled that the statement to the aunt was an excited utterance, and that the statement to the doctor was for diagnosis/ treatment.

An appeals court affirmed the defendant's conviction but interpreted the hearsay differently. It said that the statement to the aunt could not be an excited utterance because too much time had passed since the assault, and that the statement to the doctor could not be for diagnosis or treatment because the child might not have understood the purpose of the doctor's examination. Allowing the hearsay nevertheless, the appeals court explained,

"The failure of the statements to fit into the framework of the codified categories of the exceptions to the hearsay rule does not inevitably preclude their
admission. [Both statements were] made in a matter-of-fact manner . . .
which supported the trial court's conclusion that the circumstances indicated
the absence of any intellectual contrivances by the child."[51]

The appellate decision was remarkable for its hypertechnical interpretations of excited utterance and diagnosis/treatment but also instructive for its
allowing the hearsay despite those interpretations. While unwilling to adopt
the trial judge's conclusions, the appeals court felt compelled to allow the
hearsay because the statements were reliable and essential to the jury's search
for truth. Courts can use the residual exception in child sexual abuse cases
not only when no other exception fits, but also in states where specific statutory exceptions address sexual but not other forms of abuse. For example,
in 1985, the Federal Court of Appeals in *United States v. Cree* evaluated the
case of four-year-old Maurice and two-year-old Phillip, who had suffered
numerous bruises and fractures when the defendant beat them with a belt
and a stick. The children did not testify, but their clinical social worker was
allowed to tell the jury of Maurice's description of the abuse. Convicted of
assault, the defendant appealed the judge's decision to allow the social worker's testimony, but the federal court affirmed the decision under the residual
exception. It concluded:

> Maurice's age is a significant factor supporting the finding that the chal-
> lenged statements are trustworthy. . . . It is highly unlikely that a four-
> year-old child would fabricate such accusations of abuse. . . . The pro-
> priety of requiring extremely young victims of abuse to take the stand as
> the only method for putting before the jury what is, in all probability,
> the only first-hand account of abuse . . . is debatable. . . . In a more
> relaxed environment, the child in this case was able to provide his ver-
> sion of the relevant events and yet avoid a potentially traumatic court-
> room encounter.[52]

The *Cree* decision is important for several reasons. Because it interprets
the federal residual exception, it should influence many states that have
adopted the federal rule. With logic equally applicable to a sexual abuse case,
it broadened the exception to nonsexual abuse. It clarified that a social
worker as well as a doctor can relate conversations from the course of treatment. Perhaps most important, the *Cree* decision established that the reliability of a statement may actually be enhanced if made out of court by a
young witness. Because of a child's age, because of the lack of any motive or
ability to fabricate, because of the unintimidating atmosphere in which a
child describes the assault, and because of the overwhelming importance of
the child's statements for a jury, the hearsay must be allowed. Thus, within
the residual exception, the federal court articulated understanding of chil-

dren and abuse that should allow future juries to hear many child victims who otherwise would be forced to remain silent.[53]

The "Sexually Abused Child" Exception

Because traditional hearsay exceptions seemed inadequate, several states have enacted specific hearsay exceptions for child sexual abuse. Washington state's legislature created such an exception in 1982:

> A statement made by a child when under the age of ten describing any act of sexual contact . . . is admissible . . . if: (1) The court finds . . . that the time, content, and circumstances of the statement provide sufficient indication of reliability; and (2) The child either . . . (t)estifies at the proceedings; or . . . (i)s unavailable as a witness. . . .[54]

Several states have enacted similar laws, and others are considering them. Constitutional challenges to these new hearsay exceptions have failed, and prosecutors report using these laws successfully to gain admission of child hearsay.[55] Thus the sexually abused child exception may prove increasingly important. Nevertheless, the specificity of the new laws may create unintended problems. Courts tend to interpret laws that specify certain subjects to exclude all others. For example, where a hearsay exception specifies children "under the age of ten," as in the Washington statute, judges may decide that older children should not enjoy similar protection. In effect, courts say, "The legislature looked at the problem, decided what should be covered and how, and therefore implicitly excluded others from coverage."

Moreover, in their attempts to satisfy Sixth Amendment concerns, some of the new laws require the trial judge to determine unavailability as a prerequisite to allowing hearsay. For example, Indiana's law says that before hearsay can be allowed, a judge must determine a child's emotional or physical unavailability on the basis of certification by a psychiatrist or physician.[56] Such standards are illogical and outdated, particularly in light of the Supreme Court's *Inadi* decision. They may subject children to additional and unnecessary psychiatric and medical examination, and they ignore the significant value of hearsay in most child sexual abuse cases, regardless of whether the child testifies. Thus, while the new sexually abused child exceptions may be valuable where prosecutors and judges incorrectly apply other hearsay exceptions, they also may create unforeseen problems and additional injustice for children.

Technological Innovations: Videotape and Closed-Circuit Television

Because prosecution of child sexual abuse almost always requires the victim to tell what happened, the child sexual abuse trial depends on opening the competency door so children can testify and on allowing the jury to hear the child's earlier out-of-court statements. Hearsay exceptions allow the jury to hear some of the child's words, but they do not permit the jury to see the child. This often leaves prosecution, defense, and jury unsatisfied. They want to see more, to know more. For the defense, it's a matter of protecting the defendant's rights. For the prosecution, it's a matter of proving the case beyond a reasonable doubt. For the jury, it's a matter of finding the truth.

While defense attorneys have presented strenuous objections to child hearsay, law and logic compel their admission. That is not to say, however, that the defense arguments have no validity. After all, child hearsay does suffer the limitation of all hearsay: the defendant loses the chance to confront and cross-examine, and the jury loses the chance to view the child's demeanor and to assess the child's statements first-hand.

Admission of hearsay can present serious problems for both sides. Perhaps the child merely nodded agreement to a suggestive question, or perhaps an adult prompted a certain answer. Maybe an adult inadvertently elicited certain words by assuming disputed facts. Because few parents, teachers, social workers, nurses, and doctors are trained in interviewing techniques for criminal investigations, they are not likely to write adequate reports for later reference in trials. In some cases, then, the defense cannot challenge the accuracy of the witness's recall; and in others, the defense can challenge it and leave the prosecution little chance to respond.

Still, prosecutors do not want to bring children to court with counterproductive results. If a child freezes or becomes confused, such an appearance or testimony may harm the prosecution's case. Thus prosecutors may prefer to present cases with only the best available circumstantial evidence and hearsay statements. Until recently, they faced an "either-or" choice. To protect children and justify the use of hearsay, prosecutors would forego calling children as witnesses, even though their testimonies might provide the most compelling evidence.

Technology has now broadened the options. Videotape and closed-circuit television offer children the chance to testify "in court" without being in the courtroom. Videotape and closed-circuit TV have very different methods and purposes. Furthermore, two different uses of videotape—the investigative interview and the deposition—must be distinguished in order to understand their potential.

Videotape: The Investigative Interview

Many professionals who work with children now use videotape to record their interviews. Hospitals, social service agencies, and police departments train staff in proper interviewing techniques.[57] Whatever the therapeutic purpose of the interview, the resulting videotape may become evidence at a trial. The videotape brings the child's demeanor to the jury and erases most questions about whether an adult directed the child. For both the defense and prosecution, the videotape dramatically assists the jury's search for truth.[58]

The investigative videotape has other advantages. Usually prepared relatively soon after the assault, it preserves the child's statements when memory and emotions are strong. Then, as family, therapists, police, and prosecutors evaluate their options, they can review the videotape and spare the child repeated interviews.[59] In some states, the videotape can also be used before grand juries and at preliminary hearings.

Prosecutors have observed another benefit—the videotape prompts guilty pleas. "The tape may have been played for the defendant when first arrested. . . . A tape of a communicative child professionally interviewed will convince most defendants and their [attorneys] that a trial might not be in their best interest."[60] Of course, the opposite can occur if the child appears uncertain or, for therapeutic reasons, had to be prompted.

> Children's interviews are seldom straightforward, and the child may volunteer information that is detrimental to the case. . . . For example, . . . a videotape of a three-year-old who wavered on the question of whether she had a dog [could allow an] astute defense attorney [to] exploit the child's uncertainty on this apparently simple matter to discredit her entire statement. . . .
>
> Perhaps the most critical aspect of the videotaped statement is the expertise of the interviewer. . . . It is often difficult to obtain a clear story from a child without some degree of prompting. Moreover, if the child has been pressured or threatened into silence, the interviewer may feel compelled to reinforce the child as the story unfolds. These questioning techniques, though perfectly reasonable and even beneficial in a therapeutic milieu, are dangerous in a court of law. Entire videotapes have been found inadmissible where leading questions were overused.[61]

Because the investigative interview videotape shows the jury an out-of-court statement that the defendant was not able to confront, it can only be allowed at a trial as a hearsay exception. Some states have enacted new laws to assure admission of such videotapes. After two years' experience with a more limited law, the Wisconsin legislature broadened the use of videotape evidence by allowing investigative videotapes. Under the new law, the videotape will be admitted when the child is available to testify at trial, and it can still be admitted under other hearsay exceptions when the child is unavailable.[62]

Kentucky, Louisiana, and Texas also have statutes allowing such videotape evidence (1) if the videotape was of the child's first statement, (2) if the questioning was by someone other than an attorney, and (3) if both the interviewer and child are available for cross-examination at trial. These laws are interesting because they express the legislative view that questioning by non-lawyers enhances the reliability of the interview. Moreover, while these video-

tape laws require that a child still be available to testify, they do not necessarily mean that the child will be forced to testify. The defense may decide
not to call the child out of fear that cross-examination of the young witness
will be viewed unsympathetically by the jurors or that the child's in-court
testimony will bolster the evidence against the defendant.[63]

Even in states where no videotape statutes have been enacted, appellate
courts have allowed investigative interview videotapes under traditional hearsay exceptions. In Minnesota, for example, the prosecution succeeded in introducing a videotape under a rule of evidence that allows earlier statements
to be considered to refute charges of fabrication.[64] For the most part, appellate courts have permitted the investigative videotape, appreciating its fairness for both defense and prosecution, and its significance for the jury.

The investigative videotape also can be the most important evidence
when a child recants. Kee MacFarlane, director of the Child Sexual Abuse
Diagnostic Center of Children's Institute International in Los Angeles, explains:

> The intimidating environment of the courtroom, the physical proximity
> to the alleged abuser, and the succession of negatively-associated events
> predispose some child victims to take back initial statements by the time
> they get to court. The prosecution's arguments that courtroom retrac-
> tions are consistent with both the battered child syndrome and the child
> sexual abuse accommodation syndrome might be strengthened by the
> introduction of a videotape which contradicts the current denial by a
> child witness.[65]

Steve Chaney, the district attorney of Tarrant County, Texas, agrees:

> Recanting is a major problem for the legal system. Recanting is an ex-
> pected reaction of an abused child who has reported the abuse, although
> this is not well understood or accepted by the legal community. Only an
> enlightened legal system, when confronted with a recanting child, asks
> the next question, "Why is the child recanting," and seeks an answer to
> that question. Most prosecutors believe that the videotape has a major
> benefit in this area. If the child later recants, even at the time of trial,
> the case can still be prosecuted by using a good tape and psychological
> experts to explain the recanting symptoms. The [jury] is confronted with
> two opposing statements from the child and often the tape statement
> containing sufficient detail elicited by non-leading questions is the more
> compelling evidence.[66]

Thus beyond its obvious usefulness to the prosecution, the ultimate
value of the investigative interview videotape is that it helps the jury gain a
full and accurate sense of the child and whether the allegations or recantations are truthful.

Videotape: The Deposition

A few years ago in Arkansas, before the trial of a man accused of raping an eleven-year-old, the prosecutor asked the judge to order a videotape deposition of the victim that was to be used during the trial in place of the child's testimony. At the hearing to consider the prosecutor's request, the child's grandparents said that she was under a psychologist's care, that she no longer wanted to go anywhere, was easily upset, and would feel ridiculed if required to appear before a jury. The judge granted the request under an Arkansas law that authorizes "for good cause shown" the videotape deposition of any alleged victim under age seventeen.[67]

The child and defendant appeared for the videotape deposition, and the defense attorney cross-examined her. Nevertheless, the defendant appealed his conviction, claiming that the videotape procedure denied his constitutional right of trial by jury because it reduced the jury's opportunity to evaluate the demeanor and credibility of the child. The Arkansas Supreme Court affirmed his conviction and concluded that while testimony in person is almost always required in other cases, a videotape deposition provides "the best substitute" in a child sexual abuse trial.[68]

In recent years, responding to efforts to spare children the trauma of court testimony, many states have enacted laws allowing children to be "in court" through videotape depositions. Because this kind of videotape is prepared specifically for trials, the laws require the defendant's presence at the taping and the opportunity for the defense attorney to cross-examine the child.

While similar in concept, many state laws have distinct procedures reflecting somewhat different concerns. For example, laws in Kentucky, Oklahoma, and Texas specify that the child be positioned so as not to see or hear the defendant during the deposition. Some laws provide that the videotape for trial may be made by filming the child's preliminary hearing testimony. We can place these laws in two categories—those that *require* use of the video deposition at trial on the presumption that in-person testimony is always traumatic; and those that *permit* use of the video deposition at trial on the presumption that in-person testimony can be traumatic.[69]

Two distinct legal theories support the videotape deposition laws. One contends that the deposition is a specific hearsay exception created by legislatures. The other maintains that the deposition is not hearsay; rather, it is the "functional equivalent" of in-court testimony.[70] The theories need not be mutually exclusive, and each can prove useful to the prosecutor seeking admission of a videotape deposition.

Understanding just what the videotape deposition is, in legal theory, is more than an academic exercise. In fact, its admissibility may depend on which legal theory a judge favors.[71] In a two-to-one decision, the Federal Court of Appeals reversed a conviction after concluding that the trial judge had erred in granting the jury's request to replay the victim's videotape deposition during deliberations. "Videotape testimony is unique," the majority declared. "It enables the jury to observe the demeanor and to hear the testimony of the witness. It serves as the functional equivalent of a live witness."[72] Thus, the court explained, the jury's request should have been granted only as it could have been for the testimony of any other witness. The transcript of the words of the videotape could have been read back to the jury; replaying the videotape gave unfair emphasis to the child's testimony.

While this two-to-one decision scarcely resolves the issue, it does help to clarify the two theories. If the videotape is treated as being equivalent or simply a substitute for in-court testimony, then the majority is correct. It would be unfair to elevate its status during jury deliberations since it is intended only to eliminate unfair disadvantages for children in the courtroom, not to give advantage to child testimony.

On the other hand, the jury's request seems reasonable. The demeanor of a child witness is crucial. Having heard all the evidence, the jury wanted not only to hear the child's words again but to see the child. The videotape may be considered as evidence available for further scrutiny by the jury during deliberations, like documents, weapons, or other exhibits introduced in the course of a trial. The videotape is not the same as in-court testimony. It may reduce or enhance a jury's focus on demeanor. It presents a child in an atmosphere different from that of a courtroom. It therefore should be used in the way a jury sees fit.[73]

Whichever theory they espouse, many child advocates have considered the videotape deposition to be the answer to all the problems that plague the prosecution of child sexual abuse cases. Recently, however, the use of the taped deposition has lost support, particularly in states where the laws do not separate the child from the defendant during the taping. In such cases, although the deposition "removes child witnesses from the imposing milieu of the courtroom, it places them in close physical proximity to the defendant. Many prosecutors and victim advocates maintain that such a deposition can be far more harrowing to a child than giving testimony in court. . . . Prosecutors say that a videotaped deposition merely substitutes one formal proceeding for another."[74] For these reasons, the 1987 decisions of the Maine and South Carolina supreme courts are important. Affirming sexual abuse convictions, the courts approved the use of videotape depositions even though the defendants participated in the depositions from behind one-way mirrors. The defendants maintained contact with their attorneys and could see the children, but the children did not see the defendants.[75]

Whatever their limitations, videotape depositions are crucial in many cases. Like the investigative videotape, they can motivate a defendant to plead guilty. A deposition can also be made months before trial, while the

victim's memory is fresh. Because the deposition is certain to be allowed in a trial, it is better able than the investigative videotape to spare children court appearances. Even with the defendant present, a judge can conduct the videotape deposition in a sensitive manner to gain a child's statement without the trauma of court. Although they may not solve all the problems confronting child sexual abuse victims, videotape depositions often represent the difference between injustice and justice, trauma and fairness, for young witnesses.

Closed-circuit Television

A defendant was convicted of sexually assaulting his six-year-old daughter, who "when she was sworn, and before giving any testimony, stated in the presence of the court and jury . . . 'I am afraid to tell, because I am afraid of my papa.' The defendant was at this time sitting with his counsel, in front of the witness and jury; and the court . . . ordered the defendant to take a seat in the southwest corner of the court room. . . . From the place where the defendant was ordered to sit during the examination of the witness he could not see all of the jurors; neither could he see the witness, nor could he hear any of her testimony."

Far from being the innovative effort of a modern court to protect a child, this case occurred in 1899. The Utah Supreme Court sympathized with the effort of the trial judge and stressed the need for flexibility to satisfy competing concerns:

> In cases of this character, where the witness is young, the court should have considerable latitude in protecting the witness . . . but in doing so the constitutional right of the defendant must be protected. . . . The constitutional right of one accused of crime "to be confronted by the witnesses against him" was never intended as an instrument with which to defeat justice. Where the witnesses for the prosecution are present at the trial, are examined in the presence and within the hearing of the accused and jury, and an opportunity afforded the prisoner for cross-examination . . . the constitutional provision is complied with, even though the prisoner be not permitted to sit immediately in front of the witness, when such position would cause intimidation, and prevent the eliciting of testimony.[76]

If that Utah trial judge had lived eighty years later, modern technology could have enhanced his effort to protect both the child and the defendant's right to confront her. With the child in the judge's chambers or the defendant in an adjoining room, closed-circuit television could have brought victim and defendant together without the intimidation of actual, face-to-face presence. The defendant would retain the full opportunity for cross-examination and the jury could observe the child's demeanor.

Closed-circuit television is likely to become one of the most important techniques in child sexual abuse trials in the future. Technologically simple, it can be used as needed, without the separate procedures associated with videotape depositions. Courtrooms, with their adjoining chambers, provide ideal settings for closed-circuit testimony. Most important, while protecting the child, closed-circuit television most closely approximates in-person testimony. Perhaps for these reasons, several states have recently enacted laws providing for closed-circuit testimony, and courts in other states have used the same techniques even though their legislatures have not enacted such laws.[77]

By 1985, appellate courts had begun reviewing the first appeals of defendants who had confronted child witnesses through closed-circuit TV. An Arizona court affirmed convictions of two defendants who killed a young girl. They had been excluded from the courtroom when the victim's six-year-old brother became afraid to testify because of the defendants' threats. The defendants "were allowed to watch the testimony on closed circuit from an adjoining jury room. Also, breaks were taken so that the . . . attorneys could leave the courtroom to consult with them during the course of . . . testimony. . . . A procedure was established which made contact between the [defendants] and their attorneys somewhat unwieldy, but which did not limit in any way [their] ability to cross-examine the witness."[78]

In 1986, the Nebraska Supreme Court reviewed a conviction for first degree sexual assault of a four-year-old. An "attempt to examine the child in open court was frustrated by the child's failure to cooperate" and was solved by the use of closed-circuit TV. Ultimately, the court reversed the conviction because the trial proceedings did not demonstrate "that the child would be further traumatized or was intimidated by testifying in the courtroom in front of the defendant," and because "the defendant . . . was in the courtroom while his attorney was in chambers where the witness was testifying. The defendant . . . had no means of communicating with his attorney." However, while the court found the procedures employed in this trial improper, it acknowledged the constitutionality of using closed-circuit testimony, even without specific statutory authority.[79]

In 1986, the Kentucky Supreme Court considered a case in which the defendant had been convicted of sexually assaulting his five-year-old niece. During the trial, the child had become unresponsive after saying "she did not want her uncle to hurt her and did not want him present." The prosecutor had then attempted to employ Kentucky's new law that permits the use of closed-circuit testimony in a sexual abuse case of a child under age twelve.[80] In a four-to-three decision, the Kentucky Supreme Court upheld the use of closed-circuit TV. It noted "the inability to effectively prosecute child abusers where the evidence against them cannot be presented without intimidation." Recalling the fundamental purpose of jury trials, the court almost seemed to echo the Utah trial judge of the preceding century:

In the Eighteenth and Nineteenth Centuries, live testimony was the only way that a jury could observe the demeanor of a witness. The use of videotapes [and closed-circuit TV] does not represent a significant departure from that tradition because the goal of providing a view of the witness's demeanor to the jury is still achieved. A witness has never been disqualified by mere refusal or inability to look at the defendant. The testimony of a blind victim would not be invalid. The same is true for the testimony of a witness who refuses to look on the accused. By analogy a defendant would not be denied the right of confrontation when a young victim is so intimidated by his mere presence that she cannot testify unless she is unable to see or hear him.

The strength of the State and Federal Constitutions lies in the fact that they are flexible documents which are able to grow and develop as our society progresses. The purpose of a criminal or civil proceeding is to determine the truth. [The new law] provides such a statutory plan while protecting the fundamental interests of the accused as well as the victim.[81]

In 1987, the Pennsylvania Superior Court reached the same conclusion in affirming a sexual assault conviction when a five-year-old child testified by closed circuit after she "froze emotionally and was unable to testify in the presence of her father." The court explained that the "right to confront does not confer upon an accused the right to intimidate. The reliability of an abused child's testimony does not depend upon his or her ability to withstand the psychological trauma of testifying in a courtroom under the unwavering gaze of a parent who, although a possible abuser, has also been provider, protector, and parent."[82]

The Nebraska, Kentucky, and Pennsylvania decisions confirm the constitutionality of closed-circuit television. However, they also suggest that courts may use closed-circuit only when, without it, a child would be unable to testify.[83] That, in fact, was the clear message of the United States Supreme Court when, in 1988, it reviewed the use of a one-way screen in *Coy v. Iowa*, a case involving the sexual abuse of two thirteen-year-old girls.

The Iowa trial judge had allowed the two girls to testify from behind a one-way screen, according to a new Iowa statute. The defendant could see the girls, and his lawyer cross-examined them; but the girls could not see the defendant sitting in the courtroom. Unlike the trial judges in the Nebraska, Kentucky, and Pennsylvania cases, however, the Iowa judge allowed use of this special device without first reviewing whether, in fact, the two girls required the assistance of such a technique. Reversing the convictions, the Supreme Court reiterated that the Sixth Amendment right of confrontation entails at least a strong preference that confrontation between a witness and defendant be "face-to-face." Writing the court's plurality decision for four justices, Justice Antonin Scalia explained that "face-to-face presence may, unfortunately, upset the truthful rape victim or abused child; but by the same token it may confound and undo the false accuser, or reveal the child coached by a malevolent adult." In this case, he continued, because "there have been no individualized findings that these particular witnesses needed special protection," the one-way screen technique violated the defendant's Sixth Amendment rights.

While at first *Coy v. Iowa* might seem to frustrate the efforts of legislatures and judges to assist child victims, a careful reading reveals its potential value. The plurality suggests that the error was not the legislature's in providing for such special techniques to assist child witnesses, but the judge's in applying the law when it might not have been needed. In her concurring opinion for two justices, Justice Sandra Day O'Connor emphasized the limited scope of the *Coy v. Iowa* decision, and the constitutionality of such techniques, when correctly applied:

> While I agree with the Court that the Confrontation Clause was violated in this case, I wish to make clear that nothing in today's decision necessarily dooms such efforts by state legislatures to protect child witnesses. . . . I would permit use of a particular trial procedure that called for something other than face-to-face confrontation if that procedure was necessary to further an important public policy. The protection of child witnesses is, in my view and in the view of a substantial majority of the States, just such a policy. . . . if a court makes a case-specific finding of necessity, our cases suggest that the strictures of the Confrontation Clause may give way to the compelling state interest of protecting child witnesses.

Thus, in *Coy v. Iowa* (decided by eight justices, prior to the appointment of Justice Kennedy), four justices found that face-to-face confrontation could not be compromised by such a one-way technique, at least until the judge made a specific finding of necessity. Yet even these four justices decided to "leave for another day . . . the question whether any exceptions [to face-to-face confrontation] exist."[84] That day arrived just two years later when the Supreme Court decided *Maryland v. Craig* (see Chapter 7).

Expert Testimony

With videotape and closed-circuit television and proper application of hearsay law, juries will see and hear children; but that does not mean that juries will believe them. "By allowing evidence in the trial," a judge instructs a jury, "I do not imply any view on the importance or truthfulness of that evidence. That evaluation is yours."[85]

Is it not likely, then, that jurors will have misconceptions about sexual abuse and about children's credibility? After all, only recently have research and analysis exposed damaging myths about children, and many of those myths have not been dispelled in the public and legal minds. If jurors evaluate children's testimony with uninformed skepticism or irrational biases, they will not consider children's testimony with understanding and fairness.

That was the Oregon Supreme Court's conclusion in 1983 when it affirmed the decision of a trial judge to allow two social workers to testify as experts concerning recantation and the reactions of young victims of family sexual abuse:

> In the present case, eighteen of the prospective jurors questioned during voir dire were asked whether they knew a child victim of sexual abuse or if they had heard of any children who had been abused sexually by members of their families. Fifteen reported that they knew no one who had suffered from this sort of abuse; two others said they remembered hearing reports of such abuse. Because the jurors said they had no experience with victims of child abuse, we assume they would not have been exposed to the contention that it is common for children to report familial sexual abuse and then retract the story. Such evidence might well help a jury make a more informed decision in evaluating the credibility of a testifying child.[86]

Recognizing that most jurors will not have experience that allows for a fully informed evaluation of a child's behavior and credibility, courts have thus permitted experts to help juries by testifying in three areas: (1) factors affecting credibility of children, (2) factors affecting behavior of child sexual abuse victims, (3) interpretations of special forms of child communication.

Factors Affecting Credibility

In the past few years, many appellate courts have considered whether a psychiatrist, psychologist, or social worker may testify to help juries evaluate the testimony of children. For the most part, the courts have allowed experts to explain general principles of behavioral science and general patterns of child perception, memory, and communication. The courts have also allowed experts to explain behavioral patterns associated with child sexual abuse victims, such as disclosure, delay, and recantation.

However, most of the appellate decisions also prohibit the expert from giving the jury an opinion on the truthfulness of the specific child involved in the trial. The courts explain that such an opinion would "invade the province of the jury" to decide credibility. By giving an expert's stamp of approval or disapproval to the child, the expert would almost take the question of "guilty or not guilty" from the jury. For example, when one of America's leading experts on child sexual abuse testified in court that the alleged victim was believable, the conviction was reversed by the Federal Court of Appeals in *U.S. v. Azure:*

> We agree that in these types of special circumstances some expert testimony may be helpful, but putting an impressively qualified expert's stamp of truthfulness on a witness' story goes too far. . . . Dr. _____ might have aided jurors without usurping their exclusive function by generally testifying about a child's ability to separate truth from fantasy, by summarizing the medical evidence and expressing his opinion as to whether it was consistent with [the child's] story that she was sexually abused, or perhaps by discussing various patterns of consistency in the stories of child sexual abuse victims and comparing those patterns with patterns in [the child's] story. However, by going further and putting his stamp of believability on [her] entire story, Dr. _____ essentially told the jury that [the child] was truthful in saying that [the defendant] was the person who sexually abused her. No reliable test for truthfulness exists and Dr. _____ was not qualified to judge the truthfulness of that part of [the child's] story.[87]

In 1986, the supreme courts of Arizona, Iowa, North Carolina, and Pennsylvania reversed sexual assault convictions for the same reason. For example, the Iowa Supreme Court would not allow testimony from a state child abuse investigator "that children generally tell the truth when they report that they have been sexually abused." Although this testimony was cloaked in more general terms than the example above, the court decided that it was an unfair opinion about the guilt of the defendant: "[Such] opinions go a step beyond merely aiding the [jury] in understanding the evidence and actually invade the exclusive domain of the jury."[88]

The permissible range of the expert's testimony on credibility still is evolving. The supreme courts of Georgia and Hawaii offer experts greater latitude than do most states.[89] Believing that a jury can be helped, not "invaded" by an expert's view on whether a specific child is telling the truth, they do not limit the expert to testimony about general principles. Nonetheless, particularly with the recent federal decision in the *Azure* case, the Georgia and Hawaii approach may find less support in the future.[90]

Factors Affecting Behavior

Often an expert can provide important testimony to help a jury understand a child's behavior. Usually the prosecution offers such expert testimony to counter a defense based on common misconceptions. For example, if the defense cross-examines a child or parent to establish that the child did not report the assault immediately, the prosecution may want to respond with expert testimony on the child sexual abuse accommodation syndrome. However, the appellate decisions reviewing such testimony are mixed; some convictions have been affirmed and others reversed.

For example, a Pennsylvania court allowed expert testimony on the dynamics of intrafamilial sexual abuse and the behavior patterns of incest victims.[91] A Wisconsin court permitted an expert to explain why a victim may not report an assault immediately or may recant later.[92] In Kentucky, however, a conviction was reversed because of a social worker's testimony that the victim's behavior was consistent with the sexual abuse accommodation syndrome and that few children invent or exaggerate such allegations.[93] In Minnesota, the admissibility of such testimony may vary according to the age of the victim and whether the case involved incest or nonfamilial abuse.[94]

While the conflicting decisions cannot be reconciled, some patterns are emerging: (1) the more general the testimony, the more likely its admission; (2) the more necessary the testimony to answer a defense assertion, the more likely its admission; (3) the younger the child, the more likely its admission; and (4) if the alleged sexual abuse is by a family member or other person known to the victim, the more likely the admission on delayed reporting and recantation.[95]

The legal principle is that where the jury's understanding is most limited or misconceptions most likely, courts recognize that expert testimony can assist juries. This principle then allows for expert testimony if the expert opinion has sufficient scientific basis to guide the jury.[96] However, many courts have concluded that such a scientific basis is lacking. They consider the research on child sexual abuse new and tenuous, so they have not allowed expert testimony from either side.

While harmful to the prosecution in many cases, such rulings can also protect the prosecution against frivolous evidence. For example, the Utah Supreme Court, in affirming a sexual abuse conviction, rejected the defendant's claim that the trial judge should have allowed an expert to testify on the psychological profile of child sex abusers. The defendant had tried to introduce expert testimony to show his psychological differences from the "typical child molester." Knowing that such testimony could only perpetuate invalid stereotypes, the judge excluded the testimony as "confusing, misleading, and speculative."[97] Excluding such specious evidence helps juries to find the truth. But excluding legitimate expert testimony on delayed reporting and recantation has too often doomed children's cases because prosecutors have been unable to explain to uninformed juries that child victims may delay and recant and yet be truthful in their allegations of sexual abuse.

Interpretation of Child Communication

In the future, one of the most interesting areas of expert testimony may relate to alternative methods of child communication. Some children are not able to articulate a full account of sexual abuse, but they may communicate in other ways. When they do, their nonverbal communication may create a new kind of hearsay evidence that, with proper interpretation, will offer important evidence to juries. One form of this evidence—drawings by children—has already reached the courts.

In a 1985 New Jersey case, a mother sought to terminate her ex-husband's visitation rights because he allegedly had sexually abused their child. During the trial she offered expert testimony from the child's art therapist. Before accepting her testimony, the judge heard two days of testimony from other experts, including Dr. Myra Levick, one of the nation's foremost authorities on art therapy.[98] Satisfied that art therapy had a sufficient scientific basis, the judge allowed the therapist to testify. The child had prepared over one hundred drawings and told her therapist their meanings. Interpreting the drawings and repeating the child's comments, the therapist explained the overemphasis on genitalia, phallic symbols, isolation, confusion, lack of trust, regression, fright, and anger. The court concluded that although art therapy is a subjective treatment, it is reliable to the extent that its fundamental criteria allow one to draw relatively specific conclusions.

This New Jersey case was one of a growing number of family/probate court cases in which sexual abuse is alleged in a custody or visitation dispute. The judge's final comments may offer a glimpse of a more hopeful future when crucial issues of child sexual abuse will be affected by developing areas of expertise tuned to children: "The fact that there are no judicial opinions approving art therapy evidence does not . . . mitigate against the introduction into evidence of an art therapist's expert opinion. When appropriate, a court must act to introduce into the corpus juris a new vehicle to use in its never-ending search for the truth."[99]

Proving Sexual Abuse: Theory and Reality

To parents and children who have been traumatized by the legal system during a sexual abuse case, the law is hostile; but when laws are interpreted true to their traditions, they can provide special opportunities for child victims. Adept prosecutors will recognize that there are strategic options that can gain convictions in many cases that initially seem impossible to prosecute.

No longer must prosecutors assess cases only according to whether children can testify. Even when sheltered from the courtroom, their voices can be heard and their images can be seen. The evidence can be (1) the child's reaction to the assault ("excited utterance," "complaint," "tender years," or "residual" hearsay); (2) the child's statements during the examination or investigation ("diagnosis/treatment" hearsay or investigative videotape); (3) the child's testimony in preparation for trial (preliminary hearing or videotape deposition); and (4) the child's testimony in court (in person, or with closed-circuit television). Furthermore, by using appropriate language, puppets, or anatomically correct dolls, prosecutors can help children to communicate in court. Thus prosecutors have the chance to calculate the best way to offer a victim's testimony.

Skillful and determined prosecutors may also find added advantages in child sexual abuse cases because of the virtual impossibility of certain defenses and because of the defendant's own statements. While an alibi defense is among the most effective in many criminal trials, it frequently is not available to the defendant charged with child sexual abuse. Because young children rarely recall exactly when abuse occurred, prosecutors usually are not required to prove specific dates or times of assaults.[100] Hence defendants almost never can offer alibis for unspecified times. Unlike other criminal cases in which defendants sometimes claim that police are motivated to "set them up," ulterior motives can rarely be asserted against children except when the alleged abuse occurs during a divorce or custody battle.

Many child abusers confess—some out of shame, others with self-excusing but incriminating admissions. "In a surprising proportion of child sexual abuse cases, the defendant will voluntarily make damaging statements. It is common for accused molesters to tell how the children were the aggressors and they the victims; or to admit touching the child but assert that it was for nonsexual reasons."[101] Child abusers may be more likely than other criminals to confess because they do not expect that the confession will be used in a trial. Under many new state laws, however, doctors, teachers, or other professionals who have witnessed confessions must report what the abuser reveals. To be admissible as evidence, these confessions need not be preceded by Miranda warnings requiring police to inform suspects that they may remain silent and that their statements can be used against them. For example, when an Alabama social worker investigated the sexual assault of a thirteen-year-old girl and interviewed her father, the Alabama appellate court concluded that the social worker was allowed to tell the jury the defendant's admission.[102]

Finally, prosecutors can utilize other sources to help prove child sexual abuse. Medical evidence can sometimes establish that sexual abuse occurred, and experts can testify to help juries evaluate children's behavior to answer defenses based on uninformed characterizations of children and their reactions to abuse. Offering a unique set of strategies, child sexual abuse cases thus challenge the hearts and skills of the best prosecutors. While child sexual abuse prosecutions are very difficult, they also are very possible.

Then why is there so much frustration and failure? If the laws are not really hostile to child victims, why is there such horrifying injustice? If, as the United States Supreme Court could declare almost a century ago, laws are to be interpreted and applied with commonsense flexibility "simply from the necessities of the case, and to prevent a manifest failure of justice," then how can courts continue to be so uninformed and unjust? How, in the Greenbrook case, could the prosecutor and judge misunderstand the law and deny the children a chance to be heard? How, for example, could the Rhode Island Supreme Court reverse a sexual assault conviction by overturning a trial judge's decision to allow testimony from the child's counselor and doctor about statements she made to them during counseling and medical examination? In 1987 that court endangered countless children by informing the state trial courts:

> If the small child could tell the story to her mother [or counselor], she could have told it on the witness stand to the jury. . . . If the child could tell the story to the doctor, she could have told it on the witness stand to the jury.[103]

For this four-year-old child, the Rhode Island court saw no distinction between disclosing to a parent, counselor, or doctor in the privacy of home or office, and disclosing to many strangers in a courtroom. The court completely confused the law of competency and hearsay,[104] cited an obscure 1959 decision as precedent, and ignored the many recent decisions that have cautioned against such specious reasoning. The Rhode Island Supreme Court thus reduced child sexual abuse cases to standards of ignorance—ignorance about children and law.

While the Rhode Island decision is astounding in its lack of understanding of both children and law, the attitudes it reflects are not peculiar to that case or state. The prosecutor and judge in the Greenbrook case were not evil, but all too typical. In courtrooms throughout America, the discrepancy between education and ignorance, between sensitive theory and insensitive practice, between pure legal tradition and perverse legal implementation, revictimizes children.

6

Justice for Children: Meeting the Challenge

"And that's the jury-box," thought Alice, "and those twelve . . . I suppose they are the jurors." She said this last word two or three times over to herself, being rather proud of it: for she thought, and rightly too, that very few little girls of her age knew the meaning of it all.

— Lewis Carroll,
Alice's Adventures in Wonderland

AFFIRMING a child sexual abuse conviction in 1987, the Arizona Supreme Court said, "Sexual abuse of children is an old problem that society and the law have been late in recognizing and meeting. Fortunately, the rules of evidence . . . are flexible enough to meet the problem."[1] But if sound rules of evidence are not applied by sensitive and informed prosecutors and judges, legal theory will do little to gain justice for sexually abused children.

When prosecutors and judges acknowledge the need for sensitive procedures and learn the law, they will adjust language and schedules and courtroom settings to enable children to testify without trauma. In a recent case, the prosecutor and judge used a lap, dolls, and language to enable six-year-old Alexander to tell about a babysitter assaulting his younger brothers. Despite careful preparation and courtroom orientation before trial, Alexander froze when called to testify.

JUDGE: Now, Alexander . . . would you be happier right now if you were sitting on your dad's lap?

ALEXANDER: Yes.

163

JUDGE: Okay, why don't you do that. . . . You know, I've seen a lot of kids here, and sometimes their voices get bigger if they're on their mom or dad's lap, and sometimes they're just happier.

When he sat on his father's lap Alexander felt the security of a familiar arm around his body; Alexander then testified.

DISTRICT ATTORNEY: Do you know Robert . . . ?

ALEXANDER: Yes.

DISTRICT ATTORNEY: Okay, is Robert in this room, now?

ALEXANDER: Yes.

DISTRICT ATTORNEY: Can you tell me where Robert is sitting? Can you point him out to me?

ALEXANDER: He's sitting over there.

JUDGE: Alexander has pointed to Robert.

DISTRICT ATTORNEY: Have you known Robert for some time? How long have you known Robert; do you know? Does Robert come to your house and babysit?

ALEXANDER: Yes.

DISTRICT ATTORNEY: He babysits for you and who else?

ALEXANDER: My brothers.

DISTRICT ATTORNEY: Antonio and Andre?

ALEXANDER: Yes.

DISTRICT ATTORNEY: Did Robert come to your house the day your mother went to a funeral?

ALEXANDER: Yes.

DISTRICT ATTORNEY: And he came there to babysit?

ALEXANDER: Yes.

DISTRICT ATTORNEY: After your mother left the house, you were in the house with your brothers and Robert; is that right?

ALEXANDER: Yeah.

DISTRICT ATTORNEY: Did you see Robert do something to Antonio when your mother left?

DEFENSE ATTORNEY: I'm going to object. We've had a whole series of leading questions, and children are usually susceptible to leading questions. . . . I think the District Attorney has to go away from that.

JUDGE: [To the District Attorney] Lead as little as possible and as necessary. The Court will allow leading questions. If they become leading, of course, keep them so they are as nonsuggestive as possible.

DISTRICT ATTORNEY: Okay, can you tell me what Robert did to Antonio?

ALEXANDER: [Witness nods head.]

DISTRICT ATTORNEY: Tell me what he did.

ALEXANDER: He did up his butt.

DISTRICT ATTORNEY: Now, I have two dolls here. You've seen these dolls before; haven't you?

ALEXANDER: [Witness nods head affirmatively.]

DISTRICT ATTORNEY: Can you show me what the dolls—what happened? Can you do that. Okay, let's pretend that this doll was Antonio. Maybe we should—well, tell me this. Where was Antonio when Robert did this to him?

ALEXANDER: On the couch lying down.

DISTRICT ATTORNEY: Was he lying on his face or on his back?

ALEXANDER: On his face.

DISTRICT ATTORNEY: Okay, let's pretend that this doll is Antonio, okay? All right, and let's pretend that this is the couch, okay? Is Antonio lying on his face like that?

ALEXANDER: [Witness nods head.]

DISTRICT ATTORNEY: You have to answer yes or no.

ALEXANDER: Yes.

DISTRICT ATTORNEY: Was Antonio wearing pants?

ALEXANDER: No.

DISTRICT ATTORNEY: Was he wearing shorts?

ALEXANDER: Yes.

DISTRICT ATTORNEY: Okay, what happened to his shorts?

ALEXANDER: He pulled them down.

DISTRICT ATTORNEY: And after Robert—maybe we should—should pull the doll's shorts down to show that. Is that the way Antonio looked when he pulled the shorts down?

ALEXANDER: Yes.

DISTRICT ATTORNEY: The record should reflect that the anatomically correct doll's pants are pulled down below the buttocks.

JUDGE: The record will so reflect.

DISTRICT ATTORNEY: After Robert pulled his pants down, what did Robert do?

ALEXANDER: He got on top of his butt.

DISTRICT ATTORNEY: Now, we're gonna take the other doll, and I want you to show us what Robert did. Can you take the doll and show me? Will you do that for me? Can you do it? Let me ask you this. Did Robert leave his pants up or down?

ALEXANDER: Up.

DISTRICT ATTORNEY: He left them up. Okay, when Robert got on top show us what Robert did. Take the doll and show us. You can get off your father's lap if you want. He got on top of Antonio like that? That's right, one doll on top of the other? Is that what happened? You have to answer yes or no.

ALEXANDER: Yes.

DISTRICT ATTORNEY: Now, do you—can you tell us whether or not Robert's pants were up or down?

ALEXANDER: Up.

DISTRICT ATTORNEY: Now, did he have a zipper in front of his pants?

ALEXANDER: Yes.

DISTRICT ATTORNEY: Was the zipper zipped up or down?

ALEXANDER: Down.

DISTRICT ATTORNEY: Could you see anything through the zipper?

ALEXANDER: Yes.

DISTRICT ATTORNEY: What did you see?

ALEXANDER: His thing.

DISTRICT ATTORNEY: His thing? What did it look like? Can you tell us? If you look at the doll, could you tell us if the doll has something like that if you saw it?

ALEXANDER: [Witness nods head.]

DISTRICT ATTORNEY: I'll remove the pants from the anatomical dolls and let him look at the doll. Can you tell us if the doll has a thing like Robert had?

ALEXANDER: Yes.

DISTRICT ATTORNEY: Where is that. I want you to point to it. Point to it so the Judge can see.

ALEXANDER: Right there.

DISTRICT ATTORNEY: Okay.

JUDGE: All right, Alexander has pointed to the penis of the doll.

DISTRICT ATTORNEY: What did he do with this thing? What did Robert do with his thing?

ALEXANDER: Put it in his butt.

DISTRICT ATTORNEY: Put it in whose butt?

ALEXANDER: Antonio.

DISTRICT ATTORNEY: Did Antonio say anything?

ALEXANDER: Yes.

DISTRICT ATTORNEY: What did he say?

ALEXANDER: He was crying.

DISTRICT ATTORNEY: Did Robert say something?

ALEXANDER: [Witness nods head negatively.]

DISTRICT ATTORNEY: Now that same day did Robert do something to Andre?

ALEXANDER: Yes.

DISTRICT ATTORNEY: Okay, why don't you tell us what he did to Andre?

ALEXANDER: Pulled down his pants, and he got on top of him.

DISTRICT ATTORNEY: Now, again, we're gonna take this doll and pretend this is Andre, okay? Where was Andre when Robert did this to him; what room?

ALEXANDER: On the couch.

DISTRICT ATTORNEY: On the couch at your house?

ALEXANDER: Yes.

DISTRICT ATTORNEY: Was Andre face up on the couch or face down?

ALEXANDER: On the couch.

DISTRICT ATTORNEY: Was his face up or down?

ALEXANDER: Down.

DISTRICT ATTORNEY: We're gonna put the doll on the couch face down. Was Andre wearing any clothes? Do you remember?

ALEXANDER: He was wearing some shorts.

DISTRICT ATTORNEY: Did Andre have shorts on too?

ALEXANDER: Yes.

DISTRICT ATTORNEY: You're sure they weren't long pants like yours or shorts?

ALEXANDER: Shorts.

DISTRICT ATTORNEY: Did Robert do anything to Andre's butt when he did that?

ALEXANDER: Yes.

DISTRICT ATTORNEY: We're gonna remove the pants of the doll so that the buttocks are exposed. After Robert pulled down Andre's pants, what did Robert do?

ALEXANDER: Got on top of him.

DISTRICT ATTORNEY: Now, what did Robert do with his pants; do you know, with his own pants?

ALEXANDER: Pull them down.

DISTRICT ATTORNEY: Okay, we're gonna pretend this doll is Robert, okay? Show me what Robert did with his pants. Could you see Robert's thing?

ALEXANDER: Yes.

DISTRICT ATTORNEY: What did Robert do after he pulled his pants down?

ALEXANDER: He got on top of him.

DISTRICT ATTORNEY: On top of Andre?

ALEXANDER: Yes.

DISTRICT ATTORNEY: And what did he do with his thing?

ALEXANDER: Put it in his butt.

DISTRICT ATTORNEY: In Andre's butt? Okay, why don't you show me with the doll what he did. You can get off your father's lap. The record should reflect that he's placed one doll on top of the doll whose buttocks are exposed, and the doll—the pants of the first doll are down below the buttocks, and the penis is exposed.

JUDGE: The record will so reflect.

DISTRICT ATTORNEY: And did Andre say anything when Robert did this?

ALEXANDER: [Witness nods head.]

DISTRICT ATTORNEY: What did he say?

ALEXANDER: He said, he said, he said, stop Robert, and then Robert didn't stop.

DISTRICT ATTORNEY: Did Robert say anything?

ALEXANDER: No.

DISTRICT ATTORNEY: Did Robert say something to you?

ALEXANDER: Yes.

DISTRICT ATTORNEY: What did Robert say to you?

ALEXANDER: He said if I tell, he'll kick me in my balls.[2]

Alexander's testimony helped to convict the defendant of sexually assaulting Andre and Antonio.

About six months later, an Ohio man was charged with the rape of his seven-year-old stepdaughter. Just a few weeks before trial, the family court senior referee in the county where the abuse occurred attended a judicial education program in Cleveland, sponsored by the National and Ohio Councils of Juvenile and Family Court Judges.[3] New laws and techniques to assist child victims, including those employed in Alexander's case, were presented. The referee passed on the conference materials to the county's witness coordinator, who gave the information to the prosecutor in the sexual abuse case. When the prosecutor found that the seven-year-old victim was not going to testify without some special assistance, the witness coordinator suggested that the victim sit on her aunt's lap. The judge agreed, the child testified, and the jury convicted the defendant. On appeal, the defendant asserted that by allowing the victim to testify from her aunt's lap, the judge "telegraphed to the jury his belief in the credibility of the juvenile witness as well as his belief in the guilt of the [defendant and thus] tainted the jury's ability to freely evaluate witness credibility." The Ohio Court of Appeals strongly disagreed. Affirming the conviction, the court declared:

> The trial judge did what he was not only authorized, but required, to do. He made a decision to exercise reasonable control over the mode of interrogating the . . . witness with a view to making the interrogation and presentation effective for the ascertainment of truth while protecting the witness from undue embarrassment.[4]

Significantly, the Ohio court based its conclusion on an Ohio law identical to a federal law, and identical or similar to laws in almost every state:

> Mode and Order of Interrogation and Presentation—controlled by Court. The court shall exercise reasonable control over the mode and order of interrogating witnesses and presenting evidence so as to . . . make the interrogation and presentation effective for the ascertainment of truth, . . . and . . . protect witnesses from harassment or undue embarrassment.[5]

Making "interrogation and presentation effective for the ascertainment of truth" depends on the skills and sensitivities of prosecutors and judges, not on the exact formulation of evidence laws. The judge in Ohio did not wait for the legislature to enact a law before allowing a little girl to sit on her aunt's lap. Judges do not need complicated laws in order to recognize that children have limited endurance and attention spans, that they must testify according to schedules that make them most comfortable. When judges properly exercise their discretion to control when, where, and how (but not what) children testify, courts can provide justice.

Timing Children's Testimonies
Every day in trials throughout the country, lawyers approach the bench and, in whispers that juries do not hear, request recesses so that they can prepare

for the next day and catch up on other professional obligations. Understanding the complicated schedules of lawyers, judges usually adjust the time of the trial to accommodate them. Rarely, however, do they revise trial schedules to accommodate the naptime and mealtime routines and the special rhythms of children. In child sexual abuse cases, that failure can incapacitate child witnesses.

Judges should control not only the timing of children's testimonies within trials, but also the calendaring of trials. They know that in any criminal trial, delay is often a defense strategy. With the passage of time, any witness may lose interest, face intimidation, or forget; and the chance for dismissal or acquittal will increase. When children are witnesses, delays can have an even greater impact on the outcome of a trial, for in addition to the typical disadvantages of delays, there is the more compelling consideration of the amount of stress a young victim can endure. As parents envision forcing their children to relive terrifying events, they may reconsider and ask the prosecutor to drop the charges, allowing yet another perpetrator to go free. Judges regularly adjust trial calendars to assure speedy trials for defendants in custody or to accommodate out-of-town or other busy witnesses. Knowing that more than convenience may be at stake, they have an obligation to prevent delays in cases where children must testify. To enforce that obligation, in 1983 Wisconsin became the first state to enact a law requiring a speedy trial in cases involving child witnesses and victims:

> In all criminal cases and juvenile . . . hearings . . . involving a child victim or witness . . . the court and the district attorney shall take appropriate action to ensure a speedy trial in order to minimize the length of time the child must endure the stress of his or her involvement in the proceeding. In ruling on any motion or other request for a delay or continuance of proceedings, the court shall consider and give weight to any adverse impact the delay or continuance may have on the well-being of a child victim or witness.[6]

Adjusting Court Environments to Children
Courtrooms were designed for the large numbers of adults who become participants and spectators in trials. Their furniture, lighting, acoustics, and uniformed personnel assure a serious and, in some ways, intimidating atmosphere. The theory is that in such an environment, witnesses and jurors will be more likely to take their responsibilities seriously. For children, however, the courtroom can do more than encourage civic responsibility—it can terrify and silence.

Judges have always recognized that, on occasion, the courtroom is the wrong place to conduct a hearing. When necessary, they have transferred hearings to hospital rooms or crime scenes. Juvenile and family court judges have frequently sought the more informal atmosphere of chambers to help children and families discuss sensitive subjects. Unfortunately, few judges have made such commonsense efforts for children in criminal trials. Few even consider the possibility that the traditional courtroom might be modified to facilitate testimony.

With closed-circuit television, children can testify in comfortable settings that preserve appropriate court procedures. In courtrooms, child-size furniture and chairs arranged in a circular, schoollike atmosphere can reduce tension for frightened, disoriented children. Without the restraints of the conventional courtroom, they can move about freely, reassured by favorite toys or snacks. Then they may feel sufficiently secure to listen carefully to questions and answer them.

The courtroom intimidation of children can be reduced further by judges who heed the advice Jerome Frank gave forty years ago when he explained that even for adult witnesses, a judge's position and robes can have "adverse effects on the administration of justice. An ordinary, honest, citizen, unaccustomed to courthouse ways, is often disquieted by the strange garb of the judge and his elevation above the courtroom throng; called as a witness, this honest citizen may testify in a manner so constrained and awkward that he gives the impression of not telling the whole truth." Asserting that "plain dress may encourage plain speaking," Frank urged judges to shed "robe-ism," literally and figuratively.[7] The advice is especially pertinent to cases where children might be frightened by garb that they associate with witches.

At the first hint that their wardrobe or their position in the courtroom should ever change, many judges react with anger or amusement. Claiming dignity, law, and tradition, they reveal their weakness as legal historians. Fixed in neither law nor tradition, robes, courtroom arrangements, and judicial symbols evolved from shifting philosophies, none of which has any absolute legal hold on contemporary judges.

Historically, American trial judges "rode the circuit" from town to town and held court in a variety of settings to accommodate the citizens of a growing nation. In many states, they rejected European judicial trappings and attained a more democratic image by not wearing robes. In order to increase the comfort and openness of children and families, many juvenile and family court judges seldom wore robes. When judges consider the traditions that guide trial procedures and even their own appearances and positioning in courtrooms, they must do so with an accurate view of legal history. They may thus be more likely to honor the true tradition of flexibility to facilitate the search for truth.

Accommodating Children's Cognitive Abilities
It has been said that a person attends law school to "unlearn" the English language. "Car" becomes "vehicle." "Important" becomes "not unimpor-

tant." "Then what happened?" becomes "Subsequently what occurred?" Courtroom vocabulary and syntax, confusing to adults, are unintelligible to children; but lawyers continue to confuse and incapacitate child witnesses with their language. Sometimes their difficult questions are necessary and fair; but when lawyers phrase them with cognitive and language demands beyond a child's experience, they inhibit the search for truth.

Even when language is modified, some children may respond only to those with whom they have rapport. Small and anxious, impressed if not intimidated by the courtroom, cautious about talking to strangers, and distressed by having to tell about a terrible event, a child may need more help than simplified language and a familiar lap from which to testify. When a child freezes, a trusted person—even a nonlawyer—should be allowed to ask questions ruled appropriate by the judge.

That was precisely what happened in cases in Nebraska and Wisconsin, but with different results. In Nebraska, where the defendant was on trial for first degree sexual assault of a four-year-old, the child would not answer the questions of the prosecutor. The prosecutor then asked that the child's therapist present the same questions. The judge agreed, the child responded, and the defendant was convicted. The Nebraska Supreme Court reversed the conviction. Without explanation or reference to legal precedent or tradition, the court simplistically assumed that the law permits only lawyers to question witnesses: "Although it is proper . . . to allow a support person, such as a parent or therapist, to be in the room with the witness while the examination is being conducted, the actual questioning . . . must be done by persons who are authorized . . . as members of the bar."[8]

In Wisconsin, when a six-year-old victim of first degree sexual assault failed to respond to a prosecutor's questions, the judge allowed the child's victim/witness advocate to continue the questioning. The child responded and the defendant was convicted.[9] The defendant did not appeal but the Wisconsin legislature learned of the innovation and broadened a Wisconsin law to allow for this procedure: "The court shall . . . allow any questioner to have an advisor to assist the questioner, and upon permission of the judge, to conduct the questioning."[10]

While judges and bar associations have legitimate concerns about non-lawyers entering the trial process, none of those interests is threatened by court advocates who assist children. When an advocate participates in a trial, the judge still controls the substance and form of all questions. The advocate's only function is to provide security and rapport that encourage the child to participate. These nonlawyers help foster communication as a translator does for a Spanish-speaking or hearing-impaired witness. Judges who permit such innovative procedures hold true to legal tradition at its best by providing sensitive techniques to enable juries to hear children.

Prosecutors and Judges: Educating Agents for Change in the Criminal Justice System

Innovative courtroom techniques—from laps to language—seem so fair, so easy to implement. Why then do prosecutors still review sexual abuse cases with the assumption that children cannot testify? Why do judges fail to interpret law to assure juries the chance to discover truth? Why do courtrooms continue to be places of intimidation and trauma for children?

Those outside the criminal justice system assume that addressing the problems of children in court should be as natural and easy as attending a training seminar or reading a book. After all, the laws are not as unsettled as they are unknown. Sensitive judicial techniques are not as unachievable as they are unconsidered. What prosecutor would not want to know the latest developments in competency and hearsay law that allow important cases to be prosecuted? What judge would not want to ask about a child's nap schedule if that simple inquiry facilitated a child's testimony? In theory, prosecutors and judges would keep abreast of important advances in law to enable them to reach new understanding, discard old assumptions, and provide fairness for children.

Unfortunately, most remain uninformed. Law is not a commodity. Prosecutors and judges do not learn the latest law or legal technique as they do yesterday's stock market closings, today's first-place baseball team, or tomorrow's TV shows. Not all states provide prosecutors and judges with legal journals, summaries of recent appellate decisions, and continuing education programs. In too many states, judges have little opportunity or inclination to master new developments in the law.

Most prosecutors or judges are not inept, insensitive, or hostile to change. While one always hears stories of the worst (who are indeed inept, insensitive, and hostile to change), they are as exceptional as the best, who are wise, enlightened, sensitive, and innovative. All, however, probably have at least one thing in common: they are overwhelmed with cases. In any jurisdiction with a heavy criminal caseload, prosecutors and judges do all they can to stay afloat. In urban areas, daily caseloads of trials, guilty pleas, and sentencings are staggering. In smaller communities, prosecutors and judges may have more time, but they have less access to education through colleagues, libraries, and other resources.

The severity of the resource crisis for prosecutors and judges is difficult to convey to those outside the criminal justice system. No comparable crisis exists in the private sector, and in the public sector no similar crisis produces the same direct denial of justice to so many citizens. Since the 1970s prosecutors and criminal courts throughout America have been buried by an enormous, increasing, and unprecedented caseload. Cases cannot be reviewed, legal time limits cannot be met, prosecutors and judges regularly work through lunch hours and evenings to complete each day's cases. Preparation, education, and research time have disappeared. During this same period economic trends and tax-cutting political forces have produced budget cuts. Communities have reduced funding for "frills"—courtroom bailiffs, clerks, and reporters, education time and library services for prosecutors and judges, and law clerks who provide research assistance to judges.

The situation is no better in the noncriminal courts that encounter child sexual abuse issues. Juvenile courts generally receive even lower funding priority than criminal courts, and family/probate courts have been buried by an enormous increase in divorce cases with increasingly complex problems. The *Boston Globe* described the futile efforts of probate judges in Boston in 1987 who, in ten years, had seen caseloads double and, for the first time, had to evaluate "new factors at play in divorce today—tortuous calculations about the value of pension funds, custody rights of fathers, removal of the children when one of the parents moves out of state, and a growing number of abuse allegations—requir[ing] a range of skills and Solomonic sensitivity to which few people in any profession can lay claim."[11]

The image of a prosecutor carefully investigating a case, interviewing witnesses, and reading law articles to prepare an argument is, for the most part, a fantasy. And while the image of a judge pulling volumes from book-covered walls and conferring with law clerks may be reality in some appellate courts, such scenes have vanished from state trial courts. For modern prosecutors and judges, emotional burnout, physical exhaustion, and early retirement from public service have become commonplace.

The result is, to some extent, born of necessity: prosecutors and judges learn almost nothing new until they have to. In the course of a trial, when an issue is being litigated, the judge may require the lawyers to present briefs and arguments. Then, within the immediacy of that trial, the judge may learn some of the latest legal developments. When the trial ends, the judge will move on to the next case. Neither prosecutor nor judge has the luxury of learning much beyond that which is necessary to get through the case, to get through the day.

This sad reality has far-reaching implications. Because prosecution of child sexual abuse is relatively rare, few judges see cases that demand a new approach. Prosecutors, in turn, often assume that "nothing's new" in the courts and continue to evaluate cases with unfortunate but accurate assumptions about the judges. It is a vicious cycle. Hearing no advocacy that causes them to change, judges continue as always. Prosecutors remain the same. The cycle goes on, and countless children suffer. Whatever the wisdom of legal tradition and the value of recent legal developments, courtroom tragedies will continue until prosecutors and judges come to understand children and sexual abuse.

Prosecutors must learn that their usual fast pace and conventional forecasts of success are not appropriate for child sexual abuse cases. They will need patience, special investigative methods, and innovative trial techniques. They will have to understand that children, and adults aware of child sexual abuse, have powerful reasons not to report the crime, and equally powerful incentives to recant their allegations. Prosecutors, accustomed to directing cases, will have to learn to be partners with other professionals and agencies, in the specialized evaluation process required in child sexual abuse cases.

Because the damage to young victims in such cases is extraordinary and irreversible, prosecutors must not hesitate to prosecute solely because of uncertain trial results. While there may be many other valid reasons to defer prosecution, the "You do not prosecute what you cannot win" analysis must not apply just because no one can guarantee the testimony of a child or the legal and human understanding of a judge. "The probability of winning cannot be the only criterion for filing a charge. And if the more difficult cases are never filed, the opportunity to change the climate within the legal system, and within the society as a whole, will be lost."[12]

Prosecutors can change and cause changes. Robert E. Cramer, Jr., district attorney in Huntsville, Alabama, observes that child sexual abuse "requires a shift in the way the criminal justice system responds . . . and the way it interacts with other systems. . . . As a society, we will not successfully convey that sexual abuse of children is not acceptable behavior until we redesign the system responsible for helping and protecting child victims so that offenders are held responsible for their actions." He goes on to describe a crisis he and his staff encountered in 1981:

> Certain problems kept recurring. . . . The many professionals involved with the child victims were not communicating with each other. Medical exams were incomplete. They were often performed in hospital emergency rooms after the children were kept waiting for hours. The children and their families were bounced between agencies: law enforcement, protective services, hospitals, therapy, the juvenile court system, and the District Attorney's Office. The system was revictimizing the children. Few children and families could survive, much less benefit, from this approach; yet, reported cases were reaching an epidemic level.[13]

To address these problems, Cramer organized professionals from all disciplines involved with child sexual abuse. He stimulated volunteer participation from community leaders and ordinary citizens. Together, they created the Children's Advocacy Center, where professionals from child protective services, law enforcement, prosecution, mental health, medicine, and education work together. They carefully review the proper approach and method for a child's examination and initial interview in order to gain all necessary information while trying to assure the child's comfort and trust. The interviewer then presents the case at a weekly meeting where the center staff determines the best course for the child, whether that involves return to the home, a change in custody, prosecution, or diversion of the case to other persons or agencies. If prosecution is appropriate, the center assigns a victim advocate to assist the child and family through the criminal justice system. Located in a house that provides a warm, nonthreatening environment, the center and staff convey that the child is the most important focus of their work.[14]

This coordinated approach not only reduces trauma for children but increases the potential for successful prosecution. Those conducting the interviews are trained to do them properly and thus can elicit information needed for both therapeutic and legal purposes. This, in turn, enables therapists and prosecutors to select the cases appropriate for diversion as well as prosecution. The center serves about 240 sexually abused children each year. Forty percent of the cases are referred for prosecution. Almost all of those prosecuted result in convictions.[15] In Huntsville, prosecutors changed their pace, adjusted their methods, worked with other professionals, and, whether or not cases resulted in prosecution, achieved justice for children.

Change in the criminal justice system can begin with the prosecutor's initiative; but unless conventional judicial views and behaviors also change, there can be no genuine reform. Judges can change and, in turn, they can educate and change the criminal justice system. Judges must recognize their obligation to make courts more sensitive to child victims.

Some argue that judges should not be agents for change. They say that judges are supposed to be passive, waiting for others to bring issues to court. While passivity is the usual and least difficult course, judicial tradition also includes a dynamic role. In fact, codes of judicial ethics instruct judges to take initiative in informing the public, advising legislatures, and helping to improve the administration of justice.[16] Particularly when judges perceive a crucial issue to be neglected by others, they must act.

Child sexual abuse presents such a crucial issue, and judicial leaders have called on all judges to educate the criminal justice system. Meeting in 1983 at the National Judicial College, under sponsorship of the American Bar Association and the United States Department of Justice, judges from all fifty states, the District of Columbia, and Puerto Rico convened the National Conference of the Judiciary on the Rights of Victims of Crime. In its Statement of Recommended Judicial Practices, the national conference announced:

> We have concluded that it is our responsibility as trial judges not only to make improvements within the judicial system, but to take the initiative in coordinating the various elements of the criminal justice system and take the leadership role. . . . We are confident that our recommendations will greatly help victims of and witnesses to crime. . . . This can be accomplished without impairing the constitutional . . . safeguards appropriately afforded all persons charged with crime. Our goal is not to

reduce the rights guaranteed defendants but rather to assure the rights of victims and witnesses.[17]

The conference made recommendations for the protection of victims and witnesses and specifically called for special added protections for children. Among the many recommendations were those for expedited trials in child sexual abuse cases, as well as "specially designed or equipped courtrooms to protect sensitive victims" with the use of videotape depositions. The conference also called for judicial education "dealing with the needs, comforts and legal interests of crime victims" and state, regional, and national programs to educate "judges and non-judges about methods to improve the treatment of victims and witnesses."[18] The conference emphasized the unique role of the judge in assuring not only correct legal rulings, but sensitive approaches to victims: "The courtroom is the focal point of the entire criminal justice system. The judge who presides over a court becomes not only the final arbiter of each evidentiary and procedural issue, but . . . also establishes the tone, the pace, and the very nature of the proceedings. Particularly for the victim, the judge is the personification of justice."[19]

A 1986 report by the Committee of Presiding Judges presented yet another call for leadership by the judiciary. The committee represents the nation's forty largest urban areas, where over 60 percent of America's child abuse and neglect cases are heard. Adopted by the 2,000 judges and court executives of the National Council of Juvenile and Family Court Judges, its report rejects the notion that a traditional judicial role precludes activism on behalf of children. The first recommendation on judicial leadership declares: "Judges must provide leadership within the community in determining needs and obtaining and developing resources and services. . . . The judicial responsibility for impartiality does not preclude a judge from providing leadership within the community. Judges should examine their community's child protection system and process—including their own courts."[20] The report offers specific recommendations for sexually abused children and the judicial role in providing courtrooms without trauma:

Constituency for Children

Judges should take an active part in the formation of a community-wide, multi-disciplinary "Constituency for Children" to promote and unify private and public sector efforts to focus attention and resources on meeting the needs of deprived children who have no effective voice of their own.

Sensitivity to Children

All judges of all courts must ensure sensitivity in the courtroom and encourage sensitivity out of the courtroom to minimize trauma to the child victim.

The legal system must treat children with special courtesy, respect and fairness. Judges must work with attorneys, law enforcement, child protection agencies and state and local funding sources to improve facilities, services and procedures affecting children who appear in court. High priorities must be given to abuse and neglect cases, 24-hour emergency services, reduction of delays, and coordination with adult courts. Child care and counseling, child-size furniture and waiting or visitation rooms for parents and children must be available. Frequent recesses, confidentiality for name and address of the child, removal of courtroom observers during sensitive testimony, separation of victim and accused, testimony in chambers through closed-circuit television . . . should be assured to all children in court.

Evidentiary and Procedural Rules

Evidentiary and procedural rules consistent with due process must be adopted to protect the child victim from further trauma.

Reforms must be made to improve the prosecution in criminal court of child abuse and neglect to protect the abused or neglected child victim from further trauma in the courtroom. Measures for consideration include:

Expanding use of hearsay exceptions for out-of-court statements.

Granting explicit judicial authority to control the examination of child witnesses.

Presuming the competency of the child witness.

Using, where appropriate, video-taped or closed-circuit television statements by the victim.[21]

By 1987, the national council had moved the committee's report and recommendations into action by developing a "Training Curriculum on the Judicial Response to Child Sexual Abuse." The curriculum provides training by judges, prosecutors, psychologists, and pediatricians for juvenile, family, and criminal court judges and for other professionals working with sexually abused children.[22]

Thus a professional mandate clearly compels judges to learn and promote advances to assist child victims of sexual abuse. Nevertheless, the distance between that mandate and implementation is enormous. Only a small minority of judges nationwide have gained the education essential to make courts safe for children. Only a relatively small number are even aware of the recommendations of national councils of judicial leaders. Shocked by the seeming inertia of those who should be leading the struggle to establish justice for children, professionals and lay people alike face some troubling questions. How does the average judge learn? And when judges are not aware of legal advances and innovations, can citizens do anything?

Judges learn on the job. Whether appointed or elected, most trial judges often deal with laws and issues they have never before encountered. It is not

unusual for a civil lawyer with no trial experience to become a judge assigned
to a criminal trial court. It is not unusual for a judge with no background in
child development or family dynamics to be assigned to a juvenile or family
court. Some judges study hard and learn fast. Most do not. Even able and
conscientious judges, capable of making solid legal decisions, may not understand certain nonlegal issues essential to sensitive and sound decision-making
in cases involving children.

The problem of unprepared judges is not new, though it has been exacerbated by limited resources and overwhelming caseloads. As early as 1937
judicial leaders attempted to address the problem by forming the National
Council of Juvenile and Family Court Judges to provide continuing education for these specialized judges. Understanding that legal training would not
be enough for judges who evaluate cases of children and families, the council
developed multidisciplinary courses and publications. In 1963 the National
Judicial College was founded to enhance education for judges outside the
juvenile and family court specializations. Located at the University of Nevada, both the council and college offer courses at their Reno centers and
around the country, coordinating these with state judicial colleges and organizations such as the National District Attorneys Association and the American Probation and Parole Association.

Some states have mandatory judicial education with annual requirements
for all judges who are expected to take courses related to their specific assign-
ments. In addition, some courses try to make judges aware of special professional issues and personal developmental concerns. In Massachusetts and
Wisconsin, for example, judges participate in seminars with literature, phi-
losophy, and law faculty to develop a multidisciplinary focus on decision-
making and situational ethics.

It remains to be seen whether the recent attention to child sexual abuse
in the courts, and the increasing efforts in judicial education will produce
significant changes for children. However, two practical principles already
are clear. First, it is unrealistic and ineffective to try to educate all judges
about child sexual abuse because so many of them, in a variety of court as-
signments, will never encounter such cases. Second, it is realistic and essential to educate every judge who will handle such cases in juvenile, family, and
criminal courts. Without delay, therefore, every state must require specialized
education on child sexual abuse for every judge before he or she presides over
cases involving child sexual abuse.[23]

Citizen advocates can also influence judicial education, as illustrated by
the efforts of advocates for battered women. A few years ago, following the
enactment of new laws to protect battered women, the Milwaukee Task
Force on Battered Women, a volunteer group of advocates, acted to assure
that judges would know and enforce the laws. Working with supportive
judges, task force leaders developed a training seminar that awarded state
judicial education credits for judges who attended. The advocates anticipated

the less-than-enthusiastic reaction of judges to these seminars, offered in the evenings after full days of court cases, and offered by nonlawyer citizen advocates. To ensure success, they informed the media. "Battered Women to Teach Judges" was newsworthy, and every judge who read that story knew that reporters would be there and take note of judges not attending. Although it would be difficult to measure the extent to which such seminars change attitudes and practices, it is clear that determined citizens, on behalf of children, can bring the judicial horse to water and gently force it to drink.

While many view judges as entrenched and resistant to change, that image may be more apparent than real. Every state has judges who bellow, "This is my court, and I don't care what you say the law is"; but many judges are willing to listen and learn. In fact, judges may constitute a professional group unique in its readiness for change. They are not supposed to have personal allegiances to particular procedures or philosophies. Having followed a rule for years, a judge is expected to alter it immediately upon command from a higher court. In fact, that is exactly what judges frequently do with far less resistance than most outside the legal system would suspect.

The judicial profession, however, is all-too-typical in another respect that is important for child victims. Most judges are men, and most are older men. They may be loving fathers and grandfathers; but working all day as their children grew, most had limited experience at parenting. However great their devotion to their own families and the communities they serve, most lack the "sixth sense" anticipation of the needs and rhythms of children. It is a sense that women, and an increasing number of men, usually develop as they assume daily responsibility for care of their children. It is a sense desperately needed in the courts today if judges are to be genuinely knowledgeable about child victims. While most judges cannot regain that parenting opportunity, they can come to acknowledge the importance of that limitation in their experience. For many children in court, that acknowledgment may form the basis for judicial sensitivity and justice.

An educated judiciary; proper allowances for hearsay, videotape interviews, and closed-circuit testimony; child-centered court environments; in-court advocates for children—none of these is beyond immediate implementation by American criminal courts. But for Laurie Chapman and her family, the problem of children revictimized by the courts demands more than "tinkering" with legal change. After the Greenbrook trial Laurie's father, Tom, said, "There may not be much we can do to change people who abuse children, but we don't have to put up with a legal system that reabuses children. . . . If every citizen of the United States were to spend one day in a criminal court proceeding, there would be such an outcry at how outrageous the system is that the whole thing would be dismantled in a year."

Tom Chapman knows the historical reasons for the jury trial; he knows about the adversarial tradition, the constitutional rights of defendants, and the reasonable doubt standard. He also understands the concept of double jeopardy—the Greenbrook defendants could be tried only once even though his daughter and the other children did not receive their one opportunity to be heard in court with fairness. He knows his daughter was not protected or respected in court, and he is convinced that other children will suffer as other lawyers and judges misunderstand law and trial tradition and ignore the rights of children. When he says the system should be dismantled, he means it. Like other parents whose children have wrestled with the law and lost, he believes there can be no search for truth and no justice when lawyers do battle in an adversarial "game of chance" administered by judges whose training and experience are often inadequate and decided by juries whose knowledge is incomplete. Four years ago Tom Chapman would have argued that America's legal system is superior to any in the world. Today he talks wistfully of the rights and protections afforded Scandinavian, Israeli, and French—but not American—children.

Whether or not one believes that the criminal court system deserves to be dismantled, the issues raised by parents like those involved in the Greenbrook case are compelling. Ultimately, their questions lead to the larger, more disturbing—and, to some, heretical—consideration that sooner or later Americans must face: Can the criminal justice system as we know it cope with the challenge that sexually abused children present?

There are those who argue forcefully that the system has made extraordinary advances and can continue renewing itself to provide justice for children. There are others who contend with equal persuasiveness that the American criminal justice system was not designed for and thus can never respond effectively to sexually abused children. Both positions have validity. They represent the distinct and equally justified voices of a society at odds with itself over its moral and legal obligations to very different groups—defendants and child victims. They reflect the anxiety of a society frustrated by its failure to control this crime that agitates not because it is so unique, but because it is so extensive and so personally threatening.

Whether one views the criminal court system with faith and optimism or with disdain, anger, and despair, it is—for now—society's only system for supervising and restraining those who endanger children. The task it faces is formidable. Regarded by so many Americans as a symbol of trust betrayed, the criminal court system must restore public faith in its will and its ability to respond to the cries of sexually abused children.

7

McMartin:
The Final Chapter

"Well, in our country," said Alice, still panting a little, "you'd generally get to somewhere else—if you ran very fast for a long time as we've been doing."

"A slow sort of country!" said the Queen. "Now, here, you see, it takes all the running you can do, to keep in the same place. If you want to get somewhere else, you must run at least twice as fast as that!"

—Lewis Carroll,
*Through the Looking Glass
and What Alice Found There*

NO book about American courts' treatment of sexually abused children can disregard the outcome of the McMartin Preschool trials. It was the case that forced the nation to view child sexual abuse from a new perspective; to consider that even the most public and seemingly beneficent settings—both daycare centers and courtrooms—might harbor extraordinary dangers for children. By the time a jury reached a verdict, it had become America's longest and costliest criminal trial and had, in the process, forced proponents on both sides to question not only the criminal justice system's efficiency, but its competence to deal with child sexual abuse. After thirty-three months of trial, 124 witnesses, 974 exhibits, almost 64,000 pages of transcripts, and costs in excess of $13 million, no one involved in the McMartin case would ever be the same.

Not Raymond Buckey, who spent five years in jail before raising bail.

Not his mother, who spent two years in jail and deeded the school property to her lawyer to pay legal fees.

Not therapist Kee MacFarlane and the staff of Children's Institute International, whose interviews with hundreds of alleged victims became a focal point for disparagement of the prosecution's case.

Not the police or prosecutors, who were targets of criticism from the earliest to the final proceedings.

Not the defense attorneys, who, in failing to gain acquittals on all counts, were unable to establish their clients' innocence in the eyes of the public.

Not the media, which suffered accusations of bias from both sides.

Not the jurors, whose professional and personal activities were so curtailed over the endless months that the judge would feel compelled to observe, "No jury has had to endure what you had to endure."

Not Judge William Pounders, who presided over the arduous, often emotionally charged proceedings, only to concede that despite his best efforts, he had lost control of the trial he worked so hard to contain.

Not the parents, who fought for years to have the case brought to trial, who waged another campaign to have Raymond Buckey tried a second time, and who, along with MacFarlane, were cast by the defense and some of the media as the "true perpetrators."

Not the children. Perhaps most significant of all, not the children who, whatever one's opinion of their veracity, were clearly victimized by an inept criminal justice system.

After nine weeks of deliberation, the jury on January 18, 1990, acquitted Buckey and his mother, Peggy McMartin Buckey, of 52 counts of lewd and lascivious conduct with minors under the age of 14. The panel deadlocked on twelve molestation charges against Raymond Buckey and one count of conspiracy against him and his mother. The judge dismissed the conspiracy charge against Mrs. Buckey and allowed the prosecutors to decide the fate of her son. On January 31 they announced they would retry Buckey on the unresolved charges.

Angry with the decision, Buckey's lawyer moved to have Judge Pounders removed from the case, claiming that he "harbored a real and personal belief that [Buckey] was guilty." Supporters of the defendants accused prosecutors of responding to public pressure to have Buckey retried and maintained that District Attorney Ira Reiner's decision was politically motivated by his candidacy for California Attorney General. The prosecutors maintained that they had reviewed the evidence, conferred extensively with the parents and children, and concluded that "everybody—the public, the families—is entitled to resolution . . . [The parents' and children's] decision was that they wanted to stick with it one more time."

Sticking with it one more time involved the hope on all sides that the second trial would be different from the first. Just months after the initial verdict, Raymond Buckey faced yet another jury, this one charged with deciding the remaining counts on which the first jury had deadlocked. This time the trial was quicker, neater, and cheaper, but the result was as inconclusive.

When this jury also deadlocked, the judge declared a mistrial, and Deputy District Attorney Joseph Martinez announced that the prosecution would not try the case a third time. "The community has had enough," he said.

It was probably an accurate observation. McMartin had held a grip on the nation's attention far longer than the media and ordinary citizens were generally willing to tolerate. Most intolerable of all, regardless of whether a true verdict would have been guilty or not guilty, was the awareness that the legal system had failed so miserably. Even the most adamant Buckey supporters must have felt discomfort at some of the jurors' comments. Asked if they felt that the children had actually been molested, seven of the jurors who agreed to be interviewed said they believed that the children had been molested "in some sense, by someone." The problem, they asserted, was that the evidence was uncertain.

That perception was shared by the public. One Los Angeles television station that solicited viewers' responses after the verdict reported that 11,255 people called in to say that justice had not been served, whereas only 1,663 believed that it had. The public doubt and skepticism cast a cloud over both the children and the defendants, all of whom deserved and were thus denied clarity and finality. Juror Brenda Williams described herself as entering deliberations "confused and uncertain," and told reporters, "[the public] did not listen to two and a half years of testimony. I am sorry if the world is not happy. But it was me there, and I can live with it."

Ultimately, however, the issue will not be whether Ms. Williams can "live with" the McMartin result. The point may not even be whether the children, their families, and the defendants survive it. What may matter most is that the McMartin case demonstrated in the most public manner that the legal system was poorly equipped to cope with complaints of child sexual abuse. And that will never be easy for any American to live with.

What went wrong? Were the McMartin problems unique or inherent in child sexual abuse cases? Much has been written already, and much more will be offered in the years to come to answer these questions. Most insightfully, "After McMartin . . . Who Walks Point?"[1] provides thoughtful analyses by qualified professionals in several disciplines. All acknowledge the unusual factors that limit the lessons and implications of McMartin: the early emergence of the case, which brought allegations to a system with little experience; the size of the case, which defied effective investigation; the length of the trial, which prevented any clear focus for the jurors.

Virtually all McMartin participants and commentators express concern about the investigative process and acquisition of evidence. Some complain that the case was not fully investigated and that, had it been, it would never have been charged. Others contend that the investigative process doomed the case when police error allowed crucial evidence to be destroyed. All agree that if McMartin demonstrated anything, it is that those responsible for the investigation of child sexual abuse must be highly trained and extremely cautious

and thorough. All agree also that because physical or medical evidence oft
is nonexistent or problematic in such cases, justice will depend not only on the
children's testimony, but also on the quality of the children's earlier interviews, both to screen out allegations that are false and to document those that
are true.

McMartin underscored the precarious nature of the therapist's role.
Because children rarely disclose sexual abuse in the clear, direct ways the
criminal justice system demands, therapists must often ask supportive or
suggestive questions to encourage disclosure, and in so doing they risk contaminating legal cases. In effect, therapists understandably may feel that they
are forced to choose between the emotional health of a child and the evidentiary needs of a courtroom. Kee MacFarlane became a scapegoat in the
McMartin proceedings in part because an unprepared system required that
she satisfy both demands.

Jurors were especially critical of what they described as the leading questions of MacFarlane and social workers at Children's Institute International.
One juror commented, "We did not get the children's words. . . . The interviewers asked leading questions in such a manner that we never got the
children's story in their own words." Another wondered whether he received
an accurate account: "We didn't find out so much what the children knew as
what the interviewer wanted to know. . . . Once the kids started saying it, the
parents believed it. When the parents believed it, the kids started believing
it." Another doubted whether the children could distinguish fact and fantasy,
and seemed reluctant to consider the possibility that some facts may exceed
the worst adult fantasies. For him, "There seemed to be no holds barred. The
more fantastic story you could come up with the better." And another echoed
the argument about children's suggestibility: "Children believe their parents.
The parents did too much talking . . . I couldn't tell whether the children
were saying what happened to them or repeating what they had been told and
what they heard their parents telling people." MacFarlane acknowledged the
problem but suggested that the particularities of the case made the situation
far more complex than some critics seemed willing to understand:

> The children were scared. They thought they might die or their parents
> might die. When we realized that's what kept them silent, we began to
> feel we were not going to get to any of that information until they got over
> that fear. One way is to say we talked to a lot of their friends and they told
> of yucky secrets. I felt that it gave a message there may be something
> yucky they could tell. We found it relieved them. It took the onus off
> being the first one.
>
> Unfortunately, there were no adult witnesses or videotapes of the
> crime. I was naive in never having been part of a case like this. By the end
> of the first month we had 200 on a waiting list. We were seeing them
> around the clock. As more talked, I began to be reassured that the

numbers made it less important than how we got the information; they cross-corroborated each other.

Most sexual cases have only the word of the child. This case had more evidence than most cases have. What does this society require of these children? Do we need videotapes of the crime?[2]

As a result of the experience with McMartin, the Los Angeles Sheriff's Office now sends as many as three independent teams of investigators to interview children. The process has been praised by some as a significant step in improving the reliability of the investigative process because it allows interviewers to corroborate one another's observations and to correct flaws in their techniques. However, despite its commendable intentions, it is unlikely to alleviate the stress for children, who are subjected to additional strangers and increased pressure when the trauma of disclosure is at its height. Unlike the Children's Advocacy Center methods developed in Huntsville, the process may create more problems for children and courtrooms. Equally disturbing is the message that it sends to victims and their families: its protestations of concern not withstanding, the law does not respect the word of children as it does that of adults; their testimonies are, from the onset to the conclusion of the legal process, approached with suspicion and confusion.

In any final analysis, McMartin also may be considered the case that demonstrated that the criminal justice system can barely approach the possibility of ritualistic abuse of numerous children. As a result, in the future prosecutors are more likely to avoid the full scope of this horror with which, if only by virtue of the volume of evidence and potential length of trials, the system seems incompetent to cope. Don J. DeBenedictis' article in the *ABA Journal*, "McMartin Preschool's Lessons," notes that some suggest a way to deal with accusations of ritualistic abuse is "to avoid bringing [them] up . . . for fear they are too fantastic for juries to believe."[3]

McMartin was the quintessentially abusive child sexual abuse case in which everything rested on the observations, interviews, and testimonies of children, and the children's statements were always somehow judged to be suspect. Several years before the verdicts, *On Trial* forecast that judgment and maintained that "[n]o matter what the outcome, the defendants, the children, and their families will all have suffered through months of anguish, and the flaws and inability of our legal system to cope with child sexual abuse cases will have been demonstrated once again." We cite this not to praise accurate predictions, but simply to appreciate the wholly predictable results of processes that were so flawed. Whether one chooses to believe the children or not, McMartin was in the end a case about the vulnerability of both defendants and children in a legal world of adults stumbling in their search for the truth.

This is not to suggest, however, that McMartin was a typical case or that the system always stumbles so shamefully. After all, the McMartin allegations surfaced almost a decade ago, coming to a system with little knowledge or experience dealing with child sexual abuse. In fact, most professionals now dealing with child sexual abuse cases are less concerned that the mistakes of McMartin will be repeated than that a post-McMartin backlash will compromise their efforts to pursue valid prosecutions.[4]

In the past few years, many child sexual abuse cases have been prosecuted successfully, and the convictions have been reviewed by appellate courts. Most of the decisions correspond to the concepts discussed in Chapters 5 and 6. The footnotes to those chapters have been expanded to offer important details and analyses of many recent decisions.

Important Trends and Decisions

Confrontation and Closed-Circuit TV — Maryland v. Craig

The Sixth Amendment guarantees a criminal defendant the right to confront witnesses. The theory is that confrontation motivates truthful testimony, or at least reveals the demeanor of the untruthful witness. In most cases, this right does not become an issue; the accuser takes the stand, faces the defendant, and testifies. But because a sexually abused child may be too traumatized to face the accused, courtroom confrontation may not be possible.

This grim reality prompted many state legislatures to authorize courts to allow children, in certain circumstances, to testify without confronting defendants in the courtroom. By 1990, thirty-seven states permitted videotaped testimony, twenty-four authorized one-way closed-circuit television testimony completely protecting the child from any view of the defendant, and eight authorized two-way closed-circuit testimony allowing the child's view of the defendant, but on a screen from a separate room. Still, troubling issues remained. When are such techniques necessary and under what circumstances are such procedures constitutional? In 1990, these questions reached the United States Supreme Court in *Maryland v. Craig*.[5]

Sandra Ann Craig, owner of a preschool center, was found guilty of child abuse, sexual assaults, and battery in 1987. Four children, ages four to seven, testified at her trial via one-way closed-circuit television that permitted Craig and her attorney to see, hear, and cross-examine them, but spared the children any view of her. The trial judge allowed the closed circuit procedure after hearing testimony from the children's therapists, whose views were summarized in the appellate record:

> Each child would have some or considerable difficulty in testifying in Craig's presence. For example, as to one child, the expert said what "would cause him the most anxiety would be to testify in front of Mrs. Craig." . . . The child "wouldn't be able to communicate effectively." As to another, an expert said she "would probably stop talking and she would

withdraw and curl up." With respect to two others, the testimony was that one would "become highly agitated, that he may refuse to talk, or if he did talk, that he would choose his subject regardless of questions," while the other would "become extremely timid and unwilling to talk."

In authorizing the protective closed-circuit procedure, the judge relied on a 1985 Maryland statute permitting such a technique when "testimony by the child victim in the courtroom will result in the child suffering serious emotional distress such that the child cannot reasonably communicate."

Maryland's highest court reversed Craig's conviction, ruling that expert testimony was not enough to justify the use of closed-circuit TV or any other procedure that departs from face-to-face confrontation. The court said a child must face the defendant, attempt to testify, suffer "severe emotional distress," and be unable to "reasonably communicate." Then, and only then, could closed-circuit be employed.

But even then, according to the court, a child would not gain protection from confrontation. After failing to testify in the courtroom, a child must next attempt to testify via two-way closed-circuit TV; from a separate room, the child would see the defendant on a TV monitor. Only if again traumatized and unable to testify would the child be allowed to use one-way closed-circuit TV.

Why would Maryland's highest court insist that children be subjected to such an ordeal? The Maryland decision derived from its interpretation of the Supreme Court's 1988 decision in *Coy v. Iowa* (see Chapter 5), in which a defendant's sexual assault convictions were reversed because two 13-year-old girls had testified from behind a one-way screen that shielded the defendant from their view. Expressing the opinion of a four-justice plurality, Justice Antonin Scalia explained, "face-to-face presence may, unfortunately, upset the truthful rape victim or abused child; but by the same token it may confound and undo the false accuser, or reveal the child coached by a malevolent adult. It is a truism that constitutional protections have costs." This decision reiterated that a defendant's Sixth Amendment right to confront accusers includes, at the very least, a powerful preference that such confrontation be face to face. Crucial to the outcome in the *Coy* case was that the trial judge had allowed the one-way screen without learning whether the two girls needed it to testify. Thus the Supreme Court noted that the judge had made "no individualized findings that these particular witnesses needed special protection."

But what if a judge makes those findings? If a trial judge, like the one in the *Craig* case, concludes that a child needs special protection to testify, must the confrontation still be face to face? While Justice Scalia left that question open for "another day," Justice Sandra Day O'Connor addressed the issue in her concurring opinion, and concluded that face-to-face confrontation can give way if "necessary to further an important public policy." In addition, she declared "the protection of child witnesses is . . . just such a policy. . . . If a

court makes a case-specific finding of necessity, . . . the strictures of the Confrontation Clause may give way to the compelling state interest of protecting child witnesses."

Since 1988, numerous state appellate courts have considered similar issues and, until the Maryland decision, almost all applied Justice O'Connor's reasoning and allowed trial judges to permit a child to testify by closed-circuit TV or other protective procedures.[6] None required the judge to force a child first to face a defendant in order to determine whether such protection was necessary.

The significance of the Maryland case was emphasized in the Supreme Court amicus brief filed on behalf of People Against Child Abuse Inc., the Association for Child Care Excellence, and the Maryland Coalition Against Sexual Assault. Arguing that the Maryland high court decision "requires infliction on the child witness of the very trauma which the statute is meant to alleviate," the brief maintained:

> Under this procedure, a child victim is not entitled to the protection intended by the statute unless the child breaks down twice. It not only subjects children to unnecessary trauma, it also will have a devastating effect on the ability of the State to prosecute child abuses. . . . A child who has been severely traumatized twice in the courtroom will likely be in such shambles that the child will be unable to proceed even via the one-way closed-circuit television. . . . Neither responsible prosecutors nor parents will be willing to put children through this further ordeal, with a consequent loss in ability to prosecute child abusers. . . . The multiple-step procedure . . . virtually guarantees abusers immunity from prosecution by rendering the only witnesses to their crimes mute.[7]

The United States Supreme Court reversed the Maryland decision. Writing for a 5–4 majority, Justice O'Connor explained that "the word 'confront,' as used in the Confrontation Clause, cannot simply mean face-to-face confrontation. . . . Our precedents establish that 'the Confrontation Clause reflects a *preference* for face-to-face confrontation at trial,' . . . a preference that 'must occasionally give way to considerations of public policy and the necessities of the case.' "

Asserting that closed-circuit TV testimony "preserves all of the other elements of the confrontation right," the Supreme Court noted that defense attorneys can still see and cross-examine witnesses, and that defendants, judges, and juries still can view witnesses. Accordingly Justice O'Connor expressed the Court's confidence "that use of the one-way closed-circuit television procedure . . . does not impinge upon the truth-seeking or symbolic purposes of the Confrontation Clause." Thus the Court concluded that "if the State makes an adequate showing of necessity," a protective procedure can be used to avoid face-to-face confrontation. Such "necessity" can be demonstrated without requiring children to first attempt to testify face to face. The

trial judge's "determination that the child witness will suffer 'serious emotional distress such that the child cannot reasonably communicate' " was sufficient.

Most significantly for many issues arising in child sexual abuse trials, the Supreme Court posed what it termed "the critical inquiry": Is the protection of child witnesses a sufficiently "important state interest" to justify some departure from the powerful protections afforded defendants under the Sixth Amendment? The Court answered by declaring, for the first time, that "a State's interest in the protection of minor victims of sex crimes from further trauma and embarrassment and a State's interest in the physical and psychological well-being of child abuse victims" are "compelling State interests" of such importance and constitutional strength that, in some instances, they may prevail over a defendant's rights.

Confrontation and Hearsay—Idaho v. Wright

Most recent appellate decisions have affirmed child sexual abuse convictions that were based in part on hearsay accounts of children's statements. Admitting the statements under various exceptions described in Chapter 5, the decisions acknowledge the importance and fairness of such hearsay evidence and often reflect an increasing sensitivity to children and understanding of law. For example, affirming a conviction in 1989, the Massachusetts Supreme Court allowed "fresh complaint" hearsay even though the child's disclosure came eighteen months after the assault:

> There is no absolute rule of law as to the time within which a sexual assault victim must make her first complaint for that complaint to be admissible in evidence as a fresh complaint. . . . The test is whether the victim's actions were reasonable. . . . Because child sexual abusers are often related to or friends of the child victim, and because the victim's silence has been induced by threats or coercion, courts are flexible in applying the usual fresh complaint strictures. The cases involving child sexual abuse constitute a factually distinct branch of the fresh complaint doctrine that gives special consideration to the natural fear, ignorance, and susceptibility to intimidation that is unique to a young child's make-up.[8]

The courts consistently reach fair results when they recognize the vital importance of hearsay, without which the jury's search for the truth is often impossible. The courts affirm the admission of hearsay when they accurately apply traditional tenets of evidence law, including pronouncements of the Supreme Court that sometimes hearsay is admitted "simply from the necessities of the case, and to prevent a manifest failure of justice," and that such hearsay statements often "derive much of their value from the fact they are made in a context very different from trial, and therefore are usually irreplaceable as substantive evidence."[9]

For juries, the critical importance of hearsay evidence has become even clearer in recent years as an increasing number of defendants assert that the allegations are fabrications, resulting from the motives and manipulations of vengeful parents in custody disputes. In such instances jurors want to know when the child first made the allegation, to whom, and under what circumstances. If the child later recanted, the jurors want to know when, to whom, and under what circumstances. Jurors may learn that police, parents, therapists, or others interviewed the children. If the trial presents competing theories about whether those interviews were objective or manipulative, jurors should know the details—including the exact words, whenever possible—and the nature, circumstances, timing, and substance of all the child's communications. Without the admission of hearsay, such knowledge is impossible.

With more police, social workers, and other professionals audio- and videotaping their interviews with children, juries in more and more cases should gain the best evidence to evaluate the credibility of children. So, for example, in 1990 the West Virginia Supreme Court properly rejected a defendant's claim that it was unfair to show the jury the videotape of his daughter's interview by police. Testifying at the trial, she recanted her allegation of sexual abuse and claimed that the police had coerced her original statement. Perhaps only seeing the videotape of that police interview assured the jury that her recantation, not her allegation, resulted from fear; that coercion came from her father, not the police. Allowing the evidence, the court explained that sometimes "prior statements preserved on videotape possess advantages over testimony at trial. . . . We can perceive no better way . . . to decide a witness' credibility than watching an unedited videotape."[10]

Unfortunately, not all recent decisions reflect the understanding shown by the Supreme Courts of Massachusetts and West Virginia. In 1990, for example, a federal court of appeals ordered a new trial for a man convicted of sexually abusing his three-and-one-half-year-old daughter. Two times the little girl told her grandmother, "My daddy put it in my butt," and her grandmother repeated those statements to the jury. The evidence also established that the child had contracted gonorrhea and that, according to the court, there were "a dozen factors corroborating" the child's hearsay statements. However, the appeals court disallowed part of the grandmother's account and reversed the convictions. Incredibly, the court acknowledged the certainty of the assault of the child but then ignored reality:

Without making light of what certainly happened to [the child] . . . we can imagine a very young child, particularly one so bright, blithely making a sexually charged reference based on something she encountered on television or elsewhere. The reference might improperly describe an innocent contact by the father; not a detailed account of an event ordinarily beyond a child's experience.[11]

The decision implied that a preschool child, with a medically verified history of gonorrhea and a dozen other factors confirming sexual abuse, could have been "blithely making a sexually charged reference . . . improperly describ-[ing] an innocent contact" when she said, "My daddy put it in my butt." Thus, while many appellate decisions of the 1990s are sound, some still demonstrate remarkable misunderstanding. In such cases, ironically, the children become victims of judges who have fallen victim to fantasy.

In 1990, in *Idaho v. Wright,* [12] the United States Supreme Court reached several significant conclusions that should further help to establish the admissibility of almost all child hearsay in sexual abuse cases. Unfortunately, because of its very unusual and complicated factual and legal background, the case may be subject to misinterpretation and, if carelessly quoted, it could produce unintended results.

Laura Lee Wright was convicted of restraining and silencing her two- and five-year-old daughters while her younger daughter's father sexually abused them. The couple was sentenced to twenty years. In appealing only the conviction involving the younger daughter, each contended that the trial judge erred in allowing the examining physician to repeat the two-year-old's statements about the assault. Each challenged the hearsay testimony, but did so under slightly different legal theories. The Idaho Supreme Court affirmed the father's conviction but reversed Ms. Wright's. Thus only Ms. Wright's conviction for assaulting her younger daughter reached the United States Supreme Court.

The Idaho Supreme Court found the hearsay testimony very troubling. After all, the child was only two and one-half years old, and the doctor neither audiotaped nor videotaped the interview. In addition, the doctor discarded a drawing he had made and used during the interview, used leading questions, and acknowledged a preconceived view that the child had been abused by her father. Reluctant to allow a conviction to rest on statements from a child so young when the documentation of those statements was so apparently imprecise, the Idaho Supreme Court asserted, "The circumstances surrounding this interview demonstrate dangers of unreliability which, because the interview was not recorded, can never be fully assessed."

Significantly, however, the United States Supreme Court did not endorse the reasoning of the Idaho decision. Making it clear that hearsay accounts of interviews and examinations can be admitted even without audio, video, or written documentation, the Court decided to "reject the apparently dispositive weight placed by [the Idaho Supreme Court] on the lack of procedural safeguards at the interview. Out-of-court statements made by children regarding sexual abuse arise in a wide variety of circumstances, and we do not believe the Constitution imposes a fixed set of procedural prerequisites to the admission of such statements at trial." Instead, the Supreme Court explained, the issue was whether the child's statements to the doctor carried "sufficient indicia of reliability." If so, they would be reliable enough for the jury to consider. If not, the statements should not be allowed.

How should a judge measure such "indicia of reliability?" The Supreme Court first embraced the traditional view that judges should look for "particularized guarantees of trustworthiness" from "the totality of the circumstances." Then, in a drastic departure from precedent, the Court concluded that such circumstances "include only those that surround the making of the statement," and not other evidence that corroborates the statement. That is, other evidence in the trial such as medical confirmation of the assault, testimony from the other victim, the defendant's opportunity to commit the crime, would all be irrelevant to the evaluation of whether the child's statements were true. On the other hand, whether the child had a motive to fabricate, and whether, given the child's age, she would likely have made up a story of this nature, could be considered because those circumstances were "inherent." In other words, they "surrounded the making of the statement."

The distinction made little sense. In his dissenting opinion for four justices, Justice Anthony Kennedy pointed out that the majority's analysis was contrary to "the considered wisdom of virtually the entire legal community that corroborating evidence is relevant to reliability and trustworthiness." He carefully examined the Court's sharp deviation from precedent and demonstrated that even the majority's own examples quickly foundered in contradictions. For example, the majority contended that whether the child had a motive to fabricate was an "inherent" factor "surrounding" the statement. But, as Justice Kennedy explained, a judge's perception of any such motive could only derive from other corroborative evidence in the case. Thus on the very narrow issue of how to measure "indicia of reliability" of hearsay, any distinction between "inherent" and "corroborative" factors is artificial and virtually impossible to apply. On the strength of precedent, legal commentary, and Justice Kennedy's cogent dissent, this aspect of the decision may have little impact because, as Justice Kennedy concluded, it will "soon prove to be as unworkable as it is illogical."

Beyond this narrow issue, however, the Supreme Court's decision in *Idaho v. Wright* developed an analysis of hearsay that could have considerable impact on the prosecution of child sexual abuse. First, it drew a clear line between hearsay admitted under specific, "firmly rooted" exceptions, and other hearsay admitted under the "catch-all" or "residual" exception. The former, such as complaint of sexual conduct, tender years, diagnosis/treatment, excited utterance, and sexually abused child exceptions (see Chapter 5) carry the "imprimatur of judicial and legislative experience" and therefore should be admitted. The judge need not evaluate the "indicia of reliability"; the jury will decide whether the hearsay statement is reliable. If, however, the hearsay does not seem to fit one of the specific hearsay categories, then the judge must view it as "residual" hearsay, evaluating whether it is reliable before allowing it to be considered by the jury. Second, despite its confused distinction between "inherent" and "corroborative" factors, the Court provided a rather flexible standard for measuring the reliability of residual hearsay: "whether the child . . . was particularly likely to be telling the truth when the statement was made." Thus, if carefully considered, *Idaho v. Wright* should establish that residual hearsay statements are admissible in most instances because children are "particularly likely to be telling the truth" about sexual abuse, and that virtually all other hearsay statements of abuse will be admissible under specific hearsay exceptions.

Despite its conclusion that the hearsay was not properly admitted, the *Wright* decision provided little if any consolation for other defendants. Not only did it clarify the virtually certain admissibility of all hearsay offered under specific exceptions, but its restrictions on residual hearsay are just as likely to limit the defense as to limit the prosecution. After all, if the two-year-old had recanted her allegation when she talked to the doctor, his "residual" hearsay still would have been disallowed under the Court's analysis.

In a critical sense, then, the Supreme Court may have missed an excellent opportunity to explain why, in fairness to both children and defendants, virtually all hearsay in child sexual abuse cases should be admitted. Is hearsay allowed under "firmly rooted" exceptions because, as the Court maintained, it is so certainly true? No, though that has been the incorrect assumption of many lawyers and judges for years. While some hearsay assuredly is reliable (for example, the virtually involuntary exclamations that are "excited utterances"), some hearsay assuredly is not (for example, the emergency room "diagnosis/treatment" declarations of battered women that they fell down stairs). Such hearsay is properly admitted not because it is "worthy of reliance" as the Court said, but rather, worthy of evaluation by a jury. In that sense, the Idaho Supreme Court reasonably expressed concern about the hearsay evidence because, given its imprecise documentation by the doctor, it could "never be fully assessed" by the jury.

Because the *Wright* decision assures the admissibility of "firmly rooted" hearsay, it is clearer than ever before that justice in some cases will depend on whether a state's evidence laws include certain hearsay exceptions. The unfairness, of course, will be that one state will have a specific, statutory exception while another will not. One state court will allow hearsay having that firmly rooted "imprimatur of judicial and legislative experience," while another will not. In one state, highly probative hearsay evidence will be admitted, and in another the same evidence will be disallowed. In one state a child abuser will be convicted while in another, with virtually identical evidence, an offender will be acquitted or not even prosecuted. Thus the *Wright* decision may render it increasingly important for states to enact specific child hearsay exceptions if their current statutes are not adequate.

Law-Making: Protecting Children or Protecting Political Turf?
From the Supreme Court decisions in both *Craig* and *Wright*, it is apparent that state legislatures can exert powerful influence on the rules of evidence that determine whether and how child sexual abuse cases are tried in Amer-

ica's courts. State legislatures created the laws that allowed for closed-circuit TV testimony and other techniques to protect children. State legislatures enacted the "firmly rooted" hearsay exceptions that should virtually assure admission of child hearsay. Because legislatures have such power, it is crucial to understand a curious and unexpected issue that has emerged in some states. Do legislatures have the authority to enact laws regarding the trial of child sexual abuse cases or, under some circumstances, is the development of evidence law and trial procedure the exclusive domain of the judiciary?

Reviewing the constitutionality of laws enacted by legislatures in five states, courts have come to different conclusions. In Arkansas, Connecticut, and Illinois, appellate courts accepted the authority of the legislatures to enact new laws on child competency, hearsay, and videotape.[13] The supreme courts of Kentucky and Mississippi, however, declared new hearsay laws unconstitutional legislative invasions of judicial rule-making authority, in violation of separation of powers.[14] Many judges and legislators maintain that these decisions have less to do with constitutional principles than with political antagonism between the judicial and legislative branches.

For a variety of reasons such antagonism is likely to increase in the future. Legislatures have demonstrated a propensity to mandate court services and responsibilities by enacting more and more criminal statutes while refusing to allocate funds for implemention. This discouraging pattern is particularly pronounced in the area of child abuse. In a remarkably short period of years, all fifty states enacted laws requiring the prompt reporting of suspected child abuse to law enforcement or child protective services. They also required prompt response and intervention. Yet most states failed to allocate the funds for social workers, police, prosecutors, public defenders, and judges to implement the laws.

Thus we may hear the Kentucky and Mississippi message more often in the years ahead. "Don't tell us what to do," the judges may say to the legislators. "And don't you dare tell us how to be fair to kids in courts." That prospect should concern child advocates who must approach legislatures and judicial rule-making bodies if their states need new evidence laws or mandates for judicial education on child sexual abuse.[15] Squeezed in the political conflict between legislators and judges, children may be victimized by lawmakers protecting political turf rather than children.

Children in Court—Laps and Support Persons

The 1990 Supreme Court decisions in *Craig* and *Wright* focused on the constitutionality of methods to hear the words of children who can not testify in courtrooms facing defendants. Of equal significance are techniques that enable children to testify in person, facing their abusers (see Chapter 6). In fact, prosecutors increasingly report that their success in child sexual abuse trials depends not so much on special protective devices or hearsay as on their ability to prepare children to testify effectively in court. Their efforts have

been enhanced by the growing number of judges who have received training
to sensitize them to the rhythms of children and their special needs in court.
With this in mind, it is vitally important to understand the flawed reasoning
and dangerous implications of two recent Hawaii Supreme Court decisions.

In 1989, the Hawaii Supreme Court reversed a defendant's convictions for
eight counts of first degree rape, sexual abuse, sodomy, and kidnapping
because the trial judge allowed a fifteen-year-old girl to testify while sitting
near a victim-witness aide who placed her hands on the witness's shoulders.[16]
The girl had broken down and cried when she tried to testify without the aide
on the first morning of trial. The judge allowed a recess and, that same
afternoon, concluded that the supportive presence of the victim-witness aide
"would enable the complainant to continue testifying." Even with the aide's
presence the girl cried, but the aide's supportive touch enabled her to continue. The judge overruled the defense objection, agreeing with the prosecutor that the aide was "not attempting to induce any sympathy factor, but
merely trying to help the victim get through this easier and more quickly."
The judge, sensitive to the rights of both the child and the defendant, concluded, "I believe having that person here is necessary for the proceedings to
go forth and . . . give the defendant his right to confront the complaining
witness."

The Hawaii Supreme Court, however, did not agree that the aide was
"necessary," because the witness "was never asked whether she would be able
to testify alone (possibly after a longer recess), or with [the aide] sitting in the
audience of the courtroom." Moreover, the court said that the aide's presence
and touching might have "bolstered the credibility" of the witness, thereby
violating the defendant's right to a fair trial. (In a footnote, the court added
that accompaniment by a parent or close relative might be allowed, particularly for a younger witness.)

In 1990, the Hawaii Supreme Court reversed another defendant's convictions for four counts of sexual assault because an eight-year-old girl was
allowed to testify while sitting on the lap of a sexual abuse counselor.[17] The
child said she "was frightened to be there as a witness, and would feel better
if she sat on the sexual abuse counselor's lap." Declining to decide whether,
under some other circumstances, a child would be allowed to testify from a
lap, the court said that this child's fear and discomfort were not sufficient to
establish a "compelling necessity for allowing such a prejudicial scenario." In
addition, the court concluded that "the procedure followed here was fraught
with the opportunity for the accompanying person [to communicate] . . . with
the child."

Offering neither legal precedent nor factual substantiation for their conclusions, both decisions ignored essential questions:

1. How does a support person bolster the credibility of a witness? Does
it depend on whether the support person is a victim-witness aide, court

official, or relative, and on whether the jury knows the relationship to the child? Does it somehow vary according to the witness's age or distance from the aide? The court offered no answers, but speculated that the jury "might very well have . . . could very well have . . . and could have" concluded that the witness was telling the truth by virtue of the aide's mere presence. The court failed to acknowledge the equally strong possibilities that the aide's presence might have no impact on the jury's perception or might even reduce the jury's confidence in the witness's testimony. In any event, that assessment is for the jury.

2. How are these procedures "fraught with the opportunity" for aides to communicate with witnesses and prompt certain responses? Again, the court did not say. While acknowledging that judges must assure that support persons do not prompt witnesses to answer in any particular way, the Hawaii Supreme Court ignored the fact that in these two trials the judges supervised the procedures and observed nothing from the aides that prompted answers.

3. On what legal basis did the Hawaii Supreme Court conclude that "a compelling necessity" must be established before allowing such procedures? Once again, it cited no precedent. In fact, in the first case, it would not even accept the trial judge's conclusion that the aide was "necessary for the proceedings to go forth." A Spanish-speaking citizen might be able to testify in broken English. A Vietnam veteran might be able to crawl from a wheelchair to a witness stand. But no "compelling necessity" is required before providing a translator or allowing the veteran to remain seated. The court's "compelling necessity" requirement, lacking any legal basis, gives the unfortunate impression of an unreasoned bias against children.

4. On what basis did the Hawaii Supreme Court depart from evaluating these issues according to the traditional "abuse of discretion" standard? That standard provides that in matters relating to the method of testimony, including timing, location, and language, appellate courts have always deferred to the evaluation of trial judges unless there is a clear "abuse of discretion." Mere disagreement with a particular technique is not enough for an appellate court to reverse a conviction. However, without precedent or explanation, the court shed that standard, ignored the discretion of the trial judges, and placed the burden on children to prove somehow that they could not testify without such assistance.

These Hawaii decisions depart from virtually all others in which defendants challenged a trial judge's discretion to allow aides to accompany children. For example, in 1984, the Montana Supreme Court allowed a four-year-old child to testify from a prosecutor's lap. In 1985, the Texas Court of Appeals allowed a ten-year-old to testify from the lap of his guardian ad litem. In 1986, the Ohio Court of Appeals allowed an eight-year-old to testify from her aunt's lap. In 1987, the California Court of Appeals allowed an eight-year-old to testify near her mother, and the West Virginia Supreme Court allowed a

seven-year-old to testify from her foster mother's lap. In 1989, the Vermont
Supreme Court allowed a five-year-old to testify sitting with her two support
persons. And in 1990, the Minnesota Court of Appeals accepted a trial judge's
"discretion in determining the number, choice and placement of support persons" in allowing a four-year-old to testify with the supportive presence of
both her mother and the chief of police.[18]

The decisions to allow such support for children showed proper and traditional deference to the evaluations made by the trial judges. The decisions
were consistent with a rule of evidence found in many state statutes and in the
federal evidence code. These specify that the mode of questioning witnesses
should "make the interrogation and presentation effective for the ascertainment of the truth, and protect witnesses from harassment or undue embarrassment."[19] Anticipating the argument that the presence or lap of an aide
might bolster credibility of a witness, the Ohio Court of Appeals explained,
"The perceived need of the witness to sit on the lap of the aunt, her reluctance
to answer direct questions, the need for leading questions to elicit answers and
the demeanor of the witness, all could be construed by a jury as diminishing,
rather than extending, the credibility of the witness."[20]

Thus, until the Hawaii decisions, appellate courts had respected the discretion of trial judges determining whether support persons might enable
children to testify. Until these decisions, appellate courts had respected the
jury's ability to measure whether the supportive presence or comforting lap of
an aide affected the child's testimony. Until these decisions, appellate courts
had never required a demonstration of "compelling necessity" before allowing
such procedures. The tragic result is that Hawaii's parents, denied the assur-
ance that they or other trusted adults will be permitted to stay near their
children, may not allow their children to testify. Lacking any basis in fact,
logic, or law, these decisions demonstrate dangerous insensitivity to children,
and those concerned about child witnesses must understand their legal flaws
and apparent biases to assure that children in other states continue to receive
the support they need.

Civil Law

Examining the problems of sexually abused children in criminal cases is
critical to understanding the plight of children in civil cases for several reasons: (1) The civil prosecution of abuse and neglect cases in juvenile courts
discussed in Chapter 2 depends in part on knowledge of the criminal court
options. (2) The admissibility of evidence under the criminal law standards
discussed in Chapter 5 relates to criminal cases that are tried before juries
under the strictest rules of evidence. Therefore, understanding what procedures are possible and what evidence is admissible under the criminal law
should provide guidance in civil courts, where most cases are tried without

juries, before judges, under less rigid rules of evidence. Thus issues of competency, confrontation, and hearsay may not be present in civil cases; when they
are, judges can properly use criminal legal standards as reference points and
accommodate the rhythms of children with even greater ease.[21] (3) The training of criminal court judges discussed in Chapter 6 should include the same
background about child development and law that is essential for the education of juvenile and family court judges as well.

Nevertheless, civil courts often consider child sexual abuse problems in
legal contexts that are significantly different from those found in criminal
courts. Complex in both legal and human terms, many of these issues deserve
their own extensive studies. However, a brief discussion of three recent developments will contribute to a more complete understanding of the treatment of
sexually abused children in America's courts.

Private Law suits—Statutes of Limitations
"Daughters Sue Expert On Child Abuse" headlined the 1990 Associated Press
account describing a type of lawsuit virtually unknown until a few years ago.

> The adult daughters of a child abuse expert have won $1.2 million each
> in a judgment by a jury that found that the man had sexually abused and
> beaten them when they were growing up.
>
> Susan Hammond, 44, and her sister, Sharon Simone, 45, called their
> suit "a terrible act of love" to make Edward Rodgers, 72, accountable for
> years of abuse.
>
> "I feel really good that I've gone public with this," Hammond said
> after the verdict Wednesday.
>
> "My father did shameful and horrible things to me and my brothers
> and sisters. I don't believe he is a shameful and horrible man, but he has
> to be held accountable."
>
> The women sued their father for abuses suffered from 1944 through
> 1965. Rodgers is a former FBI agent, chief investigator for the district
> attorney's office in El Paso County, Colo., and a nationally known child
> abuse expert.
>
> Rodgers cannot be charged with crimes because the statute of limita-
> tions in Colorado for sexual assault on children is 10 years. The limit for
> a civil suit is two years, but jurors determined that the sisters had become
> aware of the nature and extent of their injury only within the past two
> years, during therapy.[22]

While it has always been obvious that a child sexual abuse victim is
uniquely vulnerable because of youth, it has been less obvious that some
victims may never be able to seek justice because of the passage of years. The
horror may be too great, the memory too dim, the intimidation too strong, the
therapy too slow, even the awareness of the assaults too late—and the statute
of limitations too strict—to allow for appropriate response by the courts.

While the financial interest in a lawsuit is clear, the therapeutic purpose also may be very important. Attorney Robert W. Pledl, who has litigated a number of such cases, explained, "A lot of people work on things that their parents did when they're in therapy, and for some people that is enough— they're able to resolve that. . . . But for a number of people, they need to do something in the real world. They cannot rest until they've done something to hold that person accountable. For some people, it's better to go forward with a court proceeding, even if they lose, than to remain silent. Incest is a secrecy injury. The sexual abuse obviously is terrible, but what really eats away at people is that they've been forced to keep the perpetrators secret all those years."[23]

Recently courts have accepted lawsuits from victims who have benefited from therapy and discovered their injuries years after sexual abuse occurred. As one appellate court recently declared, "The policy justifications for applying the statute of limitations to protect defendants from the threat of liability for deeds in the past is unpersuasive in incestuous abuse cases. Victims of incest have been harmed because of a most egregious violation of the parent/ child relationship. To protect the parent at the expense of the child works an intolerable perversion of justice."[24] Moreover, as if guided by the civil law concept that the discovery of harm, rather than the date of offense, should control the time limits for court action, some states have substantially revised their criminal statutes of limitations for sexual abuse. Iowa and New Jersey, for example, used to require that criminal indictments for child sexual abuse be filed within a few years of an offense. But in 1990, both states changed their statutes of limitations in order to allow charges to be filed even after many years had passed—in Iowa to the victim's age of eighteen and one-half, and in New Jersey to age twenty-three in some cases.[25]

Private Lawsuits against Government—
Joshua DeShaney and the Exile of Compassion

Adult victims of abuse are not the only ones bringing lawsuits for damages, and abusers are not the only ones being sued in the civil courts. Sometimes, relatives or guardians of abused or murdered children sue the government that should have protected them. In 1989, the United States Supreme Court decided *DeShaney v. Winnebago County Department of Social Services,*[26] a case presenting one of the most poignant legal issues involving the protection of children. While sexual abuse was not involved in this case, the tragic facts and what many consider the equally tragic decision help to expose important questions about the responsibility of government to protect children from all types of abuse.

Joshua DeShaney was born in 1979. When his parents divorced in 1980, Joshua's father was awarded custody. A second marriage soon ended in divorce, but not before the second wife told police that Joshua's father had physically abused him. The county social services department investigated but closed the case without further action until the next year when Joshua was hospitalized with multiple bruises and abrasions. The county child-protection team, consisting of a pediatrician, a psychologist, a police detective, a lawyer, and several social workers concluded that there was insufficient evidence to gain juvenile court custody over Joshua. The county did, however, intervene by gaining DeShaney's agreement to certain conditions and limited county supervision of Joshua's care.

One month later Joshua again was treated at the hospital for suspicious injuries. The county social worker concluded that there was no basis for action. Over the next six months the social worker visited the DeShaney home monthly and observed additional suspicious injuries on Joshua's head. Soon thereafter, Joshua again was treated in the hospital emergency room. Other than "dutifully recording these incidents in her files," the case worker took no action, though she later commented, "I just knew the phone would ring some day and Joshua would be dead."

A few months later DeShaney beat four-year-old Joshua so severely that he suffered serious and permanent brain damage. Brain surgery revealed a series of traumatic head injuries inflicted over a long period of time. Joshua's father was criminally prosecuted and convicted of child abuse. In addition, Joshua's mother sued the county social services department and its employees.

The lawsuit claimed that the county had denied Joshua his civil rights by depriving him of liberty without "due process of law" under the Fourteenth Amendment of the United States Constitution. Joshua's mother wanted the chance to prove that the county employees had failed to intervene to protect Joshua against a known risk of violence. The Supreme Court was not called upon to decide whether her claim was true, but rather whether such a lawsuit could be filed at all against government, under federal law.

With a complicated and subtle interpretation of the Due Process Clause, the Supreme Court concluded that although state laws might permit such a suit, nothing in the federal Constitution allowed for such a claim. Writing for a six-justice majority, Chief Justice William Rehnquist explained that the Due Process Clause protects citizens against abuse by government, not abuse by private citizens: "Its purpose was to protect the people from the State, not to assure that the State protected them from each other." Therefore, he reasoned, the Constitution did not give Joshua an "affirmative right to governmental aid," so "the State cannot be held liable under the Clause for injuries that could have been averted had it chosen to provide them."

Three justices dissented, challenging the majority's distinction between harm caused by governmental action and harm caused by a private citizen due to government's failure to act. "My disagreement," Justice Brennan explained, "arises from [the] failure to see that inaction can be every bit as abusive of power as action, that oppression can result when a State undertakes a vital duty and then ignores it." By establishing a special, protective relationship with Joshua, the county, in the opinion of the dissenters, became potentially liable for any negligent failure to protect him. By accepting responsibility for the investigation of and response to reported abuse, government also accepted responsibility to fulfill that role properly.

The dissenters did not discuss the ironic results that can develop when governments are exposed to such lawsuits. Liability for leaving a child in the parental home would undoubtedly cause caseworkers to remove children from homes where they believed a child to be at risk. While that would be good for many children, it also could lead to precipitous removal of others, reduced effort to help families stay together, and substantial pressure on overwhelmed foster care resources. Already, "the most common type of liability imposed on child protection agencies has been liability for harmful placements of children in foster homes," according to Donald Bross, legal counsel for the C. Henry Kempe National Center for the Prevention of Child Abuse and Neglect.[27] Without sufficient, excellent foster homes, removal of children can have results sometimes as disastrous as the failure to remove children from abusive parents.[28] Moreover, unwilling to accept liability when things go wrong, government might make no attempt to help things go right. In the face of increasing child abuse and decreasing social service resources, liability could lead government to abandon child protection completely, leaving children subject to private parties or charitable institutions, to be abused or protected without the involvement of government.[29]

While the results of the Supreme Court's decision may be less predictable than critics suppose, the attitude of the decision is troubling. As Justice Blackmun emphasized in his dissenting opinion, the appellate interpretation of law involves more than a scientific dissection of precedent. It involves choice, and the choices reflect attitudes about ourselves and our relation to children and their protection:

> Poor Joshua! Victim of repeated attacks by an irresponsible, bullying, cowardly, and intemperate father, and abandoned by [the county and its social service employees] who placed him in a dangerous predicament and who knew or learned what was going on, and yet did essentially nothing. . . . The question presented by this case is an open one, and our Fourteenth Amendment precedent may be read more broadly or narrowly depending upon how one chooses to read them. Faced with the choice, I would adopt a "sympathetic" reading, one which comports with dictates of fundamental justice and recognizes that compassion need not be exiled from the province of judging.

Family Court—Elizabeth Morgan and the Law of Contempt

"By now, most of you are probably familiar with Elizabeth Morgan" were Connie Chung's opening words to millions of TV viewers on January 20, 1990.[30] And indeed, millions of Americans had learned of Dr. Elizabeth Morgan, a prominent plastic surgeon who was jailed for more than two years for defying a family court order that required her five-year-old daughter, Hilary, to visit her father, who, Morgan claimed, sexually abused Hilary. Hilary's father has consistently denied the allegations.

Beginning in 1983, the legal battle over Hilary's custody and visitation has produced courtroom conflict consuming more than 4000 pages of transcripts and more than 4 million dollars in legal fees for the parents. Unfortunately, it also had left the judge uncertain about the allegations—the evidence was in "equipoise," he concluded, acknowledging a 50 percent possibility that Hilary was sexually abused by her father. Because, in the judge's estimation, the evidence fell just slightly below the "preponderance" needed for Dr. Morgan to carry her civil law burden of proof, the judge ordered her to continue making Hilary available for unsupervised visits with her father.

Instead, Dr. Morgan secretly placed Hilary in the care of her maternal grandparents who kept her in hiding in the United States, the Bahamas, Canada, England, and finally, New Zealand, where they were discovered in 1990. Meanwhile, Dr. Morgan, defying the court order to produce Hilary or disclose her whereabouts, was jailed for contempt. Only a very unusual act of Congress gained her release.

Elizabeth Morgan's cause was carried by advocates across the country who were equally appalled by the judge's refusal even to consider some evidence of abuse (particularly regarding the father's alleged abuse of his child by a previous marriage), the judge's decision permitting unsupervised visits despite his equivocal conclusion, and the jailing of the protective parent while the alleged abuser remained free. In a related case, Dr. Morgan and Hilary also sued Hilary's father and his parents for damages arising from the alleged sexual abuse. The federal court of appeals, with retired Associate Supreme Court Justice Lewis Powell sitting, reversed the trial judge's rulings in three ways: (1) the judge should have allowed a pediatrician to testify about the alleged sexual abuse of Hilary's half-sister; (2) the judge should have allowed Hilary's mother to testify about Hilary's "excited utterances"; and (3) the judge should have allowed Hilary's psychologist to testify about Hilary's "diagnosis/treatment" statements.[31] Thus there is a strong legal basis for Dr. Morgan's contention that trial courts reached wrong conclusions because they improperly restricted their own access to essential evidence.

Advocates for Hilary's father were just as incensed by what they believed to be false allegations, a failure to implement a fair visitation order, and the release of Dr. Morgan without her disclosure of Hilary's location. Who was the abuser and who was the protector? While the court failed to answer, a father searched for his daughter, a mother was confined in jail, and a little girl led a secret life in hiding.

While the Morgan case has been extremely prominent, others have presented similar circumstances, and more are certain to occur as parents choose to go underground rather than comply with court orders they fear will destroy their children. Lucy Berliner explains, "Custody or visitation disputes that involve an allegation of sexual abuse against a parent appear to be increasing. These situations are the source of significant concern in the legal and mental health communities. Intense debate has been generated about the frequency of occurrence, the validity of the complaints, and the motives of the involved parties."[32] What is known about the motives, frequency, and validity surrounding sexual abuse allegations in family courts? Although there are considerable misconceptions, recent research is beginning to offer some important answers.

The potential for false allegations is greater in the family court than in the juvenile or criminal court for at least two reasons. First, a vengeful parent may regard such an allegation as a method of gaining advantage in a custody or visitation dispute, or at least as a means to harass an ex-spouse. Second, a false allegation can enter a family court untested, without passing through the levels of investigation and review by police, social workers, and prosecutors screening juvenile and criminal cases. Thus one reasonably would expect to find more false allegations in the family courts. However, research shows that even in family courts, false allegations remain rare. Allegations of sexual abuse occur in approximately 2 percent of custody and visitation disputes, and most of those are substantiated.[33] The inference that may be drawn is that almost all of even the most antagonistic parents appreciate the emotional and legal harm they and their children could suffer from making false allegations.

What family court judges will see, therefore, is an increasing number of sexual abuse allegations resulting primarily from the increasing revelation of real abuse. Children of separated and divorced parents often are more vulnerable and likely to be abused than children living with both parents. In some cases, a parent's emotional and sexual needs, partially resulting from separation, may lead to sexual abuse. In other cases in which sexual abuse preceded the separation, a child will finally disclose the abuse to the nonabusing parent. And in still other cases, the nonabusing parent who knew of the abuse during the marriage will finally break the "code of silence" that concealed the abuse.[34]

Thus, despite the absence of the investigation and review associated with juvenile and criminal cases, most allegations of child sexual abuse in family courts are valid. The lack of such screening, however, reduces the information available to family court judges who then may be even less informed than their juvenile and criminal court colleagues. If they also hold prevalent misconceptions of children and law found throughout the courts, family court judges may deny themselves the chance to evaluate important evidence, such as that improperly excluded in the Morgan case, or they may fail to understand evidence essential to correct decision making. The tragic result may be that incorrect family court decisions will "have extremely damaging effects either by subjecting the child to continued abuse or by depriving the child of a relationship with a nonabusive parent."[35]

The responses to what some believe to be incorrect family court decisions also are almost certain to produce tragic consequences. While one may sympathize with a parent who goes into hiding with a child, or admire the courage of one who goes to jail to protect a child, that sympathy and admiration must be tempered. The child may gain protection from the abuser, but such protection is uncertain and may be short-lived. The child often lives with secrecy, anxiety, emotional uncertainty, and financial insecurity. Moving clandestinely from place to place, such children may live without adequate education, health care, and interaction with peers and family. Some, deprived of the benefits of therapy, instead live lives of deception, further complicating their mental health crises caused by an abusive parent's violation of trust. Once discovered, the "protective" parent will face the same court order that, with the passage of time, perhaps may no longer be appealed. And if that parent has taken the child into hiding, he or she now may also be criminally prosecuted for abduction or interference with custody. The agony for parents can be devastating as they choose between horrible, destructive options.

Spurred by the perceived travesty of Dr. Morgan's case, the United States Congress considered reducing the "protective" parent's burden by limiting the authority of judges to jail parents who would disobey their orders. Ultimately, while Congress enacted a law with virtually no impact other than releasing Dr. Morgan, it flirted with more sweeping limits on judicial contempt power that would have prohibited incarceration of a parent, or at least limited it to perhaps no more than six months. In hearings before the Senate Judiciary Committee, child advocates warned Congress away from such limitations.[36] They successfully argued that if Dr. Morgan had prevailed in court and her ex-husband had absconded with Hilary, she would be imploring the court to use every possible power to locate Hilary and jail her father until he disclosed her whereabouts. Thus it is crucial to remember that, despite the few horrific examples on which the media dwell, a judge's contempt power to enforce an order is always intended and almost always used on behalf of a child's best interests. To limit that authority would be to limit the judicial power to protect children.

In 1990, the United States Supreme Court reviewed such judicial authority in *Baltimore City Department of Social Services v. Bouknight*.[37] When three-month-old Maurice was alleged to have been physically abused by his mother, the Baltimore juvenile court placed him in shelter care. Later, however, he was returned to his mother under court-ordered conditions that she take part in therapy and parenting education. Eight months later, the court ordered Maurice's placement in foster care because his mother had refused to meet those conditions. When ordered to produce Maurice, she refused. The judge found her in contempt and jailed her until she "purged herself of contempt by either producing Maurice . . . or revealing his exact whereabouts."

Maurice's mother challenged the order, asserting that her refusal to tell the court was protected by her Fifth Amendment right against self-incrimination. She argued that to answer would be to confirm her actions, some of which could be prosecuted criminally. Writing for a 7–2 majority, Justice O'Connor rejected the argument explaining that because Maurice's mother "assumed custodial duties . . . as part of a noncriminal regulatory regime [under the juvenile court supervision order], . . . the Fifth Amendment privilege may not be invoked to resist compliance. . . . The court may properly request production and return of the child, and enforce that request through exercise of the contempt power, for reasons related entirely to the child's well-being."

With juvenile and family courts hearing more cases of child sexual abuse, and with potential life-saving and life-threatening decisions being made, the importance of sensitive and informed courts has become even more critical. Careful judicial decisions will produce respect for the judicial power to place children and jail those adults who would disobey. Elizabeth Morgan went to jail not only to protect her daughter, but also to expose a process that seemed to insist on remaining insensitive and uninformed. Even after her years in jail, even after Hilary was discovered, even before knowing the outcome of Hilary's case in New Zealand, Dr. Morgan wrote to her supporters not about her anger or pain, but about a legal system that had failed to learn and understand:

> Hilary first reported to me and others in 1985 that her father was sexually abusing her. She was 2½ years old. The abuse was subsequently confirmed by psychologists, psychiatrists and pediatricians. So was the abuse of her half-sister.
>
> From 1985 until the present, we have been asking the D.C. Courts to give Hilary a chance to live in safety, free from abuse. We asked the court for five things: (1) to view the videotapes of Hilary disclosing abuse; (2) to appoint a neutral expert trained in child sexual abuse to evaluate her; (3) to appoint a conscientious attorney to advocate vigorously for Hilary; (4) to consider the evidence of abuse of Hilary's half-sister, . . . (5) to rule that Hilary have no visits with the father . . . until the neutral evaluation had been completed.
>
> These things were continually denied. We did get a guardian ad litem to whom Hilary disclosed abuse. This guardian was empowered by Judge Dixon to stop the visitations if they endangered Hilary. Yet she delivered Hilary, protesting pitifully, to her father for unsupervised weekend visits, refusing to stop them even after Hilary reported resumed abuse.
>
> On February 23, 1990, Hilary was tracked down by [her father's] detectives in New Zealand. Without our even asking, Judge Mahan in New Zealand Family Court is routinely giving Hilary all five of the things we had requested for five years in the D.C. Courts.
>
> If a foreign court can grant a child interim protection and a hearing, why can't our U.S. Courts? I have been praying for many years that somewhere in this world there is a place where a child can scream for help and be heard and loved and protected. I am only sorry that for my child, if this place exists, it was not in the District of Columbia. It could be. It should be, everywhere in America.[38]

Resources

The National Resource Center on Child Sexual Abuse is a federally funded program created in 1988 for the enhancement of the knowledge and skills of professionals working with victims of child sexual abuse. With locations in both Alabama and Maryland, the Center offers information, training, technical assistance, and consultation to judges, lawyers, law enforcement officers, social and child protection workers, mental health professionals, medical personnel, educators, and others who work with child victims.

The National Resource Center on Child Sexual Abuse
c/o The National Children's Advocacy Center
Gary W. Porier, President
106 Lincoln Street
Huntsville, Alabama 35801
800/543-7006

The National Resource Center on Child Sexual Abuse
c/o The Chesapeake Institute
Jan Frohman, Project Director
11141 Georgia Avenue, Suite 310
Wheaton, Maryland 20902
800/543-7006

The National Child Abuse Hotline provides professional crisis counseling, general information, and referral services. It does not take reports of abuse for investigation or intervention. The Hotline is a part of Childhelp USA, a private, nonprofit organization. The Hotline operates throughout the United States, twenty-four hours every day.

The National Child Abuse Hotline
800/422-4453

The C. Henry Kempe National Center for the Prevention and Treatment of Child Abuse and Neglect is a multi-disciplinary clinical research center known internationally for diagnostic, treatment, and preventive programs. It provides specialized resources and programs and is available for training and contractual case consultation.

C. Henry Kempe National Center for the Prevention and Treatment of Child
    Abuse and Neglect
University of Colorado School of Medicine
1205 Oneida Street
Denver, Colorado 80220
303/321-3963

The Erikson Institute is a research center and graduate school specializing in child development with special emphasis on child abuse and child-adult communication.

The Erikson Institute
Loyola University of Chicago
25 West Chicago Avenue
Chicago, Illinois 60610
312/280-7302

The National Organization for Victim Assistance (NOVA) publishes a newsletter and offers support and training for victim advocacy related to child sexual abuse as well as victims of all ages of all crimes.

The National Organization for Victim Assistance
1757 Park Road, N.W.
Washington, D.C. 20010
202/393-NOVA

The National Association of Counsel for Children was established in 1977 to improve legal protection for children by providing training and information to child advocates from various professions. The Association includes lawyers, judges, nurses, pediatricians, psychiatrists, psychologists, teachers, social workers, police officers, private citizens, and sponsors training through conferences and a newsletter.

The National Association of Counsel for Children
Laura Freeman Michaels, Executive Director
1205 Oneida Street
Denver, Colorado 80220
303/321-3963

The National Court Appointed Special Advocate Association was established in 1982 to promote the development of programs utilizing trained volunteers as Court Appointed Special Advocates (CASA) for abused and neglected children in court. It has 286 programs operating in forty-five states, and encourages citizen volunteers to establish and expand local programs with training through the Association.

The National Court Appointed Special Advocate Association
Beth Waid, Executive Director
2722 Eastlake Avenue East, Suite 220
Seattle, Washington 98102
206/328-8588

The National Council of Juvenile and Family Court Judges provides advanced training for judges, lawyers, and other professionals who work with children in courts. Among its programs is the Child Sexual Abuse Training Program for judges and other professionals.

The National Council of Juvenile and Family Court Judges
P.O. Box 8970
Reno, Nevada 89507
702/784-4836

The National Judicial College offers specialized training for judges and other court professionals on a variety of subjects including child sexual abuse.

The National Judicial College
University of Nevada—Reno
Reno, Nevada 89557
800/25-JUDGE

The National Center for Missing and Exploited Children was established in 1984 to provide a variety of services to address issues related to both missing and exploited children. The Center works closely with numerous other nonprofit organizations attempting to locate missing children.

The National Center for Missing and Exploited Children
2101 Wilson Blvd., Suite 550
Arlington, Virginia 22201
800/843-5678

The National Center for the Prosecution of Child Abuse was founded by the American Prosecutors Research Institute in 1985 in response to dramatic increases in child abuse cases reported to law enforcement. Its mission is to promote the prosecution of child abusers and to provide advocacy on behalf of child victims. It provides training and technical assistance through workshops, regional conferences, on-site visits, and phone consultations. It also offers detailed information on case law, legislative initiatives, investigative practices, and trial strategies in its comprehensive manual, "Investigation and Prosecution of Child Abuse."

The National Center for the Prosecution of Child Abuse
Patricia A. Toth, Director
1033 North Fairfax Street, Suite 200
Alexandria, Virginia 22314
703/739-0321

The ABA Center on Children and the Law is a program of the American Bar Association Young Lawyers Division for the purpose of improving the quality of life for children through advancements in law and public policy. It conducts research and provides publications, information and training for legal and nonlegal professionals involved with children in the legal process.

The ABA Center on Children and the Law
Howard Davidson, Director
1800 M Street, N.W., Suite 300 South
Washington, D.C. 20036
202/331-2250

The National Resource Center on Child Abuse and Neglect offers information, training, consultation services, and program evaluation to improve the capability of public and private agencies to respond to child abuse and neglect. It provides a comprehensive core curriculum for child protection workers as well as specialized training in diverse subjects such as intervention with Native American families and mobilization of community resources.

The National Resource Center on Child Abuse and Neglect
American Association for Protecting Children
Patricia Schene, Director
9725 East Hampden Avenue
Denver, Colorado 80231
303/695-0811

The National Center on Child Abuse and Neglect is the federal agency responsible for awarding grants to states, public agencies, and nonprofit organizations for research, demonstration projects, and service programs designed to prevent, identify, and treat child abuse and neglect. Created by Congress in 1974, it is in the Department of Health and Human Services Administration for Children, Family, and Youth. It provides information on child abuse and neglect, and on the work of the National Center, through its Clearinghouse.

Clearinghouse on Child Abuse and Neglect
National Center on Child Abuse and Neglect
Box 1182
Washington, D.C. 20013
703-821-2086

The National Committee for Prevention of Child Abuse is a nonprofit, volunteer-based organization with chapters in all fifty states and the District of Columbia. The National Committee and its chapters provide education activities, research, and referral services for prevention of child abuse. Because different resources exist throughout the country, and because the nature and quality of medical, investigative, prosecutive, and rehabilitative services varies from one community to another, the local chapters often offer the best referral information.

The National Committee for Prevention of Child Abuse
332 S. Michigan Avenue, Suite 1600
Chicago, Illinois 60604-4357
312/663-3520

Alabama

North Alabama Chapter, NCPCA
Parents and Children Together
P.O. Box 119
Decatur, Alabama 35602
205/355-7252

Greater Alabama Chapter, NCPCA
Parents Anonymous of Alabama, Inc.
20 E. Jeff Davis Street
Montgomery, Alabama 36104
205/265-7838

Alaska

South Central Alaska Chapter, NCPCA
Center for Children and Parents
Anchorage Child Abuse Board, Inc.
3745 Community Park Loop, Suite 102
Anchorage, Alaska 99508-3466
907/276-4994

Fairbanks Chapter, NCPCA
Resource Center for Parents and Children
1401 Kellum Street
Fairbanks, Alaska 99701
907/456-2866

Arkansas

Arkansas Committee for Prevention of Child Abuse
2915 Kavanaugh Boulevard, Box 379
Little Rock, Arkansas 72205
501/371-2651

Arizona

Arizona Committee for Prevention of Child Abuse
2701 N. 16th Street, Suite 316
Phoenix, Arizona 85006
602/248-0428

California

California Consortium for the Prevention of Child Abuse
McLaren Hall
4024 N. Durfee Avenue
El Monte, California 91732
818/575-4362

California Consortium for the Prevention of Child Abuse
1401 Third Street, #13
Sacramento, California 95814
916/448-9135

Colorado

Colorado Child Protection Council
c/o American Humane Association
9725 East Hampton Avenue
Denver, Colorado 80231
303/695-0811

Connecticut

Collaboration for Connecticut's Children
60 Lorraine Street
Hartford, Connecticut 06105
203/233-4437

District of Columbia

Family Stress Services of the District of Columbia
1400 20th Street, N.W.
Washington, D.C. 20036
202/965-1900

Delaware

Parents Anonymous of Delaware, Inc.
124 D Senatorial Drive
Greenville Place
Wilmington, Delaware 19807
302/654-1102

Florida

Florida Committee for Prevention of Child Abuse
1928 Shawnee Trail
Lakeland, Florida 33803
813/683-6504

Georgia

Georgia Council on Child Abuse, Inc.
1401 Peachtree Street, N.E., Suite 140
Atlanta, Georgia 30312
404/870-6565

Hawaii

Prevent Child Abuse Hawaii
P.O. Box 2605
Honolulu, Hawaii 96803
808/951-0200

Idaho

Idaho Network for Children
P.O. Box 6032
Boise, Idaho 83707
208/322-4780

Illinois

Champaign County for Prevention of Child Abuse
2006 Winchester Drive
Champaign, Illinois 61821
217/337-1515

Quad Cities Chapter, NCPCA
Council on Children at Risk
525 16th Street
Moline, Illinois 61265
309/764-7017

Chicago Council, NCPCA
332 S. Michigan Avenue, #1600
Chicago, Illinois 60604
312/663-3520

Indiana

Indiana Committee for Prevention of Child Abuse
310 N. Alabama, Suite 300
Indianapolis, Indiana 46204
317/634-9282

Iowa

Iowa Committee for Prevention of Child Abuse
Stat Team, Inc.
City View Plaza
1200 University
Des Moines, Iowa 50317
515/281-6327

Kansas

Kansas Committee for Prevention of Child Abuse
715 W. 10th Street
Topeka, Kansas 66612
913/354-7738

Kentucky

Kentucky Council on Child Abuse
240 Plaza Drive
Lexington, Kentucky 40503
606/276-1299

Louisiana

Louisiana Council on Child Abuse, Inc.
333 Laurel Street, Suite 875
Baton Rouge, Louisiana 70801
504/346-0222

Maine

York County Chapter, NCPCA
York County Child Abuse and Neglect Council, Inc.
31 Beach Street
Saco, Maine 04072
207/282-6191

Franklin County Main Chapter, NCPCA
Franklin County Children's Task Force
32 Main Street
Farmington, Maine 04938
207/778-6960

Greater Maine Chapter, NCPCA
Maine Association of CAN Councils
P.O. Box 912
Brunswick, Maine 04011
207/874-1120

Maryland

People Against Child Abuse, Inc.
3 Church Circle
Annapolis, Maryland 21401
301/269-7816

Massachusetts

Massachusetts Committee for Children and Youth
14 Beacon Street, #706
Boston, Massachusetts 02108
617/742-8555

Michigan

Michigan Committee for Prevention of Child Abuse
32715 Dorsey
Westland, Michigan 48185
313/326-1545

Minnesota

Minnesota Committee for Prevention of Child Abuse
1934 University Avenue West
St. Paul, Minnesota 55104
612/641-1568

Missouri

Missouri Committee for Prevention of Child Abuse
1205 West 76th Street
Kansas City, Missouri 64114
816/363-2538

Mississippi

Greater Jackson Chapter, NCPCA
Exchange Club Parent/Child Center
2906 N. State, Suite 200
Jackson, Mississippi 39216
601/366-0025

Montana

Montana Committee for Prevention of Child Abuse
P.O. Box 246
Kalispell, Montana 59903
406/756-1414

Nebraska

Nebraska Committee for Prevention of Child Abuse
The Atrium, Suite 500
Lincoln, Nebraska 68502
402/477-3746

Nevada

Northern Nevada Chapter, NCPCA
Child Abuse and Neglect Task Force of Northern Nevada
415 Vagabond
Reno, Nevada 89506
702/358-4150

Southern Nevada Chapter, NCPCA
We Can, Inc.
3441 W. Sahara, Suite C-3
Las Vegas, Nevada 89102
702/368-1533

New Hampshire

New Hampshire Task Force on Child Abuse and Neglect
P.O. Box 607
Concord, New Hampshire 03301
603/225-5441

New Jersey

New Jersey Committee for Prevention of Child Abuse
35 Halsey, 2nd floor
Newark, New Jerscy 07102
201/643-3710

New Mexico

New Mexico Committee for Prevention of Child Abuse
P.O. Box 7790
Albuquerque, New Mexico 87194
505/888-4260

New York

New York State Federation on Child Abuse and Neglect
134 S. Swan Street
Albany, New York 12210
518/445-1273

North Carolina

North Carolina Committee for Prevention of Child Abuse
P.O. Box 843
Garner, North Carolina 27529
919/779-7515

North Dakota

North Dakota Committee for Prevention of Child Abuse
P.O. Box 1912
Bismarck, North Dakota 58502
701/255-3692

Ohio

League Against Child Abuse
615 Copeland Mill Road, Suite 1H
Westerville, Ohio 43081
614/899-4710

Oklahoma

Oklahoma Committee for Prevention of Child Abuse
940 N.E. 13th, Room 4N414
Oklahoma City, Oklahoma 73103
405/272-0688

Oregon

Oregon Committee for Prevention of Child Abuse
1912 S.W. Sixth Avenue, Room 120
Portland, Oregon 97201
503/725-4040

Pennsylvania

Lancaster County Chapter, NCPCA
237 W. Lemon Street
Lancaster, Pennsylvania 17603
717/399-3270

Greater Philadelphia Chapter, NCPCA
117 S. 17th Street, Suite 608
Philadelphia, Pennsylvania 19103
215/864-1080

Western Pennsylvania Committee for Prevention of Child Abuse
717 Liberty Avenue, Suite 1405
Pittsburgh, Pennsylvania 15222
412/391-2000

Rhode Island

Rhode Island Committee for Prevention of Child Abuse
500 Prospect Street
Pawtucket, Rhode Island 02860
401/521-0083

South Carolina

Midlands Chapter, NCPCA
Council on Child Abuse and Neglect
1800 Main Street, Suite 3A
Columbia, South Carolina 29201
803/733-5430

Piedmont Chapter, NCPCA
301 University Ridge, Suite 5100
Greenville, South Carolina 29601
803/240-8590

Low Country, South Carolina Chapter, NCPCA
Carolina Youth Development Center
5055 Lackawanna Boulevard
North Charleston, South Carolina 29406-4522
803/747-1339

South Dakota

Rapid City Area Child Protection Council
P.O. Box 2440
Rapid City, South Dakota 57701
605/394-2434

Tennessee

Tennessee Committee for Prevention of Child Abuse
30 White Bridge Road
Nashville, Tennessee 37205
615/356-0621/0774

Texas

El Paso Chapter, NCPCA
5837 Burning Tree
El Paso, Texas 79912
915/581-5862

Greater Houston Chapter, NCPCA
4151 S.W. Freeway, Suite 435
Houston, Texas 77027
713/621-6446

Texas Coalition for the Prevention of Child Abuse
11940 Jollyville Road, Suite 395 N
Austin, Texas 78759
512/250-8438

Laredo Chapter, NCPCA
Stop Child Abuse and Neglect, Inc.
6202 McPheeson Road, Suite 11
Laredo, Texas 78041
512/724-3177

South Plains Chapter, NCPCA
P.O. Box 10335
Lubbock, Texas 79408
806/747-2273

San Antonio Chapter, NCPCA
San Antonio CARES, Child Abuse Resources and Educational Resources
1411 N. Main Street
San Antonio, Texas 78212
512/271-3902

Utah

Utah Committee for Prevention of Child Abuse
40 E. South Temple, #395
Salt Lake City, Utah 84111
801/532-3404

Virginia

SCAN—Stop Child Abuse Now
2222 W. Main Street
Richmond, Virginia 23220
804/359-0014

Washington

Washington Association of Child Abuse Councils
P.O. Box 9602
Seattle, Washington 98109
206/624-4307

West Virginia

West Virginia Committee for Prevention of Child Abuse
P.O. Box 1949
Charleston, West Virginia 35237
304/345-6676

Wisconsin

Wisconsin Committee for Prevention and Treatment of Child Abuse and
    Neglect, Inc.
1045 E. Dayton Street, Room 202D
Madison, Wisconsin 53703
608/256-3374

Wyoming

Wyoming Committee for Prevention of Child Abuse
752 Ranger Drive
Cheyenne, Wyoming 82003
307/635-6210

Notes

Preface

1. J. Anouilh, *Antigone*, in *Contemporary Drama: Eleven Plays*, ed. E. B. Watson and B. Pressay (New York: Scribner's, 1956), pp. 125–26.

1. Children in Jeopardy

1. Statistics are available from the American Humane Association, 5351 South Roslyn Street, Englewood, Colo. 80111.

2. "Child Sexual Abuse," *Los Angeles Times Poll*, no. 98 (July 1985).

3. See D. E. H. Russell, "The Incidence and Prevalence of Intrafamilial and Extrafamilial Sexual Abuse of Female Children," *Child Abuse and Neglect* 7 (1983): 133–46.

4. See G. E. Wyatt, "The Sexual Abuse of Afro-American and White American Women in Childhood," *Child Abuse and Neglect* 7 (1985): 507–19.

5. See G. E. Wyatt and S. D. Peters, "Issues in the Definition of Child Sexual Abuse in Prevalence Research," pp. 231–40, and "Methodological Considerations in Research on the Prevalence of Child Sexual Abuse," pp. 241–51. Both articles appear in *Child Abuse and Neglect* 10 (1986).

6. The National Center on Child Abuse and Neglect, *Child Sexual Abuse: Incest, Assault, and Sexual Exploitation* (Washington, D.C.: U.S. Department of Health and Human Services, 1979).

7. A. W. Burgess et al., *Sexual Assault of Children and Adolescents* (Lexington, Mass.: Lexington Books, 1978), p. xi.

8. Wyatt, "The Sexual Abuse of Afro-American and White American Women in Childhood," p. 510.

9. Ibid., p. 511.

10. J. Crewdson and L. Emmerman, "The Culprit behind Sexual Child Abuse," *Chicago Tribune*, September 23, 1984, p. 18. See also D. Finkelhor, ed., *Child Sexual Abuse: New Theory and Research* (New York: Free Press, 1984), p. 47.

11. Interview with Donald Bross, 1987.

12. See R. C. Summit, "The Child Sexual Abuse Accommodation Syndrome," *Child Abuse and Neglect* 7 (1983): 177–93.

13. Ibid., pp. 178–79.

14. D. Whitcomb, E. R. Shapiro, and L. D. Stellwagen, *When the Victim Is a Child* (Washington, D.C.: National Institute of Justice, 1985), p. 1.

15. Information is available from the American Humane Association, the Universities of Rhode Island and New Hampshire, and the Westat Corporation, 1650 Research Boulevard, Rockville, Md.

16. V. De Francis, *Protecting the Child Victim of Sex Crimes* (Denver: American Humane Association, 1969), pp. 224–25.

17. S. Sgroi, "Introduction: A National Needs Assessment for Protecting Child Victims of Sexual Assault," in *Sexual Assault of Children and Adolescents,* p. xix.

18. F. Rush, *The Best Kept Secret: Sexual Abuse of Children* (New York: McGraw-Hill, 1980), p. 39.

19. As quoted in ibid., p. 38.

20. As quoted in ibid., p. 39.

21. Ibid., pp. 95–96.

22. As quoted in S. Brownmiller, *Against Our Will* (New York: Simon and Schuster, 1975), pp. 276–77.

23. As quoted in N. Gager and E. Schurr, *Sexual Assault: Confronting Rape in America* (New York: Gosset and Dunlap, 1976), p. 45.

24. See, for example, *Los Angeles Times Poll*, American Humane Association Child Abuse Statistics.

25. A. N. Groth, *Men Who Rape: The Psychology of the Offender* (New York: Plenus Press, 1979).

26. See P. E. Dietz, *Child Molesters: A Behavioral Analysis for Law Enforcement Officers Investigating Cases of Child Sexual Exploitation* (Washington, D.C.: National Center for Missing and Exploited Children, 1986).

27. See, for example, *Los Angeles Times Poll*, American Humane Association Child Abuse Statistics.

28. P. Eberle and S. Eberle, *The Politics of Child Abuse* (Seacaucus, N.J.: Lyle Stuart, 1986), p. 102.

29. Ibid., pp. 145–46.

30. Recently the Kentucky Supreme Court ruled that a woman who failed to take any steps to prevent her husband from raping her daughter, even though the child had told her of previous assaults, could not be convicted of complicity to rape. However, two justices dissented from the decision, and it may be the first case to consider whether criminal liability may result from such inaction. Nonetheless, such inaction certainly could result in loss of custody (*Knox v. Commonwealth*, Ky., 735 S.W.2d 711 (1987)). The Wisconsin Supreme Court recently held that the mother of two sexually abused children could be held criminally liable under Wisconsin's "Abuse of Children" law, for failing to do anything to protect them from their father (her husband). The children had reported that the father orally and anally sodomized the seven-year-old boy and eight-year-old girl. Despite their repeated reports to her, the mother not only failed to do anything about it, but continued to leave the chil-

dren alone with their father (*State v. Williquette*, 129 Wis. 2d 239, 385 N.W. 2d 145 [1986]).

31. See C. H. Kempe, "The Battered Child Syndrome," *Journal of the American Medical Association* 181 (1962): 17–24.

32. B. J. Nelson, *Making an Issue of Child Abuse: Political Agenda Setting for Social Problems* (Chicago: University of Chicago Press, 1984), p. 51.

33. Statistics are available from the Child Welfare League of America, 440 First Street, N.W., Washington, D.C. 20001.

34. W. L. Bennett and M. S. Feldman, *Reconstructing Reality in the Courtroom* (New Brunswick, N.J.: Rutgers University Press, 1981), pp. 3–4.

35. As quoted in J. Crewdson and L. Emmerman, "Children as Witnesses: Double Jeopardy?" *Chicago Tribune*, December 26, 1984, p. 1.

36. As quoted in Gager and Schurr, *Sexual Assault*, p. 129.

37. For a more detailed description of these organizations, see J. Crewdson, *By Silence Betrayed* (Boston: Little, Brown, 1988).

38. Eberle and Eberle, *The Politics of Child Abuse*, pp. 282, 141, 143. The Eberles had presented themselves as disinterested journalists but were later exposed for "having a significant interest in publication of child pornography." Donald Bross, "Law and the Abuse of Children," *Currents in Modern Thought* (June 1990): 484, citing "The Real Abusers," *National District Attorneys Association Bulletin* (March/April 1988): 1–2. In fact, the Eberles edited and contributed to *Finger*, a magazine featuring photographs and stories of children having sex with other children and adults. They also were involved in the publication of the *L. A. Star*, a tabloid devoted to advertisements for sexually related products and services. "Child Sexual Abuse," *Michigan Law Review* (May 1990): 709.

39. A. B. Russell and C. M. Trainor, *Trends in Child Abuse and Neglect: A National Perspective* (Denver: Children's Division, American Humane Association, 1984), p. 41.

40. Metropolitan Court Judges Committee, *Deprived Children: A Judicial Response* (Reno: National Council of Juvenile and Family Court Judges, 1986), pp. 13–14.

41. L. G. Arthur, "Child Sexual Abuse: Improving the System's Response," *Juvenile and Family Court Journal* 37, 2 (1986): 27.

2. Yesterday and Today

1. G. S. Goodman, "Children's Testimony in Historical Perspective," *Journal of Social Issues* 40, 2 (1984): 10.

2. L. Berliner and M. K. Barbieri, "The Testimony of the Child Victim of Sexual Assault," *Journal of Social Issues* 40, 2 (1984): 136.

3. L. M. Friedman, *A History of American Law* (New York: Simon and Schuster, 1985), pp. 24–25.

4. Ibid., p. 25.

5. Ibid., p. 43.

6. Sections 8 and 11 of the 1776 Constitution of Virginia provided for trials in "criminal prosecutions" and "controversies respecting property." The Sixth and Seventh Amendments to the Constitution of the United States provided for trials in all "criminal prosecutions" and "suits at common law, where the value in controversy shall exceed twenty dollars." See L. E. Moore, *The Jury* (Cincinnati: W. H. Anderson, 1973), pp. 101–2, 106; and R. J. Simon, ed., *The Jury System in America* (Beverly Hills: Sage Publications, 1975), pp. 31–32.

7. K. T. Erikson, *Wayward Puritans* (New York: Wiley, 1966), p. 4.

8. A. M. Platt, *The Child Savers* (Chicago: University of Chicago Press, 1969; 2d ed., 1977), p. 10.

9. S. L. Schlossman, *Love and the American Delinquent* (Chicago: University of Chicago Press, 1977), p. 57.

10. Ibid., p. 190.

11. Platt, *The Child Savers*, p. 4.

12. Ibid., p. 141.

13. Ibid., pp. 141–42.

14. Schlossman, *Love and the American Delinquent*, pp. 58–59.

15. For example, see the Order of the Wisconsin Circuit Court, Juvenile Division for Milwaukee County, August 27, 1982, Judge Leander J. Foley, Jr., presiding.

16. Schlossman, *Love and the American Delinquent*, p. 189.

17. S. A. Levitan and R. S. Belous, *What's Happening to the American Family?* (Baltimore: Johns Hopkins University Press, 1981), p. 12; see also "Breaking the Ties that Bind," *Insight* (*Washington Times*, October 13, 1986), p. 8.

18. L. J. Weitzman, *The Divorce Revolution* (New York: Free Press, 1985), pp. xvii, 352.

19. Ibid., p. xviii.

20. Ibid., p. 368.

21. *Kramer vs. Kramer*, from the novel by Avery Corman; written for screen by Robert Benton (Columbia Pictures, 1979).

22. A. J. Cherlin, *Marriage, Divorce, Remarriage* (Cambridge: Harvard University Press, 1981), p. 50.

23. "Overextending the Family," *Newsweek*, November 24, 1986, p. 76. According to a recent study, 75 percent of TV's female characters in 1987 worked outside the home, nearly 20 points higher than the real-life percentage. "Networking Women," *Newsweek*, March 13, 1989, p. 50. The new family configurations also may hold immediate dangers that researchers are just beginning to understand. According to one recent study, an American child "living with one or more substitute parents in 1976 was approximately 100 times more likely to be fatally abused than a same-age child living with genetic parents," regardless of poverty, family size, or personalities of the abusers. "How the Mind Was Designed," *Newsweek*, March 13, 1989, p. 57.

24. *Milwaukee Journal,* March 22, 1987. See also "They Hurt, They Cry," an excellent series of articles on child abuse by Mary Zahn in the *Milwaukee Sentinel,* March 30 to April 4, 1987. Ms. Zahn also authored a comprehensive series on teen pregnancy and its relation to abuse, "When the Bough Breaks," *The Milwaukee Sentinel,* January 1 to January 6, 1990. The terrible trend of child abuse was updated in another excellent series by Marilyn Marchione, "Out of Control: The Tragedy of Child Abuse," *The Milwaukee Journal,* May 6 to May 9, 1990.

25. Select Committee on Children, Youth, and Families, United States House of Representatives, March 1987.

26. See, for example, Wis. Stat. Sec. 972.11(2).

27. *People v. Barnes,* 721 P. 2d 110, 117–20 (Cal. 1986). Courts have applied the "rape shield" rule to cases of child sexual abuse. See, for example, *State v. Oliver,* 760 P.2d 1071 (Ariz. 1988).

28. *Marr v. State,* 494 So. 2d 1139, 1142 (Fla. 1986).

29. "The MacNeil/Lehrer Report," December 22, 1978; see *Battered Women: Issues of Public Policy* (Washington, D.C.: United States Commission on Civil Rights, 1978).

30. By 1987, forty-eight states provided victim compensation, forty-three states required that victims be kept informed of the status of their cases, and more than five thousand victim's rights groups had been established. See "Advocating Victims' Right to Justice," *Insight,* August 24, 1987, p. 50.

31. Wis. Stats. Sec. 950.01.

32. Friedman, *A History of American Law,* p. 24.

33. Ibid., p. 22.

34. Ibid., p. 24.

35. For an excellent and concise discussion of the rationale for criminal prosecution, even in cases of intrafamilial abuse, and a clear refutation of the false assumptions militating against prosecution, see Peters, Dinsmore, and Toth, "Why Prosecute Child Abuse?" 34 *S.D. Law Rev.* 649 (1989). In some cases, both juvenile and criminal court prosecutions may be appropriate. Double jeopardy does not bar a criminal court prosecution even when evidence failed to prove abuse in an earlier juvenile prosecution. *State v. Cleveland,* 794 P.2d 546 (Wash. App. 1990); *People v. Gates,* Michigan Supreme Court, March 5, 1990.

36. Prosecutors and others also may assume all too quickly that court will be traumatic for all children. While testifying may be a devastating experience for some children and a horrible experience for all who are treated insensitively, it can also be an empowering legal step with therapeutic value. See Berliner and Barbieri, "The Testimony of the Child Victim of Sexual Assault," 40 *J. Soc. Issues* 125 (1984); Tedesco and Schnell, "Children's Reactions to Sex Abuse Investigation and Litigation," 11 *Child Abuse and Neglect* 267 (1987); Runyan, Everson, Edelsohn, Hunter, and Coulter, "Impact of Legal Intervention on Sexually Abused Children," 113 *J. Pediatrics* 647 (1988); Goodman, Pyle, Jones, England, Port, Rudy, and Prado, "Emotional Effects of Criminal Court Testimony on Child Sexual Assault Victims" (unpublished, 1989).

3. Children's Reality

1. P. Ariès, *Centuries of Childhood: A Social History of Family Life* (New York: Jonathan Cape, 1962).

2. See L. DeMause, "The Evolution of Childhood," in his *The History of Childhood* (New York: Psychohistory Press, 1974), p. 1.

3. Ibid., p. 51.

4. Ibid., p. 25.

5. As quoted in ibid., p. 26.

6. Ibid., pp. 28, 29.

7. Ibid., p. 33.

8. As quoted in ibid., p. 31.

9. Ibid., p. 42.

10. Ibid., p. 11.

11. Ibid., pp. 43, 45; see also p. 70 n. 239 for further sources.

12. On both homosexual abuse and Petronius's account, see ibid., pp. 44–45.

13. J. E. Illick, "Anglo-American Child Rearing," in *The History of Childhood*, pp. 324–25.

14. As quoted in M. M. McLaughlin, "Survivors and Surrogates," in *The History of Childhood*, p. 129.

15. Rush, *The Best Kept Secret*, p. 37.

16. DeMause, "The Evolution of Childhood," pp. 32–33.

17. As quoted in ibid., p. 42.

18. As quoted in McLaughlin, "Survivors and Surrogates," p. 131.

19. Ibid.

20. Rush, *The Best Kept Secret*, pp. 32–33.

21. McLaughlin, "Survivors and Surrogates," p. 132.

22. As quoted in DeMause, "The Evolution of Childhood," p. 41.

23. See N. Postman, *The Disappearance of Childhood* (New York: Delacorte Press, 1982).

24. M. J. Tucker, "The Child as Beginning and End," in *The History of Childhood*, p. 233.

25. E. W. Marvick, "Nature versus Nurture," in *The History of Childhood*, p. 291.

26. Tucker, "The Child as Beginning and End," p. 244.

27. Ibid., p. 245.

28. DeMause, "The Evolution of Childhood," p. 41.

29. As quoted in ibid., pp. 11–12.

30. Ibid., p. 31.

31. Tucker, "The Child as Beginning and End," p. 252; DeMause, "The Evolution of Childhood," p. 14.

32. Marvick, "Nature versus Nurture," p. 262. Inhibition of their children's sexuality was not essential in all cases, however. Because of his position as the first legitimate heir to his father's throne, one-year-old Louis XIV was taught to cherish his sexuality by French courtiers who instructed him to present his penis rather than his hand to be kissed. The majority of children were not burdened with having to preserve a dynasty, however (ibid.).

33. DeMause, "The Evolution of Childhood," p. 48; Rush, *The Best Kept Secret.*

34. Tucker, "The Child as Beginning and End," p. 234; Illick, "Anglo-American Child Rearing," p. 331.

35. DeMause, "The Evolution of Childhood," p. 52; see also J. F. Walzer, "A Period of Ambivalence," in *The History of Childhood,* pp. 352–53.

36. Walzer, "A Period of Ambivalence," p. 358.

37. Ibid., p. 371.

38. Ibid., pp. 368, 373.

39. Ibid., p. 369.

40. Ibid., p. 369.

41. Ibid., p. 370.

42. DeMause, "The Evolution of Childhood," p. 48.

43. P. Robertson, "The Home as a Nest," in *The History of Childhood,* p. 407.

44. DeMause, "The Evolution of Childhood," p. 52.

45. Robertson, "The Home as a Nest," p. 416.

46. DeMause, "The Evolution of Childhood," p. 49.

47. Rush, *The Best Kept Secret,* p. 62.

48. Ibid., pp. 61, 63.

49. Ibid., pp. 62, 64.

50. As quoted in ibid., p. 61.

51. Postman, *The Disappearance of Childhood,* pp. 62–63.

52. DeMause, "The Evolution of Childhood," p. 52.

53. R. Farson, *Birthrights* (New York: Macmillan, 1974), p. 1.

54. G. S. Goodman, M. Golding, and M. M. Haith, "Jurors' Reactions to Child Witnesses," *Journal of Social Issues* 40, 2 (1984): 141.

55. See A. D. Yarmey and H. P. T. Jones, "Is the Psychology of Eyewitness Identification a Matter of Common Sense?" in *Evaluating Witness Evidence,* ed. S. M. Lloyd and B. R. Clifford (New York: Wiley, 1983).

56. Study cited in J. Garbarino and F. N. Stott, "Viewing the World through the Eyes of a Child: Children as Sources of Information for Adults" (Report for the Erikson Institute for Advanced Study in Child Development, 1986), pp. 10–11.

57. See studies cited in Goodman, Golding, and Haith, "Jurors' Reactions to Child Witnesses," pp. 144–45.

58. See E. Erikson, *Childhood and Society* (New York: Norton, 1963).

59. See, for example, *Los Angeles Times Poll* (see chap. 1, note 2).

60. See L. Kohlberg, "Moral Stages and Moralization: The Cognitive-Developmental Approach," in *Moral Development and Behavior: Theory, Research, and Social Issues* (New York: Holt, Rinehart and Winston, 1976).

61. Thomas Achenbach and Craig Edelbrock, "The Child Behavior Checklist," 1988; available from the Department of Psychiatry, University of Vermont, 1 S. Prospect St., Burlington, VT 05405, Attn: Dr. Thomas Achenbach's staff.

62. Summit, "The Child Sexual Abuse Accommodation Syndrome," p. 181.

63. Berliner and Barbieri, "The Testimony of the Child Victim," p. 127. In the context of divorce, custody, and visitation disputes, further research and analysis should be considered. See Chapter 7.

64. Cited in J. Crewdson and L. Emmerman, "In Sex-Abuse Cases, Child's Word Is Good," *Chicago Tribune*, December 2, 1984, p. 1.

65. Cited in ibid., pp. 1, 4.

66. M. D. Emerson and B. W. Boat, "Lying about Sexual Abuse: In the Eye of the Beholder?" (Paper presented at the Fourth National Conference on Sexual Victimization of Children, New Orleans, May 1986).

67. D. Jones and M. McQuiston, *Interviewing the Sexually Abused Child*, Kempe Center Series 6 (Denver, 1985).

68. Ibid., p. 30.

69. Ibid., p. 31.

70. Ibid.

71. E. F. Loftus and G. M. Davies, "Distortions in the Memory of Children," *Journal of Social Issues* 40, 2 (1984): 63.

72. See M. K. Johnson, M. A. Foley, and V. Neisser, "The Control of Information Pickup in Selective Looking," in *Perception and Its Development*, ed. A. D. Pick (Hillsdale, N.J.: Erlbaum, 1979).

73. G. S. Goodman, "The Child Witness: Conclusions and Future Directions for Research and Legal Practice," *Journal of Social Issues* 40, 2 (1984): 157–75.

74. See, for example, Johnson and Foley; and Loftus and Davies, "Distortions in the Memory of Children."

75. Loftus and Davies, "Distortions in the Memory of Children," p. 62.

76. Johnson and Foley, p. 45.

77. A. Skolnick, "The Limits of Childhood: Conceptions of Child Development and Social Context," *Law and Contemporary Problems* 39 (1975): 37.

78. Ibid., pp. 51, 56.

79. R. Gelman, "Preschool Thought," *American Psychologist* 34, 10 (1979): 902–3.

80. Goodman, "The Child Witness," p. 159. Goodman's research has continued to provide excellent studies. See "Children's Justice Act Grantees Meeting/November 8–9, 1989, Summary Report," National Center on Child Abuse and Neglect (1990), pp. 28–31; see also James Garbarino, Frances M. Stott et al., *What Children Can Tell Us: Eliciting, Interpreting, and Evaluating Information from Children* (San Francisco: Jossey-Bass, 1989).

81. Johnson and Foley, p. 45.

82. Skolnick, "The Limits of Childhood," p. 53.

83. See M. Montessori, *Spontaneous Activity in Education* (New York: Schocken Books, 1965).

84. Berliner and Barbieri, "The Testimony of the Child Victim," p. 132.

85. Cited in Garbarino and Stott, "Through the Eyes of a Child," p. 20.

86. See C. Chomsky, *The Acquisition of Syntax in Children from Five to Ten*, Research Monograph no. 57 (Cambridge, Mass.: MIT Press, 1969).

87. S. I. Hayakawa, "The Use and Misuse of Language," in *Science and Human Affairs*, ed. R. E. Farson (Palo Alto, Calif.: Science and Behavior Books, 1965), p. 102.

88. Skolnick, "The Limits of Childhood," p. 39.

4. There Ought to Be a Book

1. *Chicago Tribune*, 7 March 1983, 1; 3 February 1984, 15; 24 March 1984, 3; 1 April 1984, 1; 7 April 1984, 4; 10 April 1984, 9; 21 April 1984, 4; 8 May 1984, 1; 23 May 1984, 4; 11 July 1984, 7; 13 November 1984, 11; 10 January 1985, 18; 17 January 1985, 11; 18 January 1985, 18; 23 January 1985, 6; 25 January 1985, 1; 26 January 1985, 3; 17 May 1985, 1; 12 June 1985, 3; 13 June 1985, 3; 14 June 1985, 8; 15 June 1985, 4; 10 January 1986, 18; 18 January 1986, 3; 21 December 1986, 30; 21 April 1987, 12; 14 July 1987, 13; 25 February 1988, 19.

2. *Chicago Tribune*, 27 August 1984, 1; 28 August 1984, 6; 29 August 1984, 13; 30 August 1984, 1; 31 August 1984, 5; 1 September 1984, 3; 2 September 1984, 3; 6 September 1984, 22; 11 September 1984, 10; 18 September 1984, 3; 19 September 1984, 17; 20 September 1984, 1; 23 September 1984, 18; 27 September 1984, 22; 16 October 1984, 1; 17 October 1984, 4; 18 October 1984, 17; 19 October 1984, 1; 21 October 1984, 5; 22 October 1984, 8; 26 October 1984, 3; 2 November 1984, 3; 4 November 1984, 3; 15 November 1984, 13; 16 November 1984, 2; 21 November 1984, 3; 23 November 1984, 4; 28 November 1984, 4; 29 November 1984, 3; 16 December 1984, 1; 21 December 1984, 3; 25 December 1984, 5; 5 January 1985, 4; 19 January 1985, 4; 13 February 1985, 1; 14 February 1985, 4; 15 February 1985, 6; 13 March 1985, 10; 17 May 1985, 3; 12 June 1985, 3; 14 June 1985, 8; 26 July 1985, 10; 3 August 1985, 3; 8 August 1985, 5; 9 August 1985, 6; 10 August 1985, 2; 13 August 1985, 4; 14 August 1985, 10; 15 August 1985, 10; 16 August 1985, 18; 20 August 1985, 3; 21 August 1985, 8; 11 October 1985, 13.

3. J. Crewdson, *By Silence Betrayed: Sexual Abuse of Children in America* (Boston: Little, Brown, 1988), p. 18.

4. J. Hollingsworth, *Unspeakable Acts* (New York: Congdon and Weed, 1986), pp. 233, 237–38.

5. For a discussion understandable to laypersons, see B. Woodling and A. Heger, "The Use of the Colposcope in the Diagnosis of Sexual Abuse in the Pediatric Age Group," *Child Abuse and Neglect* 10 (1986): 111–14. Woodling and Heger described the procedure: "Colposcopy is a modality of magnified visual inspection which employs a binocular system with 5X to 30X magnification potential. It is primarily used

to study cervical pathology and the diagnosis of early carcinoma in situ. More recently, it has been introduced as a tool for clarifying the diagnosis of sexual abuse" (p. 112).

6. Hollingsworth, *Unspeakable Acts*, p. 231.

7. Ibid., p. 187.

8. David W. Lloyd, "Ritual Child Abuse: Understanding the Controversies," National Resource Center on Child Sexual Abuse (1990). See also Kenneth V. Lanning, "Satanic, Occult, Ritualistic Crime: A Law Enforcement Perspective" and Kathleen Coulborn Faller, "Sexual Abuse of Children in Cults: A Clinical Perspective," *RoundTable Magazine* (a publication of the National Resource Center on Child Sexual Abuse) 2, 2 (Spring 1990): 9–13.

5. The Trial

1. See Moore, *The Jury*, pp. 97–102; and Simon, *The Jury System*, pp. 24–32; as well as Simon's *The Jury: Its Role in American Society* (Lexington, Mass.: Heath, 1980), pp. 5–8; and *Duncan v. Louisiana*, 391 U.S. 145, 151–53 (1968). See also Alexander Hamilton, *The Federalist*, no. 83 (National Home Library Foundation, 1937), pp. 542–43, cited in Moore, p. 105. Hamilton wrote, "The friends and adversaries of the plan of the convention, if they agree in nothing else, concur at least in the value they set upon the trial by jury."

2. See Moore, *The Jury*, pp. 157–82.

3. Alexis de Tocqueville, "Trial by Jury in the United States Considered as a Political Institution," in *Democracy in America*, ed. Phillips Bradley (New York: Knopf, 1966), p. 297, cited in Simon, *The Jury*, p. 6.

4. *In Re Winship*, 397 U.S. 358, 361–64 (1970); see also *McCormick on Evidence*, 3d ed. (St. Paul: West Publishing, 1984), pp. 962–64.

5. *Winship*, p. 372.

6. In *Johnson v. Louisiana*, 400 U.S. 356 (1971), the United States Supreme Court explained that a unanimous jury in a criminal case is not required by the Constitution. However, almost all states do require unanimous verdicts in criminal cases.

7. J. Frank, *Courts on Trial* (Princeton: Princeton University Press, 1949), pp. 80–81.

8. "Several courts have followed the prevailing trend of admitting evidence of a defendant's commission of a related but uncharged crime in child molestation cases. While evidence of this sort is generally inadmissible, such an independent incident has been allowed into evidence to show a common scheme or course of conduct" ("Child Molestation Admissibility and Competency," *Journal of Juvenile Law* 8 [1984]: 450). See also *Luce v. United States*, 469 U.S. 38 (1984). Recent decisions also have allowed evidence of uncharged conduct. See *State v. Friedrich*, 135 Wis. 2d 1 (1987); *Pounds v. United States*, 529 A.2d 791 (D.C. App. 1987); *Getz v. State*, Del. Supr., 538 A.2d 726 (1988); *State v. Parker*, 545 A.2d 512 (Vt. 1988); *State v. Champagne*, 422 N.W. 2d 840 (S.D. 1988); *People v. Porterfield*, 772 P.2d 638 (O. App. 1988); *Adrian v. People*, 770 P.2d 1243 (Colo. 1989); *State v. Shamsid-Deen*, 379 S.E.2d 842 (N.C. 1989).

9. *Dutton v. Evans*, 400 U.S. 74, 89 (1970).

10. Goodman, "The Child Witness," pp. 12–13.

11. *Wheeler v. United States*, 159 U.S. 523, 524–26 (1895).

12. See Whitcomb, Shapiro, and Stellwagen, *When the Victim Is a Child*.

13. Ibid., p. 31, quoting Professor Irving Prager, University of La Verne College of Law, as cited in Mary Ann Galante's "New War on Child Abuse," *National Law Journal*, June 25, 1984, p. 26.

14. Whitcomb, Shapiro, and Stellwagen, *When the Victim Is a Child*, p. 32.

15. E.g., in *State v. Williams*, 729 S.W. 2d 197 (Mo.banc 1987), the Missouri Supreme Court declared such a law constitutional.

16. See, for example, *State v. Davis*, 66 Wis. 2d 636, 648 (1974); *Walls v. State*, 166 Ga. App. 503 (1983); *State v. Ross*, 451 N.W.2d 231 (Minn. App. 1990); *People v. Summit County District Court*, Colorado Supreme Court, May 14, 1990. For a comparable ruling in a civil case terminating parental rights, see *Waeltz v. Dept. of Human Services*, 768 S.W.2d 41 (Ark. App. 1989).

17. 6 Wigmore, *Evidence*, sec. 1827, pp. 413–14.

18. D. D. Blinka, *Wisconsin Bar Bulletin* 59, 1 (1986): 15.

19. *State v. Superior Court, Pima County*, 719 P. 2d 283 (Ariz. App. 1986).

20. *Kentucky v. Stincer*, 96 LEd 2d 631, 647 (1987). See also *State v. Jones*, 367 SE2d 139 (N.C. App. 1988). See also *State v. Smith*, 765 P.2d 742 (Mont. 1988).

21. Whether "fairness" will continue to be the standard, and whether *Kentucky v. Stincer* will be applicable to trial procedures may have been placed in doubt by the 1988 decision of the Supreme Court in *Coy v. Iowa*. See discussion in note 84 below.

22. Wisconsin Jury Instructions—Criminal, no. 300 (1986). Some states also provide specific jury instructions regarding child witnesses. For example, Wisconsin Jury Instructions—Criminal, no. 340 provides: "A child is a competent witness and his testimony should be weighed in the same manner as testimony of any other witness. Considerations of age, intelligence, ability to observe and report correctly, ability to understand the truth, conduct on the witness stand, interest, appearance, and other matters bearing on credibility apply to a child witness in common with all witnesses."

23. *Ohio v. Roberts*, 448 U.S. 56 (1979).

24. Recently, the Kansas Supreme Court allowed a child's hearsay statement, distinguishing between physical and testimonial unavailability. The court explained that testimonial unavailability may be based on potential psychological trauma when expert testimony establishes that (1) psychological injury from further testimony appears probable; (2) the degree of such injury appears substantial; (3) the injury is expected to continue for a substantial duration; and (4) the injury would be substantially greater than that resulting from the experience of the average victim who would testify. *State v. Kuone*, 757 P.2d 289 (Kan. 1988).

25. *United States v. Inadi*, 475 U.S. 387 (1986).

26. Ibid., p. 399.

27. *State v. Robinson*, 735 P. 2d 801, 814 (Ariz. 1987). See also *State v. Allen*, 755 P.2d 1153 (Ariz. 1988), where the Arizona Supreme Court distinguished the facts of *Robinson* from a situation in which hearsay would not be allowed because, under the circumstances, the child's statements did not have the "ring of truth." The child's knowledge of sexual matters, possible motives to lie, as well as the lack of spontaneity of the child's disclosure, all led the court to conclude that the child's account had to be tested by cross-examination to assure a fair trial.

28. *Johnson v. State*, 732, S. W. 2d 817 (Ark. 1987); see also *Cogburn v. State*, 732 S.W. 2d 807 (Ark. 1987); *State v. Gallagher*, 554 A.2d 221 (Vt. 1988); *Tucker v. State*, Del. Supr., 564 A.2d 1110 (1989); *State v. Palomo*, 783 P.2d 575 (Wash. 1989). Other appellate courts also have reached the same conclusion in applying *Inadi*. See *People v. Rocha*, 547 N.E.2d 1335 (Ill. App. 2 Dist. 1989); *Nelson v. Farrey*, 874 F.2d 1222 (7th Cir. 1909).

29. *Inadi*, p. 399.

30. *Mattox v. United States*, 156 U.S. 237, 244 (1894).

31. *State v. Campbell*, 705 P. 2d 694, 701–2 (Or. 1985).

32. Whitcomb, Shapiro, and Stellwagen, *When the Victim Is a Child*, p. 70. See also *Commonwealth v. Amirault*, 535 N.E.2d 193 (Mass. 1989), allowing a mother to tell of her child's "fresh complaint" made eighteen months after the assault, quoted in chapter 7.

33. See M. H. Graham, "Child Sex Abuse Prosecution: Hearsay and Confrontation Clause Issues," in *Papers from a National Policy Conference on Legal Reforms in Child Sexual Abuse Cases* (Washington, D.C.: American Bar Association, 1985), p. 186.

34. Other recent decisions hinge on whether the "fresh complaint" was "self-motivated" or "extracted by interrogation." See *State v. Middleton*, 657 P.2d 1215 (Or. 1983); *Smith v. State*, 686 P.2d 247 (Nev. 1984); *State v. J.S.*, 536 A.2d 769 (N.J. Super. 1988); *State v. Bethune*, 557 A.2d 1025 (N.J. Super. A.D. 1989), affirmed, New Jersey Supreme Court, August 1, 1990; *State v. Hill*, New Jersey Supreme Court, August 1, 1990. Some disclosures, of course, initially may be "self-motivated" and then elaborated through investigation. The Texas Court of Appeals considered a social worker to whom a child was brought for investigation to be the "first person" to whom the child disclosed even though the child first broached the subject of abuse with a teacher. *Garcia v. State*, 792 S.W.2d 88 (Tex. Cr. App. 1990).

35. *People v. Gage*, 28 N.W. 835, 835–36 (Mich. 1886).

36. Ibid., pp. 836–37.

37. See, for example, *State v. Mueller*, 344 N.W. 2d (Iowa App. 2d Dist., 1983); and Whitcomb, Shapiro, and Stellwagen, *When the Victim Is a Child*, p. 70.

38. *United States v. Renville*, 779 F. 2d 430, 435–38 (8th Cir. 1985).

39. *State v. Robinson*, p. 810; see also *State v. Clements*, 734 P. 2d 1096 (Kan. 1987), which broadened the scope of "diagnosis/treatment" statements to those given to "mental health therapists." This is consistent with many recent appellate decisions that have allowed "expert" testimony from counselors of various professions. The decisions implicitly acknowledge that although such testimony usually has been of-

fered in court by psychiatrists and psychologists, other kinds of therapists frequently are involved with child sexual abuse victims. See, for example, *People v. Beckley*, 409 N.W.2d 759 (Mich. App. 1987), in which a rape counselor's testimony was allowed to rebut the defense assertion that the child's post incident behavior was inconsistent with that of an actual victim of sexual abuse. See also *State v. Deanes*, 303 N.C. 508 (1988). In noncriminal custody cases, some states have enlarged the potential for hearsay testimony by allowing "diagnosis/treatment" testimony about a child's statements from any person to whom the child would normally turn for "sympathy, protection, or advice." See *State v. Nordstrom*, 244 A. 2d 837 (R.I. 1988); *In re Jean Marie W.*, 559 A.2d 625 (R.I. 1989).

40. In recent years, numerous appellate courts have reviewed the diagnosis/treatment identification issue and applied the *Renville* ruling. See *State v. Nelson*, 138 Wis. 2d 418 (1987); *State v. Maldonado*, 536 A.2d 600 (Conn. App. 1988); *Johnson v. State*, 770 S.W.2d 128 (Ark. 1989); *People v. Meeboer*, 449 N.W.2d 124 (Mich. App. 1989); *People v. Gaffney*, 769 P.2d 1081 (Colo. 1989); *Drumm v. Commonwealth*, Ky., 783 S.W.2d 380 (1990); *Morgan v. Foretich*, 846 F.2d 941 (4th Cir. 1988). A few other decisions have criticized the *Renville* decision. See *Cassidy v. State*, 536 A.2d 666 (Md.App. 1988); *People v. LaLone*, 437 N.W.2d 611 (Mich. 1989).

41. Federal appellate decisions are not binding on state courts. However, they do have substantial influence on the decisions of state appellate courts. This is particularly true in evidentiary issues because many states have evidence rules identical or similar to the Federal Rules of Evidence. See J. Yun, "A Comprehensive Approach to Child Hearsay Statements in Sex Abuse Cases," *Columbia Law Review* 83 (1983): 1748, n. 31.

42. For example, Wis. Stats. Sec. 908.03(2).

43. Berliner and Barbieri, "The Testimony of the Child Victim," p. 133.

44. *Bertrang v. State*, 50 Wis. 2d 702, 707–8 (1970); *State v. Boston*, 46 Ohio St. 3d 108 (1989); see also *In re Interest of R.A.*, 403 N.W. 2d 357 (Neb. 1987); and "A Tender Years Doctrine for the Juvenile Courts: An Effective Way to Protect the Sexually Abused Child," 61 U. Det. J. Urb. L. 249 (1984).

45. *Brown v. United States*, 152 F. 2d 138 (D.C. Cir. 1945).

46. Whitcomb, Shapiro, and Stellwagen, *When the Victim Is a Child*, p. 71, citing *Lancaster v. People*, 615 P. 2d 720 (Colo. 1980), and *People v. Ortega*, 672 P.2d 215 (Colo. App. 1983). Even when a child's "spontaneous" disclosure comes in response to adult questions, it can be admitted as an excited utterance. See *In the Interest of O.E.P.*, 654 P.2d 312 (Colo. 1982).

47. Yun, "A Comprehensive Approach to Child Hearsay Statements," p. 1759.

48. Ibid., p. 1755.

49. *Black's Law Dictionary*, 5th ed. (St. Paul: West Publishing, 1979), p. 1173; under a slightly different theory, if an utterance is considered a "verbal action" or "gesture" courts may conclude that it is not hearsay. Recently, for example, two foster mothers were allowed to testify that they heard children cry out words such as "Arne, stop," while sleeping. The court found such nightmare statements to be "involuntary verbal reactions" rather than hearsay. *State v. Stevens*, 794 P. 2d 38 (Wash.App. 1990).

50. Fed. R. Ev. 803(24).

51. *People in Interest of W.C.L.*, 650 P. 2d 1302, 1303–1305 (Colo. App. 1982); see also *W.C.L. Jr. v. People*, 685 P.2d 176 (Colo. 1984); and *Oldsen v. People*, 732 P.2d 1132 (Colo. 1986).

52. *United States v. Cree*, 778 F. 2d 474, 475–79 (8th Cir. 1985).

53. Three recent state supreme court decisions further emphasize the importance of the residual exception. The New Jersey Supreme Court reversed a sexual assault conviction because the New Jersey evidence code did not include a residual exception, and the trial court had allowed testimony about a child's statements by a psychologist under a "heretofore unstated" hearsay exception. In reversing the conviction, the New Jersey Supreme Court stressed the need for the legislature to enact such an exception so that such reliable evidence could be admitted. *State v. D.R.*, N.J. Sup. Ct., no. A-12/13, 3/2/88. By contrast, the Wisconsin Supreme Court affirmed a sexual assault conviction based on the admission of testimony by a social worker, under Wisconsin's residual exception: "We conclude there is a compelling need for admission of hearsay arising from young sexual assault victims' inability or refusal to verbally express themselves in court when the child and the perpetrator are sole witnesses to the crime. . . . the residual exception is an appropriate method to admit these statements . . . ." *State v. Sorenson*, 421 N.W.2d 77 (Wis. 1988). See also *State v. Deanes*, 374 S.E.2d 249 (N.C. 1988).

54. 1982 Wash. Legis. Serv., chap. 128 s 2 (West).

55. Whitcomb, Shapiro, and Stellwagen, *When the Victim Is a Child*, pp. 72, 75–77, citing *State v. Slider*, 688 P.2d 538 (Wash. App. 1984), and *State v. Rodriguez*, 657 P. 2d 79 (Kan. App., 1983). See also ibid., p. 77, note 10.

56. Ind. Code s 35-37-4-6.

57. See K. McFarland, "Diagnostic Evaluations and the Uses of Videotapes in Child Sexual Abuse Cases," in *Papers from a National Policy Conference on Legal Reforms*, pp. 121–26; and P. Langelier, "Interviewing the Child Victim of Sexual Abuse" (paper presented at the Seventh National Conference on Child Abuse and Neglect, Chicago, November 13, 1985), reprinted in *Pretest Training Curriculum on the Judicial Response to Child Sexual Abuse* (National Council of Juvenile and Family Court Judges, August 1986).

58. See G. S. Goodman and V. S. Helgerson, "Child Sexual Assault: Children's Memory and the Law," in *Papers from National Policy Conference on Legal Reform*, p. 55. See also the 1988 Missouri Supreme Court decision, affirming a child rape and sodomy conviction, that explained that investigative interviews are admissible particularly because they provide "a species of evidence distinct from the declarant's trial testimony; they possess unique strengths and weaknesses." *State v. Wright*, 751 S.W.2d 48 (Mo. banc 1988). See Chapter 7 and the discussion of *State v. King*, West Virginia Supreme Court, June 28, 1990.

59. D. A. Haas, "The Use of Videotape in Child Abuse Cases," *NOVA Law Journal* 8 (1984): 373–76.

60. S. Chaney, "Videotaped Interviews with Child Abuse Victims," *Papers from a National Policy Conference on Legal Reform*, p. 214; see also Whitcomb, Shapiro, and Stellwagen, *When the Victim Is a Child*, p. 60.

61. Ibid., pp. 61–62.

62. Wis. Stat. Sec. 908.08(1); Judicial Council Note 4/30/86.

63. Whitcomb, Shapiro, and Stellwagen, *When the Victim Is a Child,* pp. 61–62. But see *Long v. State,* 742 S.W.2d 302 (Tex. Cr. App. 1987), in which a sharply divided court reviewed the Texas law. Concluding that the law violated the defendant's Sixth Amendment right of confrontation, the court relied heavily upon *Ohio v. Roberts,* and the unavailability/reliability criteria. That portion of the decision, therefore, seems inadequate in light of the United States Supreme Court's subsequent decisions in *United States v. Inadi* and *Kentucky v. Stincer.*

64. *Hennepin Co. v. Sullivan,* Minn. Ct. App. CX-84-807, 1/8/85, cited in Whitcomb, Shapiro, and Stellwagen, *When the Victim Is a Child,* p. 61.

65. McFarland, "Diagnostic Evaluations," pp. 127–28.

66. Chaney, "Videotaped Interviews," p. 215.

67. Ark. Stat. Ann. s 43–2036 (Supp. 1985).

68. *McGuire v. State,* 706 S.W. 2d 360, 362 (Ark. 1986). However, if the statute does not allow the defendant to cross-examine the child at the videotaping, it is not constitutional. *People v. Bastien,* 541 N.E.2d 670 (Ill. 1989). A videotape of a child's preliminary hearing testimony also may be admissible at the trial. *State v. Tarantino,* 458 N.W.2d 582 (Wis. App. 1990).

69. Whitcomb, Shapiro, and Stellwagen, *When the Victim Is a Child,* p. 63.

70. Ibid., p. 64.

71. See D. W. Lloyd, "Practical Issues in Avoiding Confrontation of a Child Witness and the Defendant in a Criminal Trial," in *Papers from a National Policy Conference on Legal Reform,* pp. 277–80.

72. *United States v. Binder,* 769 F. 2d 595, 600 (1985).

73. Since the decision in *Binder,* other courts also have reversed child sexual abuse convictions because juries were allowed to review videotape testimony during deliberations. See *Chambers v. State,* 726 P. 2d 1269 (Wyo. 1986); *Martin v. State,* 747 P.2d 316 (Okl.Cr. 1987). More recently, however, a conviction was affirmed because the appellate court concluded that the videotape review "simply enabled the jury to take greater care in evaluating the evidence." *State v. Ross,* 451 N.W.2d 231 (Minn. App. 1990).

74. Whitcomb, Shapiro, and Stellwagen, *When the Victim Is a Child,* p. 65.

75. *State v. Twist,* 528 A. 2d 1250 (Me. 1987); *State v. Cooper,* 353 S.E. 2d 441 (S.C. 1986). In 1984 the New Jersey Superior Court reached the same conclusion, upholding the use of videotape testimony by a ten-year-old sexual abuse victim. The court explained:

> The confrontation clause is not implacable in its demands. Nearly every authority agrees that it is subject to exceptions. In reaching the conclusion . . . that the use of videotaped testimony . . . is permissible, it is accepted as a fact that only a modest erosion of the clause, if any, will take place. The child, through the use of video, will not be obliged to see the defendant or to be exposed to the usual courtroom atmosphere. Nevertheless, the defendant as well as the judge, the

jury, and the spectators, will see and hear her clearly. Adequate opportunity for cross-examination will be provided. This is enough to satisfy the demands of the confrontation clause. If it is not, it represents a deserved exception. (*State v. Sheppard*, 484 A. 2d 1330, 1342–1342 [1984])

Other decisions upholding the use of videotaped testimony of a child despite constitutional or statutory provisions for the right of "face to face" confrontation include *People v. Johnson*, 497 N.E. 2d 308 (Ill. 1986); *Chambers v. State*, 504 So. 2d 476 (Fla. Ct. App. 1987); *Altmeyer v. State*, 496 N.E. 2d 1328 (Ind. App. 1986); *State v. Strable*, 313 N.W. 2d 497 (Iowa 1981); *People v. Henderson*, 503 N.Y.S. 2d 238 (1986).

76. *State v. Mannion*, 57 Pac. Rpt. 542, 544 (court opinion) and 545 (concurring opinion) (1899).

77. Whitcomb, Shapiro, and Stellwagen, *When the Victim Is a Child*, p. 50. Most recently, such a statute was found to be constitutional by the Maryland Court of Appeals in *State v. Wildermuth*, case no. 2-1987, decided September 10, 1987.

78. *Matter of Appeal in Pinal County Juvenile Action*, 709 P. 2d 1361 (Ariz. App. 1985).

79. *State v. Warford*, 389 N.W. 2d 575, 581–82 (Neb. 1986).

80. KRS 421.350.

81. *Commonwealth v. Willis*, 716 S.W. 2d 224, 230–31 (Ky. 1986); see also *Commonwealth v. Siegfriedt*, 522 N.E.2d 970 (Mass. 1988).

82. *Commonwealth v. Ludwig*, Sup. Ct. Pa., no. 02883 (Philadelphia, 1987), p. 13. The court also cited the United States Supreme Court's clarification that the "main and essential purpose of confrontation is to secure for the opponent the opportunity of cross-examination. The opponent demands confrontation, not for the idle purpose of gazing upon the witness, or of being gazed upon by him, but for the purpose of cross-examination." (*Davis v. Alaska*, 415 U.S. 308 [1974].)

83. See K. K. Coppel, "An Analysis of the Legal Issues Involved in the Presentation of a Child's Testimony by Two-Way Closed-Circuit Television in Sexual Abuse Cases," in *Papers from a National Policy Conference on Legal Reform*, pp. 241–51. See also the Missouri Supreme Court's recent consideration of videotape procedures in *State v. Seever*, 733 S.W. 2d 438 (Mo.banc 1987), and the Connecticut Supreme Court's decision that a defendant may be excluded from the presence of the victim during the videotaping when "the state has demonstrated a compelling need. . . . The state must show that the minor victim would be so intimidated, or otherwise inhibited, by the physical presence of the defendant that the trustworthiness of the victim's testimony would be seriously called into question" (*State v. Jarzbek*, 529 A. 2d 1245, 1255 [Conn. 1987]).

84. *Coy v. Iowa*, 487 U.S. 1012 (1988). The plurality opinion is remarkable in one other respect. While the court in *Kentucky v. Stincer* went out of its way to emphasize that its "fairness" standard and analysis was not limited to pretrial proceedings, the *Coy* decision briefly implies such a limitation on *Stincer* by Justice Scalia's reference to "confrontation at some point in the proceedings other than the trial itself, *Kentucky v. Stincer.*" Surprisingly, neither the concurring nor dissenting justices

commented on that apparent alteration of *Stincer*. Thus, future appellate litigation in child sexual abuse cases may probe the relative merits of the "fairness" standard of *Stincer*, and the "necessity" standard of *Coy*.

85. See, for example, Wisconsin Jury Instructions–Criminal, no. 215 (1983).

86. *State v. Middleton*, 657 P. 2d 1215, 1220 (Or. 1983).

87. *United States v. Azure*, 801 F. 2d 336, 340–41 (8th Cir. 1986); the physician who testified was Dr. Robert ten Bensel.

88. *State v. Myers*, 382 N.W. 2d 91, 92–95 (Iowa 1986). See also *State v. Moran*, 728 P. 2d 248 (Ariz. 1986); *Commonwealth v. Seese*, 517 A. 2d 920 (Pa. 1986); *State v. Lindsey*, 720 P. 2d 73 (Ariz. 1986); *Tevlin v. People*, 715 P. 2d 338 (Colo. 1986); *State v. Heath*, 341 S.E. 2d 565 (N.C. 1986). While this principle most often limits the prosecution, it may also aid their case. See, for example, *State v. Tafoya*, 617 P. 2d 151 (N.M. 1980), in which the defense was not allowed to offer expert testimony that the victims were lying.

89. *State v. Kim*, 645 P. 2d 1330 (Hawaii 1982); *State v. Butler*, 349 S.E. 2d 684 (Ga. 1986). See also *State v. Jensen*, 432 N.W.2d 913 (Wis. 1988). However, in 1990 Hawaii abandoned this approach, overruling its decision in *Kim*. *State v. Felomino Batangan*, Hawaii Supreme Court, September 27, 1990.

90. See R. J. Roe, "Expert Testimony in Child Sexual Abuse Cases," in *Papers from a National Policy Conference on Legal Reform*, pp. 295–304; see also D. McCord, "Expert Psychological Testimony about Child Complaintants in Sexual Abuse Prosecutions: A Foray into the Admissibility of Novel Psychological Evidence," *Journal of Criminal Law and Criminology* 77, 1 (1986). McCord explains, "Courts do not always begin their analyses at the obvious starting point: whether the testimony 'will assist' the trier of fact. Courts are often beguiled by easily-cited case law stating the principle that ordinarily a jury does not need expert assistance in determining the credibility of witnesses, without ever examining whether the expert testimony assisted the jury in the case before it" (p. 25).

91. *Commonwealth v. Baldwin*, 502 A. 2d 253 (Pa. Sup. 1985).

92. *State v. Haseltine*, 120 Wis. 2d 72 (App. 1984).

93. *Lantrip v. Commonwealth*, 713 S.W. 2d 816, 817 (Ky. 1986).

94. *State v. Hall*, 392 N.W. 2d 285 (Minn. App. 1986).

95. The supreme courts of Alabama, Delaware, Georgia, Michigan, South Dakota, Vermont, and Wisconsin recently decided to allow expert testimony on child sexual abuse accommodation syndrome, delayed reporting, and recantation. See *Ex parte Hill*, 553 So. 2d 1138 (Ala. 1989); *Wheat v. State*, 527 A.2d 269 (Del. Sup. 1987); *Allison v. State*, 353 S.E.2d 805 (Ga. 1987); *People v. Beckley*, 456 N.W.2d 391 (Mich. 1990); *State v. Bachman*, 446 N.W.2d 271 (S.D. 1989); *State v. Dunbar*, 566 A.2d 970 (Vt. 1989); *State v. Jensen*, 432 N.W.2d 913 (Wis. 1988). Other state appellate courts recently disallowed similar evidence. See *State v. Rimmasch*, 775 P.2d 388 (Utah 1989); *Commonwealth v. Higby*, 559 A.2d 939 (Pa. Super. 1989); *State v. York*, 564 A.2d 389 (Me. 1989); *People v. Leon*, California Court of Appeals, 2d Dist., October 31, 1989; *Commonwealth v. Garcia*, Pennsylvania Supreme Court, Philadelphia, June 4, 1990. Some of the most interesting and analytical decisions come from Colorado. Affirming most convictions from trials in which experts testified about

behavioral manifestations of sexually abused children, the decisions also allowed the experts to describe behavioral patterns of other members of incestuous families. See *People v. Vollentine*, 643 P.2d 800 (Colo. App. 1982); *People v. Roberts*, 722 P.2d 443 (Colo. App. 1986); *People v. Koon*, 724 P.2d 1367 (Colo. App. 1986); *People v. Lucero*, 724 P.2d 1374 (Colo. App. 1986); *People v. Daninger*, 772 P.2d 674 (Colo. App. 1989).

96. See McCord, "Expert Psychological Testimony," pp. 24–34.

97. *State v. Miller*, 709 P. 2d 350, 352–53 (Utah 1985). A Maryland court recently applied the same rationale to exclude testimony from a social worker that a defendant's responses to her questions were consistent with "classic indicators" of a child abuser (*Sloan v. State*, 522 A. 2d 1364 [Md. App. 1987]). See also *Haakenson v. State*, Alaska Ct. App., no. A-1641, 8/5/88; and *State v. Clements*, 770 P.2d 447 (Kan. 1989); California, however, allows defense experts to testify that defendants "show no obvious psychological or sexual problems [as] circumstantial evidence which bears upon whether they committed sexual acts upon children, and [as] admissible 'character' evidence on their behalf." *People v. Stoll*, 783 P.2d 698 (Cal. 1989); see also *People v. Ruiz*, 272 Cal. Rptr. 368 (Cal. App. 1 Dist. 1990).

98. Dr. Myra Levick, *Mommy, Daddy, Look What I'm Saying: What Children Are Telling You through Their Art* (New York: M. Evans, 1986).

99. *Wilkerson v. Pearson*, 210 333, 338–39 (N.J. Super. 1985). Recently, the United States Court of Appeals analyzed child communication through "play therapy" with an anatomically correct doll. *U.S. v. Gillespie*, CA. 9, no. 87–5067, 7/22/88.

100. Some specificity may be required, however, depending on the issues involved in each case. Recent decisions include: *People v. Keindl*, 68 N.Y.2d 410 (1986); *People v. Slaughter*, 259 Cal. Rptr. 437 (Cal. App. 3 Dist. 1989); petition for review granted, 261 Cal. Rptr. 704 (1989); *State v. Mulkey*, 560 A.2d 24 (Md. 1989); *People v. Jones*, 270 Cal. Rptr. 611 (Cal. 1990); *People v. Fernandez*, 263 Cal. Rptr. 139 (Cal. App. 6 Dist. 1989); *State, V. Dunbar*, 566 A.2d 970 (Vt. 1989).

101. Berliner and Barbieri, "The Testimony of the Child Victim," p. 69.

102. *Fain v. State*, 462 So. 2d 1054 (Ala. Cr. App. 1985). In this case, the social worker was carrying out a routine investigation without focusing on the father as the suspected abuser. However, when a social worker interviews a suspect as part of what is or will be a police investigation, *Miranda* usually will apply. See *Cates v. State*, 776 S.W.2d 170 (Tex. Cr. App. 1989).

103. *State v. Paster*, 524 A. 2d 587, 590–91 (R.I. 1987). Another recent decision reflecting ignorance of children and the law of hearsay exceptions is *Commonwealth v. Haber*, 505 A. 2d 273, 275–76 (Pa. Sup. 1986), in which the court said, "We are not impressed by the fact that the legislatures in a handful of states have enacted statutes that permit the state to introduce the out-of-court assertions of children. . . . We do not believe that the out-of-court assertions of children, particularly four- and five-year-old children, . . . merit exception to the hearsay rule."

104. The Rhode Island Supreme Court carelessly concluded that if a child is found incompetent to testify at the trial, earlier hearsay statements of the child should not be admitted. The ability of a child to testify at a trial has little if any relationship to the reliability of the child's prior statements. Intended to measure a witness's

capacity to testify at the trial, competency laws provide no legal or logical measurement of hearsay. Even if a child doesn't understand an oath, earlier statements to parents, police, therapists, or doctors may be, in the words of *Inadi*, "irreplaceable as substantive evidence." In 1989, the supreme courts of Ohio and Colorado explained that very point, correctly distinguishing the law of competency from the law of hearsay. See *State v. Boston*, 46 Ohio St. 3, 115 (1989); *People v. District Court of El Paso County*, 776 P.2d 1083 (Colo. 1989). See also *State v. Townsend*, 556 So. 2d 817 (Fla. App. 1990). In 1990 the United States Supreme Court also distinguished the two concepts, correcting the same error made by the Idaho Supreme Court, *Idaho v. Wright* (Case No. 89-260, June 27, 1990, slip opinion, p. 17).

6. Justice for Children

1. *State v. Robinson*, 735 P. 2d 801, 813 (Ariz. 1987).

2. *In the Interest of R.B.*, Wisconsin Circuit Court, Branch 1, Milwaukee County, no. 03219308, 9/21/84 (transcript, pp. 52–62). See also Gronik, *Journal of Juvenile Justice*, pp. 449–50, regarding use of dolls; and R. H. Passman and L. A. Lautmann, "Fathers', Mothers', and Security Blankets' Effects on the Responsiveness of Young Children during Projective Testing," *Journal of Consulting and Clinical Psychology* 50, 2 (1982): 310–12. Use of anatomical dolls has been affirmed consistently by many appellate courts. See, for example, *State v. Tuffree*, 666 P.2d 912 (Wash 1983); *State v. Madden*, 472 N.E.2d 1126 (Ohio 1984); *State v. Eggert*, 358 N.W.2d 156 (Minn. App 1984); *Vera v. State*, 709 S.W.2d 681 (Tex. App. 1986); *State v. Fletcher*, 368 S.E.2d 633 (N.C. 1988); and *State v. Deanes*, 323 N.C. 508,520 (1988) in which the North Carolina Supreme Court commented that "by using the dolls, the children can demonstrate what they want to communicate but find hard to put into words." See also Sue White and Gail Santilli, "A Review of Clinical Practices and Research Data on Anatomical Dolls," *Journal of Interpersonal Violence* 3, 4 (December 1988): 430–42.

3. The Ohio Association of Juvenile and Family Court Judges, "Implementing Social Policies/A Multidisciplinary Approach" (Cincinnati, August 28–29, 1985; Columbus, August 29–30, 1985; Cleveland, September 11–12, 1985; Toledo, September 12–13, 1985).

4. *State v. Johnson*, 528 N.E.2d 567, 569 (Ohio App. 1986). See Chapter 7 for more recent decisions regarding children testifying from laps or with the supportive presence of aides and relatives.

5. Federal Rules of Evidence 611(a). A judge's discretion is broad but not limitless. For example, when a trial judge escorted a child from outside the courtroom to the witness stand, the conviction was reversed because the appeals court concluded that the jury could have construed that as the judge's "endorsement of the child's credibility." *People v. Rogers*, Colorado Court of Appeals, April 5, 1990.

6. Wis. Stats. Sec. 971.105.

7. Frank, *Courts on Trial*, pp. 254–59.

8. *State v. Warford*, 389 N.W. 2d 575, 582 (Neb. 1986).

9. *In the Interest of C.N.*, case no. 03219866, Wisconsin Circuit Court, Branch 1, Milwaukee County, 1984.

10. Wis. Stats. Sec. 967.04(8) (b) (6).

11. "Probate Judges Beset by Demands," *Boston Globe,* December 7, 1987.

12. Berliner and Barbieri, "The Testimony of the Child Victim," p. 135; see also Goodman, "The Child Witness," p. 6.

13. R. E. Cramer, Jr., "The District Attorney as a Mobilizer in a Community Approach to Child Sexual Abuse," *University of Miami Law Review* 40, 1 (November 1985): 209–10.

14. Brochure, Children's Advocacy Center, 106 Lincoln St., Huntsville, Alabama.

15. Cramer, "District Attorney as Mobilizer," p. 310.

16. For example: "A judge should contribute to the public interest by advising, suggesting and supporting rules and legislation which, from his or her judicial observation and experience, will improve the administration of justice." (Wisconsin Code of Judicial Ethics, SCR 60.01[14]).

17. Conference Statement, National Conference of the Judiciary on the Rights of Victims of Crime, NCJ 93208 NIJ, pp. 5–6.

18. Ibid., p. 12.

19. Ibid., title page, quoting *Final Report, President's Task Force on Victims of Crime,* December 1982, p. 73.

20. Metropolitan Court Judges Committee, *Deprived Children,* p. 10.

21. Ibid., pp. 12, 14, 16–17.

22. *Child Sexual Abuse—Issues and Actions: A Training Curriculum to Improve Judicial Response* (National Council of Juvenile and Family Court Judges, Reno, Nevada, 1987).

23. However, such a requirement, even by statute, will not necessarily accomplish its purposes. Recently, for example, the New York legislature enacted Judiciary Law 211, which provides: "The chief judge . . . shall establish standards and administrative policies for general application . . . throughout the state . . . relating to: [t]he continuing development and implementation of methods and techniques designed to reduce significantly the trauma to child witnesses likely to be caused by testifying in court proceedings [and t]he appropriate education and training of judges and nonjudicial courtroom personnel concerning the social and psychological stages of child development to ensure that they adopt or modify, where appropriate, courtroom procedures, including the questioning and treatment of a child witness by the parties, to protect the child from emotional or psychological harm." Unfortunately, the law has a sunset provision terminating its mandates in 1991. It has not been implemented to produce the intended training and remains unknown to most New York judges. The viability of such a law also may be doubtful as some state judiciaries jealously guard their authority to establish their own training agendas. See Chapter 7.

7. McMartin

1. "After McMartin . . . Who Walks Point?" videotape, produced by the National Children's Advocacy Center and Independent Media Network (1990); available

from the National Children's Advocacy Center, Audio/Visual Dept., 106 Lincoln St., Huntsville, AL 35801.

2. R. Reinhold, "McMartin Case: Swept Away in Panic on Child Molestation," *New York Times*, January 24, 1990, p. A 12.

3. D.J. DeBenedictis, "McMartin Preschool's Lessons," *ABA Journal* 76 (April 1990): 29.

4. See: "McMartin: Anatomy of a Witch-hunt," *Playboy* (June 1990), 45–48; "From the Mouths of Babes to a Jail Cell," *Harpers* (May 1990), 52–63; "Letters," *Harpers* (July 1990); *RoundTable Magazine* 2, 3 (Summer 1990).

5. *Maryland v. Craig*, U.S. Sup. Ct., no. 89–478, June 27, 1990.

6. See *Glendening v. State*, 536 So. 2d 212 (Fla. 1988); *State v. Vincent*, 768 P.2d 150 (Ariz. 1989); *State v. Bonello*, 554 A.2d 277 (Conn. 1989); *State v. Eaton*, 769 P.2d 1157 (Kan. 1989); *State v. Thomas*, 442 N.W.2d 10 (Wis. 1989); *State v. Conklin*, 444 N.W.2d 268 (Minn. 1989); *State v. Dunbar*, 566 A.2d 990 (Vt. 1989). Only the New York Court of Appeals also imposed overwhelming trauma on a child, concluding that after a five-year-old child was unresponsive for approximately two hours on the witness stand, that still was not enough for the judge to decide that closed-circuit TV was necessary. *People v. Cintron*, N.Y. Court of Appeals, January 11, 1990. For a state supreme court application of the Craig decision, see *State v. Crandall*, 577 A.2d 483 (N.J. 1990).

7. Brief Amici Curiae, p. 7.

8. *Commonwealth v. Amirault*, 535 N.E.2d 193, 198–199 (Mass. 1989).

9. *Mattox v. United States*, 156 U.S. 237 (1894); *United States v. Inadi*, 475 U.S. 387 (1986).

10. *State v. King*, W. Va. Sup. Ct., June 28, 1990.

11. *Gregory v. North Carolina*, 900 F.2d 705 (4th Cir. 1990); Justice Wilkinson declared in his dissenting opinion, "If this verdict is unreliable, then I fear reliability in prosecutions for the sexual abuse of very young children is beyond our grasp."

12. *Idaho v. Wright*, U.S. Sup. Ct., June 27, 1990. See also *State v. Wright*, 775 P.2d 1224 (1989), and *State v. Giles*, 772 P.2d 191 (1989).

13. *Curtis v. State*, 783 S.W. 47 (Ark. 1990); *State v. James*, Conn. Supreme Ct., June 20, 1990; *People v. Rocha*, 191 Ill. App. 3d 529 (1989).

14. *Drumm v. Commonwealth*, Ky. Sup. Ct., January 18, 1990; *Hall v. State*, Miss. Sup. Ct., February 9, 1989.

15. See Chapter 6, note 23.

16. *State v. Suka*, 777 P.2d 240 (Hawaii 1989).

17. *State v. Rulona*, 785 P.2d 615 (Hawaii 1990).

18. *State v. Rogers*, 692 P.2d 2 (Mont. 1984); *Mosby v. State*, 703 S.W.2d 714 (Tex. App. 13 Dist. 1985); *State v. Johnson*, 528 N.E.2d 567 (Ohio App. 1986); *People Disandra*, 239 Cal. Rptr. 9 (Cal. App. 3 Dist. 1987); *State v. Jones*, 362 S.E.2d 330 (W.Va. 1987); *State v. Dunbar*, 566 A.2d 970 (Vt. 1989); *State v. Ross*, 451 N.W.2d 231 (Minn. App. 1990).

19. Fed. R. Evid. 611(a). See also Fed. R. Evid. 102, adopted by thirty states, which provides, "These rules shall be construed to secure fairness . . . and promotion of growth and development of the law of evidence to the end that the truth may be ascertained and proceedings justly determined."

20. *State v. Johnson*, 528 N.E.2d 567, 569–571 (Ohio App. 1986).

21. For example, parents have no Sixth Amendment right to confront their children who testify in a family court hearing, *In re Michael C.*, 557 A.2d 1219 (R.I. 1989); in a juvenile court hearing, *Castellanos v. DHRS*, 545 So. 2d 455 (Fla. App. 1989); in a termination of parental rights hearing, *Matter of Juvenile Action No. JS-7499*, 786 P.2d 1004 (Ariz. App. 1989).

22. *St. Louis Post-Dispatch/* Associated Press, May 18, 1990.

23. "Daughters seek justice for childhood abuse, "*Milwaukee Journal*, December 3, 1989; see also C. L. Mithers, "Incest and the Law," *New York Times Magazine*, October 21, 1990, pp. 44–63.

24. *Hammer v. Hammer*, 418 N.W.2d 23 (Wis. App. 1987); see also *Johnson v. Johnson*, 701 F. Supp. 1363 (N.D. Ill. 1988).

25. Iowa Stat. Sec. 802.2; N.J.S.A. 2C:1–6.

26. *DeShaney v. Winnebago County Department of Social Services*, 109 S. Ct. 998 (1989).

27. D. Bross, "Law and the Abuse of Children," *Currents in Modern Thought* (June 1990), 482.

28. See "Foster Care System Reeling, Despite Law Meant to Help," *New York Times*, September 21, 1990, p. A1.

29. Attorney Curry First, who represented Joshua DeShaney's interests as his guardian ad litem, made the same point explaining the complexities of the issues and acknowledging that had Joshua's appeal succeeded, the victory could have become a "double-edged sword"; interview of Curry First, July 29, 1990.

30. "Saturday Night With Connie Chung," CBS Television, January 20, 1990.

31. *Morgan v. Foretich*, 846 F.2d 941 (4th Cir. 1988).

32. L. Berliner, "Protecting or Harming? Parents Who Flee with Their Children," *Journal of Interpersonal Violence* 5, 1 (1990): 119.

33. N. Thoennes and J. Pearson, "Allegations of Sexual Abuse in Custody and Visitation Cases: An Empirical Study of 169 Cases from 12 States," (Denver: The Association of Family and Conciliation Courts, 1988), cited in D. Bross, "Law and the Abuse of Children" (note 27), pp. 483–484. See also K.M. Quinn, "The Credibility of Children's Allegations of Sexual Abuse," 6 *Behav. Sci. & L.* 181 (1988), reporting that a survey of the American Federation of Conciliation Courts found that 2.5 percent of all contested custody and visitation cases include a sexual abuse allegation, of which 22 percent were assessed probably not to have occurred. See also L. Berliner, "Deciding Whether a Child Has Been Sexually Abused," in *Sexual Abuse Allegations in Custody and Visitation Cases* 48, ed. E.B. Nicholson and J. Bulkley (1988); Corwin, Berliner, Goodman, Goodwin, and White, "Child Sexual Abuse and Custody Disputes: No Easy Answers," 2 *J.Interpersonal Violence* 91 (1987).

34. See Chapter 2, and Chapter 2, note 23.

35. Corwin, et al (note 33).

36. Hearings, U.S. Senate Committee on the Judiciary, May 16, 1989. See also H.J. Pennington and L. Woods, *Legal Issues and Legal Options in Civil Child Sexual Abuse Cases: Representing the Protective Parent* (New York: National Center on Women and Family Law, 1990).

37. *Baltimore City Department of Social Services v. Bouknight*, U.S. Sup. Ct., February 20, 1990.

38. "Friends of Elizabeth Morgan" (newsletter) 2, 2(Spring 1990), 1. In November 1990 the New Zealand court granted custody of Hilary to Elizabeth Morgan. "New Zealand Gives Custody to Morgan," *Washington Post*, November 30, 1990.

Select Bibliography

Agtion, O. *Sexual Assault among Adolescents.* Lexington, Mass.: Lexington Books, 1983.

American Bar Association. *Papers from a National Policy Conference on Legal Reforms in Child Sexual Abuse Cases.* Washington, D.C., 1985.

Anderson, L., and G. Shafer. "The Character-Disordered Family: A Community Treatment Model for Family Sexual Abuse." *American Journal of Orthopsychiatry* 49 (1979): 436–45.

Ariès, P. *Centuries of Childhood: A Social History of Family Life.* New York: Jonathan Cape, 1962.

Armstrong, L. *The Home Front: Notes from the Family War Zone.* New York: McGraw-Hill, 1983.

———. *Kiss Daddy Goodnight.* New York: Hawthorn Books, 1978.

Arthur, L. G. "Child Sexual Abuse: Improving the System's Response." *Juvenile and Family Court Journal* 37, 2 (1986): 27.

Bender, L., and A. Blau. "The Reactions of Children to Sexual Relations with Adults." *American Journal of Orthopsychiatry* 7 (1937): 500–518.

Bennett, W. L., and M. S. Feldman. *Reconstructing Reality in the Courtroom.* New Brunswick, N.J.: Rutgers University Press, 1981.

Bode, J. *Fighting Back: How to Cope with the Medical, Emotional, and Legal Consequences of Rape.* New York: Macmillan, 1978.

Bolton, F. G., and S. R. Bolton. *Working with Violent Families.* Newbury Park, Cal.: Sage, 1987.

Bross, D. C. *Multidisciplinary Advocacy for Mistreated Children.* Denver: National Association of Counsel for Children, 1984.

———, ed. *Legal Representation of the Maltreated Child.* Denver: National Association of Counsel for Children, 1979.

Browning, D. H., and B. Boatman. "Incest: Children at Risk." *American Journal of Psychiatry* 134 (1977): 69–72.

Brownmiller, S. *Against Our Will.* New York: Simon and Schuster, 1975.

Bulkley, J., ed. *Child Sexual Abuse and the Law.* Washington, D.C.: National Legal Resource Center for Child Advocacy and Protection, American Bar Association, 1981.

245

——. *Innovations in the Prosecution of Child Sexual Abuse Cases.* 2d ed. Washington, D.C.: National Legal Resource Center for Child Advocacy and Protection, American Bar Association, 1982.

——. *Recommendations for Improving Legal Intervention in Intrafamily Child Sexual Abuse Cases.* Washington, D.C.: National Legal Resource Center for Child Advocacy and Protection, American Bar Association, 1982.

Bulkley, J., and H. Davidson. *Child Sexual Abuse—Legal Issues and Approaches.* Washington, D.C.: American Bar Association, 1980.

Burgess, A. W. *Child Pornography and Sex Rings.* Lexington, Mass.: Lexington Books, 1984.

——, ed. *Rape and Sexual Assault.* New York: Garland Publishing, 1985.

Burgess, A. W., A. N. Groth, and L. L. Holmstrom. *Sexual Assault of Children and Adolescents.* Lexington, Mass.: Lexington Books, 1978.

Burgess, A. W., and L. L. Holmstrom. "Rape Trauma Syndrome." *American Journal of Psychiatry* 131 (1974): 981–86.

——. "Sexual Trauma of Children and Adolescents: Pressure, Sex, and Secrecy." *Nursing Clinics of North America* 10 (1975): 551–63.

Butler, S. *Conspiracy of Silence.* San Francisco: New Glide Publications, 1978.

Chappel, D., et al., eds. *Forcible Rape.* New York: Columbia University Press, 1977.

Chomsky, C. *The Acquisition of Syntax in Children from Five to Ten,* Research Monograph no. 57. Cambridge, Mass.: MIT. Press, 1969.

Cohen, R. L., and M. A. Harnick. "The Susceptibility of Child Witnesses to Suggestion." *Law and Human Behavior* 7 (1980): 56–65.

Constantine, L. L., and F. M. Martinson, eds. *Children and Sex: New Findings, New Perspectives.* Boston: Little, Brown, 1981.

Conte, J. R. "The Effects of Sexual Abuse on Children: A Critique and Suggestions for Future Research." *Victimology* 10 (1986): 110–30.

——, ed. *Journal of Interpersonal Violence.* Beverly Hills, Cal.: Sage, 1987–89.

Conte, J. R., and L. Berliner. "Sexual Abuse of Children: Implications for Practice." *Social Casework* 62 (1981): 601–6.

Conte, J. R., and J. Schverman. "Factors Associated with an Increased Impact of Child Sexual Abuse." *Child Abuse and Neglect* 11 (1987): 201–11.

Crewdson, J. *By Silence Betrayed: Sexual Abuse of Children in America.* Boston: Little, Brown, 1988.

Daro, D. *Confronting Child Abuse.* New York: Free Press, 1988.

De Francis, V. *Protecting the Child Victim of Sex Crimes Committed by Adults.* Denver: American Humane Association, 1969.

DeMause, L., ed. *The History of Childhood.* New York: Psychohistory Press, 1974.

De Young, M. *The Sexual Victimization of Children.* Jefferson, N.C.: McFarland, 1982.

Dietz, P. E. *Child Molesters: A Behavioral Analysis for Law Enforcement Officers In-*

vestigating Cases of Child Sexual Abuse. Washington, D.C.: National Center for Missing and Exploited Children, 1986.

Eberle, P., and S. Eberle. *The Politics of Child Abuse.* Secaucus, N.J.: Lyle Stuart, 1986.

Erikson, E. *Childhood and Society.* New York: Norton, 1963.

Farson, R. *Birthrights.* New York: Macmillan, 1974.

Feild, H. *Jurors and Rape.* Lexington, Mass.: Lexington Books, 1980.

Finch, S. M. "Adult Seduction of the Child: Effects on the Child." *Medical Aspects of Human Sexuality* 7 (1973): 170–87.

Finkelhor, D. *Sexually Victimized Children.* New York: Free Press, 1979.

———. *A Sourcebook on Child Sexual Abuse.* Beverly Hills, Cal.: Sage, 1986.

———, ed. *Child Sexual Abuse: New Theory and Research.* New York: Free Press, 1984.

Finkelhor, D., and G. T. Hotaling. "Sexual Abuse in the National Incidence Study of Child Abuse and Neglect: An Appraisal." *Child Abuse and Neglect* 8 (1984): 23–33.

Flowers, R. B. *Children and Criminality.* New York: Greenwood Press, 1986.

Fontana, V. *Somewhere a Child Is Crying.* New York: New American Library, 1973.

Fortune, M. *Sexual Violence: The Unmentionable Sin.* New York: Pilgrim Press, 1983.

Forward, S., and E. Buck. *Betrayal of Innocence.* New York: Tarcher, 1978.

Fuller, K. E. "Is the Child Victim of Sexual Abuse Telling the Truth?" *Child Abuse and Neglect* 8 (1984): 473–81.

Gager, N., and E. Schurr. *Sexual Assault: Confronting Rape in America.* New York: Grosset and Dunlap, 1976.

Gagnon, J. "Female Child Victims of Sex Offenders." *Social Problems* 13 (1965): 176–92.

Gallagher, V. *Speaking Out, Fighting Back.* Seattle: Madrona Publishers, 1985.

Garbarino, J., and G. Gilliam. *Understanding Abusive Families.* Lexington, Mass.: Lexington Books, 1986.

Garbarino, J., F. Stott et al. *Children as Sources of Information.* San Francisco: Jossey-Bass, 1989.

Garbarino, J., et al., eds. *Troubled Youths, Troubled Families.* New York: Aldine, 1986.

Geiser, H. *Hidden Victims.* Boston: Beacon Press, 1978.

Gelinas, D. J. "The Persisting Negative Effects of Incest." *Psychiatry* 46 (1983): 312–32.

Gelman, R. "Preschool Thought." *American Psychologist* 34, 10 (1979): 900–905.

Goodman, G. S. "The Child Witness: Conclusions and Future Directions for Research and Legal Practice." *Journal of Social Issues* 40, 2 (1984): 157–75.

Goodwin, J., ed. *Sexual Abuse: Incest Victims and Their Families.* London: John Wright, 1982.

Groth, A. N. *Men Who Rape: The Psychology of the Offender*. New York: Plenus Press, 1979.

Halliday, L. *The Silent Scream: The Reality of Sexual Abuse*. Sexual Abuse Victims Anonymous, R.R. No. 1 Campbell River, B.C. Canada V9W 3S4, 1981.

Hawkins, P. *Children at Risk*. Bethesda, Md.: Adler and Adler, 1986.

Hayakawa, S. I. "The Use and Misuse of Language." In *Science and Human Affairs*, ed. R. E. Farson. Palo Alto, Cal.: Science and Behavior Books, 1985.

Heifer, R. "The Epidemiology of Child Abuse and Neglect." *Pediatric Annals* 10 (1984): 745–51.

Helfer, R. E., and R. S. Kempe, eds. *The Battered Child*. Chicago: University of Chicago Press, 1987.

Herman, J. L. *Father-Daughter Incest*. Cambridge, Mass.: Harvard University Press, 1981.

Hollingsworth, J. *Unspeakable Acts*. New York: Congdon and Weed, 1986.

Hotaling, G. T. et al. *Coping with Family Violence*. Newbury Park, Cal.: Sage, 1988.

Hotaling, G. T. et al. *Family Abuse and Its Consequences: New Directions in Research*. Newbury Park, Cal.: Sage, 1988.

Hyde, M. O. *Sexual Abuse—Let's Talk about It*. Philadelphia: Westminster Press, 1984.

Jampole, L., and M. K. Weber. "An Assessment of the Behavior of Sexually Abused and Nonsexually Abused Children with Anatomically Correct Dolls." *Child Abuse and Neglect* 11 (1987): 187–92.

Jones, D., and M. McQuiston. *Interviewing the Sexually Abused Child*. Kempe Center Series 6. Denver, 1985.

Justice, B., and R. Justice, *The Broken Taboo*. New York: Human Sciences Press, 1979.

Katz, S., and M. Mazur. *Understanding the Rape Victim*. New York: Wiley, 1979.

Kempe, C. H. "The Battered Child Syndrome." *Journal of the American Medical Association* 181 (1962): 17–24.

Kempe, R. S., and C. H. Kempe. *Child Abuse*. Cambridge, Mass.: Harvard University Press, 1978.

Kepler, V. *One in Four*. Mansfield, Ohio: Social Interest Press, 1984.

Lederer, L., ed. *Take Back the Night*. New York: William Morrow, 1980.

Libia, D. "The Protection of the Child Victim of a Sexual Offense in the Criminal Justice System." *Wayne State Law Review* 15 (1969): 977–84.

Lindberg, M. "Is Knowledge Base Development a Necessary and Sufficient Condition for Memory Development?" *Journal of Experimental Child Psychology* 30 (1980): 401–10.

Lister, E. D. "Forced Silence: A Neglected Dimension of Trauma." *American Journal of Psychiatry* 139 (1982): 867–72.

Loftus, E. F. "The Malleability of Human Memory." *American Scientist* 67 (1979): 312–20.

MacFarlane, K., B. Jones, and L. Jenstrom, eds. *Sexual Abuse of Children: Selected Readings*. Washington, D.C.: National Center on Child Abuse and Neglect, 1980.

MacVicar, K. "Psychotherapeutic Issues in the Treatment of Sexually Abused Girls." *Journal of Child Psychiatry* 18 (1979): 342–53.

Marin, B. V., B. Holmes, M. Guth, and P. Kovac. "The Potential of Children as Eyewitnesses." *Law and Human Behavior* 3 (1979): 295–305.

Marquis, K. H., J. Marshall, and S. Oskamp. "Testimony Validity as a Function of Question Form, Atmosphere, and Item Difficulty." *Journal of Applied Social Psychology* 2 (1972): 167–86.

Marsh, J. *Rape and the Limits of Law Reform*. Boston: Auburn House, 1982.

Martin, H. P. *The Abused Child*. Cambridge, Mass.: Ballinger, 1976.

Massey, J. D., O. R. Garcia, and J. R. Emich, Jr. "Management of Sexually Assaulted Females." *Obstetrics and Gynecology* 38 (1971): 29–36.

Mayhall, P., and K. E. Norgard. *Child Abuse and Neglect*. New York: Wiley, 1983.

Medea, A., and K. Thompson. *Against Rape*. New York: Farrar, Straus and Giroux, 1974.

Mehta, M. N., et al. "Rape in Children." *Child Abuse and Neglect* 3 (1979): 671–77.

Meiselman, K. *Incest*. San Francisco: Jossey-Bass, 1978.

Melton, G. B. "Children's Competency to Testify." *Law and Human Behavior* 5 (1981): 73–85.

Metropolitan Court Judges Committee. *Deprived Children: A Judicial Response*. Reno: National Council of Juvenile and Family Court Judges, 1986.

Mrazek, P. B., and C. H. Kempe, eds. *Sexually Abused Children and Their Families*. Oxford: Pergamon, 1981.

Muldoon, L., ed. *Incest: Confronting the Silent Crime*. Saint Paul: Minnesota Program for Victims of Sexual Assault, 1979.

Myers, J. E. B. *Child Witnesses: Law and Practice*. New York: Wiley Law Publications, 1987.

National Center on Child Abuse and Neglect. *Child Sexual Abuse: Incest, Assault, and Sexual Exploitation*. Washington, D.C.: Department of Health, Education, and Welfare, 1978.

———. *Study Findings: National Study of the Incidence and Severity of Child Abuse and Neglect*. Washington, D.C., 1981.

National Conference of the Judiciary on the Rights of Victims of Crime. *Statement of Recommended Judicial Practices*. Washington, D.C.: United States Department of Justice, 1984.

National Council of Juvenile and Family Court Judges. *Child Sexual Abuse—Issues and Actions*. Reno, 1988.

Neisser, V. "The Control of Information Pickup in Selective Looking." In *Perception and Its Development*, ed. A. D. Pick. Hillsdale, N.J.: Erlbaum, 1976.

Nelson, B. J. *Making an Issue of Child Abuse: Political Agenda Setting for Social Problems*. Chicago: University of Chicago Press, 1984.

O'Brien, S. *Child Abuse, A Crying Shame*. Provo, Utah: Brigham Young University Press, 1980.

———. *Child Pornography*. Dubuque, Iowa: Kendall Hunt, 1983.

O'Carroll, T. *Paedophilia: The Radical Case*. London: Peter Owen, 1980.

Parton, N. *The Politics of Child Abuse*. New York: St. Martin's Press, 1985.

Perker, J. "The Rights of Child Witnesses: Is the Court a Protector or Perpetrator?" *New England Law Review* 17 (1982): 643–717.

Perlmutter, M. *Children's Memory*. New Directions in Child Development, no. 10. San Francisco: Jossey-Bass, 1980.

Peters, J. J. "Children Who Are Victims of Sexual Assault and the Psychology of Offenders." *American Journal of Orthopsychiatry* 30 (1976): 398–421.

———. "The Psychological Effects of Childhood Rape." *World Journal of Psychosynthesis* 5 (1974): 11–14.

Peterson, C., and M. E. P. Seligman. "Learned Helplessness and Victimization." *Journal of Social Issues* 39 (1983): 103–16.

Postman, N. *The Disappearance of Childhood*. New York: Delacorte Press, 1982.

President's Task Force on Victims of Crime. Washington, D.C.: U.S. Government Printing Office, 1982.

Rodabaugh, B., and M. Austin. *Sexual Assault*. New York: Garland STMP Press, 1981.

Rush, F. *The Best Kept Secret: Sexual Abuse of Children*. New York: McGraw-Hill, 1980.

Russell, A. B., and C. M. Trainor. *Trends in Child Abuse and Neglect*. Denver: American Humane Association, 1984.

Russell, D. E. H. "The Incidence and Prevalence of Intrafamilial and Extrafamilial Sexual Abuse of Female Children." *Child Abuse and Neglect* 7 (1983): 133–46.

———. *The Politics of Rape*. New York: Stein and Day, 1975.

———. *Sexual Exploitation*. Beverly Hills: Sage, 1984.

Salter, A. C. *Treating Child Sex Offenders and Victims*. Newbury Park, Cal.: Sage, 1988.

Sanford, L. *The Silent Children: A Book for Parents about the Prevention of Child Sexual Abuse*. New York: McGraw-Hill, 1981.

Schultz, L. G. "The Child Sex Victim: Social, Psychological, and Legal Perspectives," *Child Welfare* 52 (1973): 147–57.

———. *The Sexual Victimology of Youth*. Springfield, Ill.: Charles C. Thomas, 1979.

Sgori, M., ed. *Handbook of Clinical Intervention in Child Sexual Abuse*. Lexington, Mass.: Lexington Books, 1982.

Skolnick, A. "The Limits of Childhood: Conceptions of Child Development and Social Context." *Law and Contemporary Problems* 39, 3 (1975): 37–77.

Summit, R. "The Child Sexual Abuse Accommodation Syndrome." *Child Abuse and Neglect* 7 (1983): 177–93.

Summit, R., and J. Kryo. "Sexual Abuse of Children: A Clinical Spectrum." *American Journal of Orthopsychiatry* 48 (1978): 231–51.

Tedesco, F., and S. V. Schnell. "Children's Reactions to Sex Abuse Investigation and Litigation." *Child Abuse and Neglect* 11 (1987): 267–72.

Tyler, A. H., and M. R. Brassard. "Abuse in the Investigation and Treatment of Intrafamilial Child Sexual Abuse." *Child Abuse and Neglect* 8 (1984): 47–53.

U.S. Department of Health and Human Services. *Sexual Abuse of Children: Selected Readings.* Washington, D.C., 1980.

VanderMey, B. J., and R. L. Neff. *Incest as Child Abuse.* New York: Praeger, 1986.

Walker, M., and S. Brodsky, eds. *Sexual Assault.* Lexington, Mass.: Lexington Books, 1976.

Warner, C. W., ed. *Rape and Sexual Assault.* Germantown, Md.: Aspen Systems, 1980.

Weiss, E. H., and R. F. Berg. "Child Psychiatry and the Law: Child Victims of Sexual Assault—Impact of Court Procedures." *Journal of the American Academy of Child Psychiatry* 21 (1982): 513–18.

Weitzman, L. J. *The Divorce Revolution.* New York: Free Press, 1985.

Whitcomb, D., E. R. Shapiro, and L. D. Stellwagen. *When the Victim Is a Child.* Washington, D.C.: National Institute of Justice, 1985.

White, S., et al. "Interviewing Young Sexual Abuse Victims with Anatomically Correct Dolls." *Child Abuse and Neglect* 10 (1986): 519–29.

Woodling, B., and A. Heger. "The Use of the Colposcope in the Diagnosis of Sexual Abuse in the Pediatric Age Group." *Child Abuse and Neglect* 10 (1986): 111–14.

Wyatt, G. E. "The Sexual Abuse of Afro-American and White American Women in Childhood." *Child Abuse and Neglect* 7 (1985): 507–19.

Wyatt, G. E., and S. D. Peters. "Issues in the Definition of Child Sexual Abuse in Prevalence Research." *Child Abuse and Neglect* 10 (1986): 231–40.

———. "Methodological Considerations in Research on the Prevalence of Child Sexual Abuse." *Child Abuse and Neglect* 10 (1986): 241–51.

Wyatt, G. E., and G. J. Powell. *Lasting Effects of Child Sexual Abuse.* Newbury Park, Cal.: Sage, 1988.

Yarmey, A. D. *The Psychology of Eyewitness Testimony.* New York: Free Press, 1979.

Yarmey, A. D., and H. P. T. Jones. "Is the Psychology of Eyewitness Identification a Matter of Common Sense?" In *Evaluating Witness Evidence,* ed. S. M. Lloyd and B. R. Clifford. New York: Wiley, 1983.

Yun, J. "A Comprehensive Approach to Child Hearsay Statements in Sex Abuse Cases." *Columbia Law Review* 83 (1983): 1745–66.

Supplement to the Second Edition

In recent years, hundreds of articles, books, and videotapes on child sexual abuse and related subjects have been published. The following are among the most significant:

Braga, J., and L. Braga. *When Children Are Witnesses*. New York: Guilford Publications, Inc., 1989.

Garbarino, J., F. M. Stott, et al. *What Children Can Tell Us: Eliciting, Interpreting, and Evaluating Information from Children*. San Francisco: Jossey-Bass, 1989.

Toth, P. A., and M. P. Whalen, eds. *Investigation and Prosecution of Child Abuse*. Alexandria, Va.: National Center for the Prosecution of Child Abuse, American Prosecutors Research Institute, 1987.

Several excellent journals provide the most current research and developments:

Journal of Interpersonal Violence. Jon R. Conte, ed. Sage Publications, Inc., 2111 West Hillcrest Drive, Newbury Park, CA 93120.

Child Abuse & Neglect/The International Journal. Richard D. Krugman, ed. Kempe National Center, 1205 Oneida Street; Denver, CO 80220.

Protecting Children, a publication of the American Association for Protecting Children, a division of the American Humane Association. Kathern Bond, ed. 9725 East Hampden Ave., Denver, CO 80231.

RoundTable Magazine, a publication of the National Resource Center on Child Sexual Abuse. Kathleen Broyles, managing ed. 106 Lincoln Street, Huntsville, AL 35801.

The National Resource Center on Child Sexual Abuse also publishes comprehensive bibliographies on specific subjects including the following:

Selected Bibliography on Expert Testimony
Selected Bibliography on Child Sexual Abuse for U.S. Attorneys
Selected Bibliography on Interviewing Children for Attorneys and Guardians Ad Litem
Selected Bibliography on Adolescent Child Sexual Abusers
Selected Bibliography on Children As Witnesses
Selected Bibliography for Therapists of Adult Survivors of Sexual Abuse
Selected Bibliography for Adult Survivors of Sexual Abuse
Selected Bibliography on Legal Issues in Multi-Disciplinary Approaches to Child Sexual Abuse

The bibliographies are available from The National Resource Center on Child Sexual Abuse:

Alabama Office	Maryland Office	Information Service
106 Lincoln Street	11141 Georgia Avenue	800-KIDS-006
Huntsville, AL 35801	Wheaton, MD 20902	
205/533-KIDS	301/949-5000	

Index